The Ezra 7^{10} Plan - Book 1

A Heart to Understand

This is the first book in a three-part discipleship series called the Ezra 7^{10} ™ Plan. The three books are: Book 1 - **First Love:** *A Heart to Understand*, Book 2 -**Faithful Life:** *Eyes to See*, and Book 3 - **Free at Last:** *Ears to Hear*. For more information about this discipleship series please go to the program web site at http://www.ezra710plan.org.

The Ezra 7^{10}™ Plan

A guide to discovering and sharing life's greatest treasure

The Word of God

through
PERSONAL STUDY

by
PERSONAL APPLICATION

in
PERSONAL OUTREACH

Seeing God as never before

As He personally directs our life and the lives that we touch

Unless otherwise indicated all Scripture quotations are taken from the New American Standard Bible ®© 1960,1962, 1963, 1968, 1971, 1972, 1973, 1975, 1977, 1995 by the Lockman Foundation. Used by permission. (www.Lockman.org)

Cover Graphic: Heart_sweetheartValentine –by Jouni Paavilainen: www.ChristianPhotos.Net

Editor-in-Chief: Judy Kissinger

The Ezra 7$\underline{10}$ Plan – Book 1
First Love: *A Heart to Understand*
Copyright© 2011 Geoseff Doulos
Front Royal, VA 22630

Ezra 7$\underline{10}$ publications
ISBN–13: 978-0-6154-249-72
ISBN–10: 0-6154-249-7x

All rights reserved. No part of this publication may be reproduced, stored in a retrieval system, or transmitted in any form or by any means – electronic, mechanical, digital, photocopy, recording, or any other – except for brief quotations in printed reviews, without the prior permission of the author.

The Ezra 7:10™ Plan

"For Ezra

had

set his heart to

STUDY the law of the Lord,

and to

PRACTICE it,

and to

TEACH

His statutes and ordinances in Israel"

NASB95

The Ezra 7:10™ Plan

STUDY

Examining the Bible thoroughly and effectively

We Master the Word

PRACTICE

Applying God's Word to everyday life

The Word Masters Us

TEACH

Instructing others so well that they can teach others

The Master Multiplies the Word through Us

To the Glory of God

TABLE OF CONTENTS

Ezra 7:10 Plan - Book 1
First Love: A Heart to Understand

Introduction	xiii
Overview	01
Suggested Syllabus	03
Disciple Skill	05
Quiet Time	
Ammo	51
Prayer & Petition	
Armor	95
What You Wear:	
Belt, Breastplate and Helmet	
Study	109
Context is the Key:	
Looking at the Forest	
Practice	151
Making Good Applications:	
Exercising the Truth	
Teach	161
Developing Questions:	
Preaching the Word	
Discovery	173
God's Love for Me	

TABLE OF CONTENTS

Ezra 7:10 Plan - Book 2
Faithful Life: Eyes to See

Overview

Disciple Skill
Reading & Memorizing

Ammo
Sword of the Spirit

Armor
What You Bear:
Shield

Study
Key Observations:
Looking at the Trees

Practice
Standing on Principle:
Destroying the Lie

Teach
Developing the Message:
Here I am... Send Me

Discovery
God's Will for Me

TABLE OF CONTENTS

Ezra 7:10 Plan - Book 3
Free at Last: Ears to Hear

Overview

Disciple Skill
Witnessing

Ammo
Gospel of Peace

Armor
What you Dare:
Shoes

Study
Turnkey Studies:
Verse, Topic and Book

Practice
Overcoming Obstacles:
Bearing our Cross

Teach
Tools of the Trade:
The Harvest

Discovery
God's View of History

Appendices

The Ezra 7:10 Plan

INTRODUCTION

The Unique Plan

In today's global Biblical community there is a vast multitude of resources available to help Christians begin and sustain their walk with the Lord. In order to prevent an increase in this surplus population, a number of questions were asked about the Ezra 7:10 Plan by its author. Will this work meet a need that is already being met by other resources? Will this work build on a foundation, or build the same foundation? Is it timely? Is it ageless? Does this resource seek to promote authors or organizations, or is this a true prophetic message, so to speak?

As the Ezra 7:10 Plan (Plan) is further detailed below in the following paragraphs, perhaps only the reader can be the final arbiter of the usefulness of this work. While it is certainly true that there is nothing new under the sun, the unique way in which this Plan seeks to foster the growth of Christians will make its own case. This discipleship series is indeed needed today.

The Plan is split into three books, that is levels, each increasing in maturity, but each level contains the same basic working format. The books are titled as follows: Book 1 - **First Love:** *A Heart to Understand*, Book 2 - **Faithful Life:** *Eyes to See*, and Book 3 - **Free at Last:** *Ears to Hear*.

Each book has a *Disciple Skill* section that helps to build a solid foundation of Christian disciplines, such as having a quiet time, reading and memorizing Scriptures, and witnessing that are meant to last a lifetime. These actions are to be practiced daily — yes, daily.

In addition, each book contains additional lessons titled *Ammo* and *Armor*. Each Ezra 7^10 Plan level discusses pieces of the *Armor of God* mentioned in Ephesians chapter six. *Ammo* covers at least one offensive spiritual weapon that we can employ as we continue our journey with the Lord Jesus. In *Armor* we discuss primarily defensive weapons to be used in our walk with God. Both the *Ammo* and *Armor* topics tie in extremely well with the other themes of each Plan level.

There is a *Study* section on learning keys to studying and interpreting the Bible, a *Practice* section on how to apply what we have learned, and lastly, a *Teach* section on how to teach others what we have just learned and are practicing. This last emphasis on teaching is what sets this Plan apart from many other courses.

Finally, each Plan level contains a Bible study to complete and discuss. This Bible study follows the *Study, Practice, Teach* sections, and thus we will be well equipped not only to complete the Bible study, but to make practical applications from it, and to teach others what we have just learned. Book one's Bible study, *God's Love for Me*, contains an in-depth study of the Biblical definition of God's love as described in 1 Corinthians chapter thirteen. After going through the study perhaps for the first time we, *...being rooted and grounded in love, may be able to comprehend with all the saints what is the breadth and length and height and depth, and to know the love of Christ which surpasses knowledge, that you may be filled up to all the fullness of God.* (Ephesians 3:17-19). The other books contain Bible studies on *God's Will for Me* and on *God's View of History*.

Study, Practice and <u>*Teach*</u>

One major goal of this discipleship series is to provide a framework for studying, applying and cementing the truths of the Bible into our life. That should be a goal of any Bible study that we may attend. But this Plan seeks to propel the disciple into taking further steps that are so often missing in other studies. These missing steps include teaching others what we have learned, while we continue to develop the spiritual eyes and ears to discern what the Lord is doing in our life and in the world around us.

The Ezra 7:10 Plan

INTRODUCTION

We do not want to become like those mentioned in Isaiah 6:9 quoted by the apostle Paul in Acts.

Acts 28:26,27 *Go to this people, and say, You shall indeed hear but never understand, and you shall indeed see but never perceive. For this people's heart has grown dull, and their ears are heavy of hearing, and their eyes they have closed; lest they should perceive with their eyes, and hear with their ears, and understand with their heart, and turn for me to heal them.*

Too often the actual accomplishment of Bible studies ends up being the temporary storage of information. This is so far — so far — from what the Lord intended. In one of His final statements to His disciples, often called "The Great Commission," He stated,

Matthew 28:19, 20 *Go therefore and make disciples of all the nations, baptizing them in the name of the Father and the Son and the Holy Spirit, teaching them to observe all that I commanded you; and lo, I am with you always, even to the end of the age.*

The process of making disciples may as well be stated as making duplicates, not in the sense of reproducing our character, but in reproducing Christ's character and mission in others. One key thing that seems to be missing in the process of making disciples is teaching others how to teach others. In addition, disciples need to perceive that the Lord is indeed with them, and constantly working with and through them, as He develops their character and faith. Remember — God is always the Father, and we are always the children, even when we grow up. God will never stop encouraging and disciplining us as we move toward the goal of being like Him. For those senior disciples out there, this is an exhortation to continue the race and finish well. For others, the message is clear: start well, and continue with perseverance the race that is before us, looking to Jesus, the pioneer and perfecter of our faith.

Hebrews 12:1-3 *Therefore, since we have so great a cloud of witnesses surrounding us, let us also lay aside every encumbrance and the sin which so easily entangles us, and let us run with endurance the race that is set before us, fixing our eyes on Jesus, the author and perfecter of faith, who for the joy set before Him endured the cross, despising the shame, and has sat down at the right hand of the throne of God. For consider Him who has endured such hostility by sinners against Himself, so that you will not grow weary and lose heart.*

The Time is now

Are we seeing a proliferation of (non-professional) teachers and solid disciples? Today we have more access to the Word and Bible resources than ever before. It is clear that we are losing the battle for the hearts and minds of these young (and old) disciples. We are not advocating more action in the sense of just more Bible study attendance or perhaps leading a Sunday school class. To be an effective disciple of Christ, we must begin and end our day with the Lord. It means spending enough time with God on a daily basis that it forces us to give up useless time — what the Bible calls *labor that does not satisfy* (Isaiah 55:2). This does not mean being a full-time monk, but rather, following Jesus' example, which included spending a significant portion of each day with the Father. It is hoped that this Plan will give us a framework for accomplishing this by showing us how to invest our time with the Lord effectively.

What is needed today, especially as it is very apparent that *...the time is near...* (Revelation 1:3), is for men and women to take seriously the study of God's Holy Word and be committed to making disciples. There has been a veritable explosion of books, magazines, CDs, DVDs, radio and TV programs where knowledgeable and unknowledgeable people espouse their insights into the Word of God. And perhaps some, like sheep, mindlessly take in this massive amount of information, always learning yet never coming to any personal convictions about God's truths contained in the Scriptures. And having itching ears, they simply choose which authors they like, or which TV or radio preachers they like, that preach what they like to hear, never knowing if in fact the Bible really teaches what these people claim. These lost sheep have no conviction, only the author's conviction. They have no authority, only their preacher's authority. They have no courage, only their radio teacher's courage. They have no light, but can only wait until these others shed light on their path. These sheep think the Bible is so hard to understand, too difficult for mere church goers like themselves. They rationalize that they simply do not have the time it takes to figure it all out. This is why they think they need all these pre-packaged insights,

The Ezra 7:10 Plan

and quick and easy applications. "Just tell me what to do and I'll try to fit it into my schedule."

Proverbs 29:18 says,

Where there is no vision a people are unrestrained, but happy is he who keeps the law.

This vision can be defined as a fresh word from God, or insights into His Word that we get from God. These are not warmed over, micro-waved insights from somebody else. Our major source of learning needs to be only from the Bible. Our interpreter is none other than the Holy Spirit Himself. All this proliferation of books can be tossed aside, save for a few choice reference books. We need men and women who can quote and teach from the Bible: "Thus says the Lord," not "my pastor says," or "this book says," or the "TV preacher said." When we decide to align ourselves with Jesus' definition of disciple, which in the simplest sense is that of a student being taught by <u>one</u> Teacher, we will begin to grow past infancy, and on into maturity.

John 8:31,32 *You are my disciples if you continue in my word ....*

It is our earnest prayer that the Ezra 7:10 Plan will illustrate the great truth contained in Colossians 2:10, *and in Him you have been made complete...*, which teaches that total sufficiency can be found in Christ alone. We pray that as Ezra did, we will set our hearts ... *to study the Law of the Lord, and to practice it, and to teach His statutes and ordinances...* (Ezra 7:10); and as the apostle Paul encouraged we would, *Let the word of Christ richly dwell within you, with all wisdom teaching and admonishing one another...* (Colossians 3:16). Most of all, we pray that our relationship with *Abba,* Father, would be deepened beyond measure and we would see God as never before as He personally directs our life and the lives we touch!

Freely you have been given, freely give

The Ezra 7^{10} ™ Plan is copyrighted material, 1998 — 2011. However, it is our desire not to prevent its duplication in any form. We only ask that our permission is requested first and the material used is referenced in the following way:

"Ezra 7^{10} ™ Plan © 1998 – 2011 by G. Doulos. Used by permission." Our desire is that this Plan and any portion of it may be used for individual personal growth and for the growth of others.

Please let us know if we can be of any additional help!

We may be contacted via Email: help@ezra710plan.org

The Ezra 7:10 Plan - Book 1

First Love

A Heart to Understand

The Ezra 7:10 Plan *1st Love*

Book 1 – First Love: A Heart to Understand

OVERVIEW

Welcome to the first book in the three-part discipleship series called the Ezra 7:10 Plan. *First Love* has a two-fold symbolism. For new believers it sets our hearts right from the beginning on what is most important in life. Our first love is, and always will be, the Lord. For older believers *First Love* is the reminder to the church at Ephesus:

Revelation 2:4, 5 *But I have this against you, that you have left your first love. Therefore remember from where you have fallen, and repent and do the deeds you did at first...*

Every section in *First Love* represents key building blocks for our spiritual foundation. Our relationship with God, the cornerstone, is the most important thing in our life. Deeds will follow, but as the verse above states, we need to keep our *first love*. As we grow in our relationship with God we will begin to embark on the spiritual disciplines that are contained in the Scriptures. That discipline is the cement between the blocks.

Every section has a chapter devoted to teaching others what we have just learned. Thus not only will we be learning these new spiritual disciplines, but we will learn how to get others started and excited about them as well. This is a hallmark of every Ezra 7:10 publication. Over the next four months we will *Study*, *Practice* and *Teach*. The homework after each section will reinforce these themes.

The Lord is looking forward to spending time with us, for we are *His First Love!*

The Ezra 7:10 Plan — 1st Love

OVERVIEW

First we will start off by learning about Quiet Time, which is the single most important activity of our life. If we put a priority each and every day on our time alone with the Lord we will be off to a great start. This one activity can completely change our life and we can bet that the enemy will try and prevent us from making this a habitual part of our life. We call this a *Disciple Skill* because every disciple of God must master it.

This is followed by a discussion of different aspects of the *Armor of God* as mentioned in Ephesians chapter six. In *Ammo* we discuss Prayer and Petition. If we fully grasp the potential we have in prayer, like Quiet Time, we will be well on our way to a close lifelong relationship with the Lord and we will always be in His service. In *Armor* we discuss the belt, the breastplate and the helmet. It is interesting to note that the apostle Paul wrote to the Ephesians about the *Armor of God,* and yet it is this same church mentioned in the book of Revelation that had *lost its first love.* Perhaps if we grasp the truths mentioned in the *Armor of God* we will not lose our *first love.*

The next three sections, *Study, Practice* and *Teach,* help us lay the foundation for properly studying the Scriptures, making personal applications, and preparing ourselves to teach others. In the *Study* section we will learn how to properly search the Scriptures by understanding how the surrounding context may influence its meaning. Our *Practice* section will show us how to make resolutions that will last, and will change our behavior to become more Christ-like. The *Teach* section will begin to get us thinking of how we can help others by passing on what we have just learned. We will learn how to develop questions that we can use for our own personal study, but also for leading others to discover the *Truth*.

Finally, we have a Bible study to complete and discuss. *God's Love for Me* contains a wonderfully in-depth study of the biblical definition of God's love as described in 1 Corinthians chapter thirteen. The Bible study is placed after the *Study, Practice, Teach* sections so that we will be well equipped to get the most out of it.

The Ezra 7:10 Plan — 1st Love

OVERVIEW

Suggested Syllabus

The following table represents a suggested order of the course material.

Section	Pages	Assignment	Time frame
Quiet Time	46	Read – prepare lesson on some aspect of Quiet Time	2 weeks
Prayer & Petition	44	Read – prepare lesson on some aspect of Prayer & Petition	2 weeks
Armor: Belt	3	Read – do written work	1 week
Armor: Breastplate	4	Read – do written work	
Armor: Helmet	3	Read – do written work	
Study			
Grammatical Context	11	Read – do written work	1 week
Geographical Context	6	Read – do written work	1 week
Cultural Context	6	Read – do written work	1 week
Historical Context	10	Read – do written work	1 week
Biographical Context	4	Read – do written work	1 week
Practice	8	Read – do written work	1 week
Teach	9	Read – do written work	
Bible Study			
16 - on love's character / 1 – optional assignment	~8 ea.	Read – do written work assumes 2 studies per week	8-9 weeks

    The basic format would be to assign material to read and homework to be done a week ahead of time. Homework? Absolutely! It will be fun and most of all, life-changing. The following week, the material and the homework would be discussed, and the next week's assignment would be given out. The sections on *Quiet Time* and *Prayer & Petition* have homework in addition to reading the

The Ezra 7:10 Plan — 1st Love

material. The homework requires that we prepare a teaching on some aspect of quiet time and prayer. *Quiet Time* and *Prayer & Petition* will usually take more than one week to finish for each of them. For these sections, we can discuss the insights we have gained from the material during the first week's meeting. During the second week's meeting we can continue our discussion of the material and also present our lesson plans. By the second week we can also discuss the amazing things we have received from our quiet times and our prayer times! One week is suggested for each of the other sections.

Thus *First Love* can be covered and all assignments completed in around twenty weeks or in about four and a half months.

First Love can also be tailored to the needs of the group. For example, if the group is made up of veteran Bible studiers, perhaps the Bible study on love should be completed first. If the group is composed of mostly new believers, then extra time can be devoted to *Quiet Time* and *Prayer & Petition*. There is no rush. For those extra eager disciples out there, be ready to add even more assignments to challenge them!

Help for leaders can be found at *http://www.ezra710plan.org*. Individual questions can be sent via e-mail to *help@ezra710plan.org*.

May God richly bless our time with Him.

Disciple Skill

Quiet Time

Setting our Heart on God

The Ezra 7:10 Plan *1st Love*

DISCIPLE SKILL

Quiet Time
Setting Our Heart on God

The single most important thing that we will ever do in our life will be to spend time with the Lord. The term "Quiet Time" has been coined in relatively recent Christian circles to describe this time alone with the Lord. If we make it the number-one priority of our life each day, our life will be blessed, we will be a blessing, and we will experience a relationship with God as never before. We will also experience a peace, a purpose, and a plan for our life that will instill in us a quiet yet bold confidence to face whatever may lie ahead.

The next five sections will prepare us to begin (or re-energize) our lifelong relationship with the Lord. First we look at why this time is so important and so exciting. *Our Father* discusses not just why we need to do this, but also the fact that the Lord Himself has done everything He can to make having a close relationship with Him possible. *Our Failures* candidly talks about some common pitfalls and distractions that prevent us from a quality relationship with God. Next, *Our Fruit* is basically a mini Bible study of the *Parable of the Sower*. In this section we will learn about the fruits of spending time with the Lord. *Our Fruit* is both inspiring and sobering. In the following section, *Our Focus,* we relay some very tangible ways to get the most out of our time with the Lord of Glory.

The Ezra 7:10 Plan *1st Love* DISCIPLE SKILL Quiet Time

Finally in the last section, *Our Field,* we teach how to pass this knowledge onto others who may be in our field of view and in our sphere of influence. We become equipped to teach others in our own words how to experience Quiet Time.

As in all Ezra 7:10 publications, we will be informed, we will be given ways to practice this new knowledge and we will be equipped to teach others what we have just learned.

The Ezra 7:10 Plan *1st Love*   DISCIPLE SKILL Quiet Time

Our Father

Experiencing God

Do we realize that God is our Father in the truest sense of the word? He not only created us physically, but He also provided the way by which we can be born again spiritually, and abide with Him for all eternity. From day one, He has desired the best for us. Even though we stray from Him, He always holds out His hand to guide us back. One of the amazing things to remember about our Father is that *He never gives up on people.*

His first goal after He brought us into this world was to provide a means whereby we can fellowship with Him. Even though we stubbornly went our own way apart from Him, He kept nudging us to realize the error of our ways so we could yield ourselves completely to His perfect plan for us. As in the *Parable of the Lost Sheep,* He went out to search for one little lost lamb to bring him to a place where life could be lived to the fullest.

That clearly shows how much *He cares about us*. Now this is the kind of person we want to get to know.

By now, perhaps we are somewhat familiar with the doctrine of sin and salvation, but let us go over this again, to understand fully and appreciate how great is our God. Of course everyone in the world has been originally separated from our true Father because of sin and the desire to do things his own way. We might not have thought of ourselves as particularly evil or sinful, but in God's eyes whatever does not proceed from the truth or faith in His word is sinful. We do not have to think of sin in terms of evil, but in terms of incompatibility with God. God cannot be in the presence of sin; therefore anything sinful must be separated from Him. God's way of providing sinful man a way to approach a holy God is through atonement. He recognized that we were incapable of being sinless, but if our sin could be atoned for we would have the ability to approach Him. *It is clear that the Lord cherishes communing with us and blessing us.*

The Ezra 7:10 Plan — 1st Love   DISCIPLE SKILL Quiet Time

One place this atonement or salvation message is contained is in Isaiah chapter 53.

Isaiah 53:6 *All of us like sheep have gone astray, Each of us has turned to his own way; But the LORD has caused the iniquity of us all To fall on Him.*

So we see this verse describes the state that we were in before we received an actual pardon for our sins. The verse does not describe our condition as evil. It uses the terms *gone astray* and *turned to his own way*. Nevertheless this condition is evil and idolatrous to the Lord. Why dwell so long on this particular discussion?

First of all, as we have said before, it shows us the great lengths that God has taken for our benefit (i.e., His plan for our redemption from day one, culminating in the death of His own Son Jesus Christ).

Second, it shows that since He has taken such care to save us from the penalty of our sins, He must want to show the same care in guiding and blessing us. How can anything compare to spending time with a person such as this?

Finally, *since God has gone to great lengths for us, we should go to great lengths with Him.*

Let us now go back to the beginning of our spiritual journey. To some that is not too long ago and for some it is ancient history. By going back to our spiritual start we can check to see if our spiritual priorities are still where they should be or if we need to make any changes.

When we became a follower of Christ through our profession of faith, we probably were baptized, and joined a fellowship of believers, doing Bible study, etc. We may have experienced quite a few character changes, and have made some lifestyle changes as well. Rebirth leads to re-growth, and all is well and exciting. But amidst these Christian activities we must remember that at the heart of everything is God. Our new life is not just a life of new activities and new

The Ezra 7:10 Plan *1st Love* DISCIPLE SKILL Quiet Time

relationships. At the core of it all we need to let it sink in that God truly is our Father, and we are his children. *Do we need to break away from the hustle and bustle and rejuvenate our relationship with our heavenly Father?*

Depending on what age we were when we first became believers, this concept (God as our Father) may be easy or it may be difficult to grasp. Also, our family background — such as whether we had a good father or a father who abandoned us — may make a difference in how we initially handle our new relationship with our Father God. Make no mistake about this point though, "God is good all the time and all the time, God is good." We can also exchange "good" with "love." If we grasp this one single principle, we will be well on our way to developing a close personal relationship with our Father. *Do we need to remind ourselves again of the deep love God has for us?*

Changing leadership or instructors can be difficult (for example at work or school). As a new Christian we have the ultimate change of leadership. We ourselves are no longer in charge; someone even better, the Lord, is now in charge. We are no longer following our old ways but are seeking to follow God's ways. The great thing about being a child of God though, is just that — we have God as our Father! *Do we need to give God back the reins of leadership we may have subtly taken back?*

When we meet with the Lord each day we are not just meeting with a friend, or a general, or a task master, or a physician, or a judge, or a farmer, or a master designer, or a physical therapist, or a counselor (the list is endless); in fact, we are meeting with all of these in one Person, who also happens to be our Father. This should inspire reverence, joy and yes, a little fear (in a good way). *Do we need to remind ourselves that God is our source of total supply?*

It is hoped this review was helpful and we can implement any needed changes. Now it is time to end with an exhortation to keep running the race well with our relationship with God as the number-one priority in our lives.

The Ezra 7:10 Plan 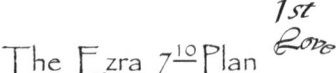 1st Love   DISCIPLE SKILL Quiet Time

Quiet Time helps ensure that we will not stray too far from God and His ways. The apostle Paul, in the Book of 2 Timothy chapter two, likens hardships we will face to different occupations such as a soldier, a farmer and an athlete. Yet amidst these adversities of life we must always remember that God is guiding us as a Father who is raising his children (our age does not matter). Ultimately the goal is to know God Himself fully and to be able to recognize God's fingerprints in our lives and the lives we touch. We will be able to discern God's will, God's voice and God's unmistakable handiwork. *We will view with awe not just his handiwork in creation, but in re-creation — that would be us!*

It is not the intent of this exhortation on Quiet Time to fill the pages with Bible verses so that it becomes a Bible study in itself. We can do that on our own time (which would be an excellent investment of time). Suffice to say, there are many verses that talk about the need for us to spend time with the Lord every single day. This will help us learn His ways and to walk in them and to have a close personal relationship with God.

From the beginning of time until the present, our knowledge of God has been given to us in different ways. But even those folks who lived before Moses and the written Law had learned plenty from the Lord through a variety of sources. We can be sure that Enoch, Noah, Job and of course David, had Quiet Times with the Lord. Even a cursory reading of Job makes it clear that he knew the Lord well, not perfectly of course, but very well. Where did his knowledge of God come from? Read the Book of Job for the answer. The Bible as we know it was not in existence way back then, but the need to spend time with the Lord and learn about his ways was obviously as important then as it is now. David is one of the best examples. He had a very close and insightful relationship with the Lord, even though he had access to just the first five books of the Bible (The Pentateuch). If we read the Psalms of David we can get a glimpse of where he discovered the ways and teachings of God. From the Psalms it is very clear that he meditated on the Scriptures that were available to him, but he also discovered other aspects about God through other experiences. Those same experiences are available to us today. Read the Psalms to discover these wonderful (and sometimes not so wonderful) experiences that God uses to manifest Himself to us.

The Ezra 7:10 Plan 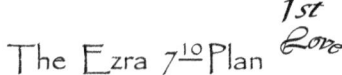   DISCIPLE SKILL Quiet Time

So often new Christians become lax in their time and allow the things of the world to creep in, and they lose their ability to distinguish what is of the Lord and what is not. Too often they cannot see or hear the Lord any more. This may be especially true as believers get older. The Old Testament has numerous examples of this (e.g., Solomon, Lot, Jereboam, etc.).

It is difficult to start out well and to finish well. But the Bible was written to give us a roadmap for spiritual success. That is why our Quiet Time is the single most important thing we can do. Every spiritual decline in the Bible is initially due to spending less and less time with God. Conversely, every spiritual revival begins with a renewal to spend time with God on a daily basis to learn His Word and His ways.

If we can commit ourselves to spending some time with our Father God every single day of our lives without fail, we will have prepared ourselves adequately for the long haul, for finishing well. *To cross the finish line with joy, looking forward to spending the rest of eternity with the Lord, our true Father forever, to not fear death, will be a great feeling.* How sad for some, who perhaps in their last few days on earth, spend it in *sackcloth and ashes* repenting of their past complacencies and their worldly entanglements. While *better late than never* is certainly true with respect to our salvation and our service to the Lord, yet why not take a spiritual performance review now and every year to make sure we are on the right track? Let us leave this world with no regrets or as few regrets as possible.

Why talk about the end of life on earth now, when this is supposed to be an exhortation on how to run the race well? Simply put, the end goal determines our plan of action. Even if we are young, it does not hurt to attend a few funerals, or to visit a courtroom. We will realize with certainty that life on earth has a sure end, and that judgment once pronounced is final. Can we live each day as if it is our last?

The Ezra 7:10 Plan 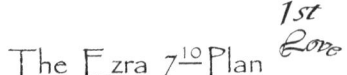 DISCIPLE SKILL Quiet Time

Ecclesiastes 7:2-5 It is better to go to a house of mourning Than to go to a house of feasting, Because that is the end of every man, And the living takes it to heart. Sorrow is better than laughter, For when a face is sad a heart may be happy. The mind of the wise is in the house of mourning, While the mind of fools is in the house of pleasure. It is better to listen to the rebuke of a wise man Than for one to listen to the song of fools.

Yes, too often we can become complacent about how much time we have even though the Bible is full of exhortations to make the most of our time. How do we fall into this trap? You guessed it. Our daily time with the Lord slips and is gradually replaced by something else. Seems so simple, yet the ways of the world are subtle. We must guard our hearts and minds so we mimic the Lord's ways and not the world's ways. The side paths off the straight and narrow are many and we must wear blinders to a certain extent to make sure we do not step to the left or to the right.

Psalm 44:18 *Our heart has not turned back, And our steps have not deviated from Your way,*

To start off well in the Christian life is vital for a successful finish. We do not want to sow any tares (weeds) among the wheat so early (or at any time for that matter) in our Christian walk.

We must remember the single most important thing about being a Christian is having a deepening relationship with our Father God. Quiet Time is the key. As each year passes, we should keep asking ourselves whether or not our actions and activities are drawing us closer to God or farther away. When God seems far away guess who moved? The next section, *Our Failures*, helps us stay close to God by showing us what to avoid!

The Ezra 7:10 Plan *1st Love* DISCIPLE SKILL Quiet Time

Our Failures

Extinguishing God

This section details some traps to avoid, thus making the most of our time here on earth while we are *in the world* but not *of the world*.

So if one of the keys to the Christian life is to spend quality time with the Lord, then what do we think the enemy of God (read: Satan) is going to do about this? He is going to try and sidetrack us and subtly distract us by getting us *hooked* on other activities that compete for this time that we have devoted to the Lord.

A look at two simple words, *amusement* and *entertainment*, and their word origins will help us see this plan of the enemy. All definitions in this section are from *Merriam-Webster, I. (1996, c1993)*.

The word *amusement* literally means *to not think*. The word *muse* means to *think* or *ponder*, and combined with the negative prefix *"a"* means *not thinking, no thinking,* or *without thinking*.

So we see that amusement literally means to not think, to not meditate, and to not think deeply. This is the total opposite of what we are supposed to do while we live our life and especially with the Scriptures. Now the *accuser* (i.e., Satan) knows that if we develop a habit of seriously meditating on God's Word, and we develop a habit of focusing on the Word and its meaning and application, we will become stronger. He is against that and will throw many amusements our way.

As a side note, it is extremely interesting that today's worldly marketing strategy is not just to provide a good product, but to get people hooked on their *favorites*, so that they will spend an ever-increasing amount of time involved in enjoying and pursuing their favorite amusements. This is done in many ways. Just think how people get hooked on (also read – addicted to) their favorites: sports, web sites, TV shows, video games, foods, drinks, music groups, etc., not to mention the pursuit of material things and self-recognition. The list is seemingly endless.

While healthy diversions can be refreshing, we should make sure that *we* are in control of our amusement time and not vice versa.

We need to be careful to make sure that our amusements do not prevent us from spending quality time with the Lord and quantity time in ministering to others using our gifts and talents. In the case of some addictions, we may be literally fighting for our lives. If a journey of a thousand miles begins with one step, so it is with the gradual enslavement of our minds. It just does not happen overnight. And we cannot play the *victim card* here; because we are not suddenly at the mercy of amusements, we have the choice each day.

We have stated before, "If God seems far away, guess who moved?" *If our time with God is not exciting, we may not be just living in the world, but we may be living like the world.* Pray that this will not happen.

Let's move on to *entertainment*.

The meanings of the two basic parts, *enter* and *tain*, are as follows: *enter* means *to be interlocked* or *connected*; and *tain* means *to hold*. Putting those together we get a picture of the mind being completely held and locked in place, not being able to do anything else but being fixated on that which entertains it.

The Biblical term lust actually shares the same idea in principle as entertainment. Lust is when we direct our minds to focus on one thing that we want. Entertainment is when we allow something to control our minds. Both activities trap the mind, and make it difficult for us to hear the voice of our Father God. Both are choices we make.

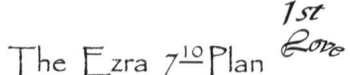

The Bible describes lusting as a battle, as a war against our very soul.

1 Peter 2:11 *Beloved, I urge you as aliens and strangers to abstain from fleshly lusts which wage war against the soul.*

Also as the following verses state, *we must be careful that the world does not dilute our most precious possession – the love of God.*

1 John 2:15,16 *Do not love the world nor the things in the world. If anyone loves the world, the love of the Father is not in him. For all that is in the world, the lust of the flesh and the lust of the eyes and the boastful pride of life, is not from the Father, but is from the world.*

Therefore we must understand that the battle is for our mind (also read heart, soul, mind, and strength). Thus, whether we are being amused (diverted from musing on the Lord's ways), or entertained (our mind being held captive), both can prevent us from serving the Lord to our fullest capacity. The choice is ours. As we will see in the next section, how much fruit we bear for Christ is determined, in large part, by how *free* we truly are in Christ. We were not pardoned from sin so that we can indulge ourselves, but rather we were freed to serve others, as a true child of our Father.

Galatians 5:13 *For you were called to freedom, brethren; only do not turn your freedom into an opportunity for the flesh, but through love serve one another.*

The Ezra 7¹⁰ Plan *1st Love* DISCIPLE SKILL Quiet Time

Our Fruit

Ever-increasing in God

As we follow His Word more closely, we enhance our friendship with the Lord. Our level of obedience to the Word does not make the Lord love us any more or any less. His love is unconditional. Our fellowship with Him, however, is much sweeter when we follow His Word and His Ways. If God seems far away — guess who moved? Seems we have heard that before!

Keep this in mind as we become familiar with His Word and His ways. Our goal is to develop a great lifelong eternal friendship with the Lord of Glory. We are not just learning rules and regulations, or facts and figures. We are getting to know the Person responsible for these words, and the one who created us, and thought we were so special that He would die for us, so that He could have the pleasure of our company!

To understand the diversity of responses to the Word of God throughout the world, let us look at the Parable of the Sower. Read Matthew 13:1-23, and then consider the following comparisons and commentary. These are nothing more than making some common-sense observations, and asking and answering some simple questions. This exercise will help us see the importance of Quiet Time and begin to teach us how to glean insights from the Word. Since the Gospels of Mark (chapter 4) and Luke (chapter 8) also carry this story, with slight but interesting differences, we have included a few insights from their versions as well.

This parable is applicable for both seekers and believers. For seekers, those who are searching for the truth about God, this parable illuminates how it is possible to appear to be a born-again Christian while never having truly repented of sinful ways and never having confessed Jesus as Lord and Savior. For believers, this parable contains amazing principles for starting and finishing the race well and for maximizing our fruitfulness.

The Ezra 7:10 Plan — 1st Love

DISCIPLE SKILL — Quiet Time

A few times in this section, we will note that fruit is the ultimate outward sign of true belief. That said, the ultimate reason we bear fruit is due to the indwelling Holy Spirit. We cannot see the wind, only the effect it has on things. Thus we cannot see the indwelling Spirit in others, only the effect He has on them. *A person controlled by the Holy Spirit will produce fruit. It will be unavoidable and unmistakable.*

Our own fruitfulness is determined by many things. Read on!

The Ezra 7:10 Plan *1st Love*

DISCIPLE SKILL *Quiet Time*

Jesus speaks to the Crowds Matthew 13	**Jesus speaks to the Disciples** Matthew 13
1 That day Jesus went out of the house and was sitting by the sea. *2 And large crowds gathered to Him, so He got into a boat and sat down, and the whole crowd was standing on the beach.* *3 And He spoke many things to them in parables, saying, "Behold, the sower went out to sow;* *4 and as he sowed, some seeds fell beside the road, and the birds came and ate them up.*	*18 Hear then the parable of the sower.* *19 When anyone hears the word of the kingdom and does not understand it, the evil one comes and snatches away what has been sown in his heart. This is the one on whom seed was sown beside the road.*

Commentary:

Even if we were not privy to the interpretation given by Jesus to the disciples, we could glean some things from just meditating on what Jesus said to the crowds, and by asking questions. Why were the birds able to eat the seeds? Two obvious reasons are that they could see them; and they were able to pick them up without anyone or anything getting in their way. So we could come to the conclusion that if the seeds were completely buried in the soil the birds would not have been able to even see them, let alone snatch them up. Or, if the seeds were only partially buried, but still visible, perhaps if someone or something would be there to protect the seeds from the birds, then the seeds would also be safe from being snatched away.

The spiritual application of this would be obvious if we relate the Word to the seed and the heart to the soil. When the sower (God or one of His messengers) preaches the Word (the seed), we must make sure that our heart (the soil) is receptive to the Word, so that it goes deep into our heart. Even if we have doubts, which could be representative of the seed not completely buried, we must guard

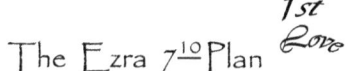

DISCIPLE SKILL   Quiet Time

ourselves from those doubts (the birds); otherwise the Word (seed) will be removed from our heart (soil).

Jesus says essentially the same thing in principle. The evil one who will play on our doubts and our misunderstandings will try and get us to dismiss what was sown in our heart. If the Word is about salvation, and it is removed from our heart, we will miss an opportunity for salvation. If the Word is about spiritual growth, we will miss an opportunity to grow and bear fruit in a particular area.

Note that Mark (chapter 4) and Luke (chapter 8), which also carry this story, contain essentially the same thoughts. Luke adds that in addition to the birds eating the seeds, the seeds were trampled underfoot first. This trampling could be an illustration of how the Word may be corrupted or doubted even before it has a chance to get into the soil (heart).

In Jesus' discussion with His disciples, Luke adds that not only does the devil take away the Word from the heart of those who have heard it, but he does this so that they will not believe and be saved. This puts a specific evangelistic emphasis on the parable.

The Ezra 7:10 Plan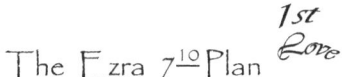

DISCIPLE SKILL Quiet Time

Jesus speaks to the Crowds Matthew 13	**Jesus speaks to the Disciples** Matthew 13
5 Others fell on the rocky places, where they did not have much soil; and immediately they sprang up, because they had no depth of soil. *6 But when the sun had risen, they were scorched; and because they had no root, they withered away.*	*20 The one on whom seed was sown on the rocky places, this is the man who hears the word and immediately receives it with joy;* *21 yet he has no firm root in himself, but is only temporary, and when affliction or persecution arises because of the word, immediately he falls away.*

Commentary:

Without hearing Jesus' special insights to His disciples, we can glean a few things by asking questions. Why do seeds falling on rocky places with little soil spring up so quickly? Well, if we think about it, most seeds when they germinate spend some time underground developing their root system before they pop out of the ground. So we do not see them immediately but only after a few days to a week or so. But for the seeds sown without much soil, the resulting plant will be visible right away. This is what it means that they immediately sprang up. Follow this up with another question: Why is it helpful to stay underground for awhile? Before the plant is subjected to the sun, wind and beating of the falling rain, it needs to make sure it is anchored to the soil securely and has a steady supply of water so that its stem and leaves have the strength to withstand whatever comes their way. The spiritual application to this is obvious. Growth is a long process and takes commitment. *The long haul cannot be fueled just by emotion, but by devotion.*

While Mark parallels Matthew, Luke again tends to summarize things, by saying only the ...*seed fell on rocky soil, and as soon as it grew up, it withered away, because it had no moisture.* Notice it does not say anything about a root or the sun, but the picture is still clear.

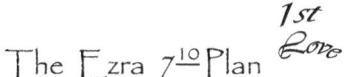

Greek Speek:

temporary - the Greek word is πρόσκαιρος *(proskairos)*. The word *temporary* in verse 21, in the Greek means *for a time,* or *for a season*; thus the root exists for only a specified time.

affliction - the Greek word is θλῖψις *(thlipsis)*, other verses where this word is used (cross references) include Acts 7:10, 11:19, 14:22, Romans 8:35.

persecution - the Greek word is διωγμός *(diōgmos),* cross references include Mark 10:30, Acts 8:1, Romans 8:35.

falls away - the Greek word is σκανδαλίζω *(skandalizo)*, note that the words *he falls away* literally mean *to be offended by.*

    This brings a slightly different connotation to the verse. Without knowing the Greek, you might think that the person is falling away because his new-found faith is too weak to hold up to the affliction and persecution. But in reality, the Greek suggests that the person is *unwilling* (not unable) to associate with being a Christian if it means that he will be afflicted or persecuted for his belief. He (immediately) does not like it one bit.

    It is extremely interesting to read Paul's statement in Romans 8:35 in light of this.

Romans 8:35 *Who will separate us from the love of Christ? Will tribulation* (thlipsis*), or distress, or persecution* (diogmos), *or famine, or nakedness, or peril, or sword?*

    Note that Paul says that tribulation and persecution (among other things) cannot separate us from the love of Christ; and yet, it is these very things that cause the person with no root to fall away. So what determines our response to persecution and affliction? That, my friend, is a question to ponder.

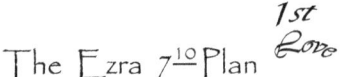

Final Thoughts:

While Mark again parallels Matthew in verse 21, Luke adds a thought, *...and these have no firm root; they believe for a while, and in time of temptation fall away.*

The question to ask with Luke's narrative is: Is temporary belief, really belief at all? If you will follow the Word when it is convenient and not embarrassing, are you really a follower of the Word and a true disciple? It is interesting to note that Luke is basically equating the root with belief; in other words, no lasting root – no true belief.

Again this has applications for both seekers and believers. For seekers it explains why it may appear that they may have found the faith but really they do not possess a true saving faith. For believers, it is a warning to have our roots firmly established as in the teaching found in the book of Colossians.

Colossians 2:6,7 *Therefore as you have received Christ Jesus the Lord, so walk in Him having been firmly rooted and now being built up in Him and established in your faith, just as you were instructed, and overflowing with gratitude.*

The Ezra 7:10 Plan — 1st Love

DISCIPLE SKILL Quiet Time

Jesus speaks to the Crowds Matthew 13	**Jesus speaks to the Disciples** Matthew 13
7 Others fell among the thorns, and the thorns came up and choked them out.	*22 And the one on whom seed was sown among the thorns, this is the man who hears the word, and the worry of the world and the deceitfulness of wealth choke the word, and it becomes unfruitful.*

Commentary:

Note that Matthew 13:7 and the corollary in Luke state that the thorns choked the seed(s) *out*. Mark however, states that the thorns choked the seed and specifically mentions that it yielded no crop. This zero crop yield is implied in Matthew and Luke. Let us now look collectively at what Matthew, Mark and Luke say about what causes the Word to be choked out of our life.

Causes of choking

Matthew: worry of the world; deceitfulness of wealth

Mark: worries of the world, deceitfulness of riches, the desires for other things

Luke: worries and riches and pleasures of this life

Taking all three Gospels together, the main causes of choking are: Worry, wealth, riches, desire for other things, and pleasures.

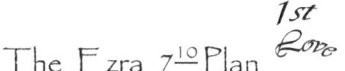

The Ezra 7:10 Plan — 1st Love   DISCIPLE SKILL Quiet Time

A question to ponder: What do entertainment, amusement, worry, pursuit of wealth and pleasure, and the desire for other things have in common? Look at the following list and ponder this.

<u>Action</u>	<u>Effect on the Mind</u>
Worry	strangle, constrict
Pursuit	blocks out
Amuse	prevent, restrict
Desire	captivate
Entertain	lock, trap

Greek Speek:

Choke

There are three different words for *choke* used in the three gospels for this passage.

πνίγω *(pnigō)*, the generic word for *choke*.

ἀποπνίγω *(apopnigō),* uses a more descriptive form of the verb using the preposition *apo* implying choking off, smothering, i.e., choking unto death.

συμπνίγω *(sumpnigō),* a more descriptive form of the verb employing the preposition *sun* (written as *sum* before the consonant *p*) implying choking together, or the idea that the thorns are ganging up on (crowding around) the plant.

All three Gospels use *sumpnigō* for the word *choke* <u>when Jesus is talking to His disciples.</u> This probably signifies that worry, the pursuit of wealth, and pleasure will collectively *gang up* on us to choke out the Word. Interestingly <u>when Jesus is</u>

The Ezra 7:10 Plan 1st Love

DISCIPLE SKILL Quiet Time

talking to the crowds, Matthew uses *pnigō* for *choke*, Luke uses *apopnigō*, and Mark uses *sumpnigō*.

Now let us look at a few more words from the passage: Worry, wealth and unfruitful.

Worry

μέριμνα *(merimna)* is the Greek word and it is generally translated as *worry, care or anxiety*. It is interesting to note that our English word "worry" had its early origins as a verb meaning to strangle or constrict. This is exactly what the thorns are doing to us.

Wealth

πλοῦτος *(ploutos)* is the Greek word and refers to *wealth, riches, abundance, fullness*; with respect to the abundance of one's possessions, it would thus equate to one's personal wealth.

Unfruitful

ἄκαρπος *(akarpos)* is the Greek word that Matthew and Mark use which is a negative noun. The alpha *(a)*, at the beginning is the negative meaning *no* or *without*. The Greek word καρπος *(karpos)* means *fruit*. So the meaning is *no fruit, without fruit*, or *fruitless*.

Luke uses *bring no fruit to maturity*. Luke puts a slightly different meaning into this part of the story. He indicates that the thorns gang up and choke the seed/plant (the Word) so that the fruit does not come to maturity or completion. Now the purpose of a plant is to bear fruit, so if the fruit never matures it is essentially worthless. The point is clear: thorns will spur the development of only immature fruit or prevent fruit from growing altogether. Perhaps Luke's description of immature fruit could also be a good analogy of someone who could appear as a Christian bearing fruit, but in reality the fruit is not genuine, not useful, and not produced by the Holy Spirit.

Final thoughts:

For seekers this means that despite an initial outward appearance of growth, there was no solid belief that could outlast the surrounding trappings. Isaiah says many times in his book that the people had eyes to see but did not see, and ears to hear but did not hear. It is no wonder, as their quest of worldly pleasures and the anxieties that are associated with that pursuit completely captivated their mind, making it impossible for the Holy Spirit to convict them of sin, righteousness and judgment (see John 16:8). For believers, we must be on guard, since we will be attacked on our weakest front. Thus we will not bear much fruit if we allow the things of the world to choke the Word. We may need to do some serious "weeding" in our lives.

The Ezra 7:10 Plan *1st Love*   DISCIPLE SKILL Quiet Time

Jesus speaks to the Crowds Matthew 13	**Jesus speaks to the Disciples** Matthew 13
8 And others fell on the good soil and yielded a crop, some a hundredfold, some sixty, and some thirty. 9 "He who has ears, let him hear."	*23 And the one on whom seed was sown on the good soil, this is the man who hears the word and understands it; who indeed bears fruit and brings forth, some a hundredfold, some sixty, and some thirty.*

Commentary:

Both Matthew 13:8 and its parallel in Mark 4 mention the increase as 30-, 60- and 100-fold; while Luke just mentions a 100-fold increase. Also in the explanation in Matthew 13:23 and in Mark 4, the 30-, 60-, and 100-fold increase is mentioned, while Luke does not even mention a specific increase, but states that the seed bore fruit *with perseverance*. It is interesting to note in the Gospels how the soil (hearts of people) received the seed (Word), as summarized below:

Matthew: Hear and Understand
Mark: Hear and Accept
Luke: Hear (in an honest and good heart) and Hold it Fast

All of the Gospels mention *hear*, but the next word describing how they received the Word is different among the Gospels. Matthew uses almost a neutral description of how they received it (i.e., *understand*), that by itself does not necessarily imply acceptance or belief. Mark states the acceptance, but does not indicate the level of commitment.

Luke 8:15 seems to make it crystal clear, *But the seed in the good soil, these are the ones who have heard the word in an honest and good heart, and hold it fast, and bear fruit with perseverance.*

While Luke does make it more clear how the Word was received, we already know how it was received, by the action that it produced. Thus even if the

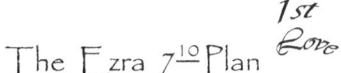

Scripture had only said, "this is the man who hears the Word and bears fruit," we would already know a lot by meditating on "bears fruit." We would know that the Word was sown deep into the heart of the individual. In all likelihood strong roots developed, and a continual supply of faith was turned into practice that yielded much fruit of the Spirit.

The ultimate outward sign of true belief has and always will be bearing fruit. This discussion on Quiet Time does not permit a lengthy discussion of fruit. However, please look at the following list (taken from Galatians 5:22, 23): *love, joy, peace, patience, kindness, goodness, faithfulness, gentleness, self-control.* Since the first fruit mentioned in the verse is love, and since Paul mentions in 1 Corinthians 13 that love is the *greatest*, we have also included in the Ezra 7:10 Plan (Book 1) an in-depth study of love, to encourage our personal growth in this area.

Another aspect of fruit is that it contains seeds. These seeds can then be planted to grow even more fruit, for an ever-increasing abundance of fruit. When we get to the point where God is using us to spread the seeds of our fruit, and we see this fruit reproduced in others, then truly our harvest will be plentiful. We will see new plants grow (new believers), and existing plants flourish (growing disciples), all as a result of God blessing our fruitfulness.

The following tables sum up the passage that we have been studying. It is quite clear from this summary, as we have stated before, that fruit is the true outward indicator of saving faith, and of a true believer. For seekers, the Word that is being snatched, burnt or choked is the Word of salvation that is able to atone for their sin and make them born again as a true child of God.

But also for believers, this is a good picture of how some branches in our life seem to take forever to bear fruit. The key is the interest and the initial response. We may put some of the Word deep into our hearts, but other parts of Scripture we may struggle with applying.

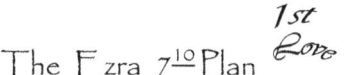

The Ezra 7:10 Plan DISCIPLE SKILL Quiet Time

These are the seeds that are being snatched away, scorched or choked, before they have a chance to grow or bear fruit. We need to break up the hardened soil of our lives in those weak areas in order to have the seed (Word) planted deep into our heart. Yes, the key is getting the seed deep into good soil.

Summary of the Parable of the Sower

Seed Sown	Interest	Initial Response	Final Response
Path (Hard Soil)	Hear Only	No desire to understand	Stays away
On Rocky Places	Hear Only	Emotional	Quickly falls away
In Thorns	Hear Only	Intellectual	Pursues other things
In Good Soil	Hear, Understand, Obey, Teach	Willful, Intellectual, Emotional	Follows the Word

Seed Sown	Final condition of seed or plant	Reasons
Path (Hard Soil)	Snatched away	Hard Hearted
On Rocky Places	Scorched	Offended by Trouble And Persecution
In Thorns	Choked	Worries, Pursuit of Wealth, Pleasure
In Good Soil	Growing, Fruit bearing	Faith, Obedience

The Ezra 7:10 Plan *1st Love*   DISCIPLE SKILL Quiet Time

Believers bear fruit and mature believers bear much fruit. As we may discern from the list of fruit in Galatians mentioned above, it does not mention money, business success, and personal skills as fruit. As believers, we must be aware that the fruit of the Spirit *is the list that counts!* All of the things that we have achieved in this world will pale in comparison to achieving (bearing) fruit. It is the fruit in our life, these character qualities that emulate the person of God, that will bless us, and more importantly, will make us a true blessing to others.

Jesus says that we can tell where a person stands by watching for the fruit. In the following passage Jesus talks about how we can discern between true and false prophets, but it is also applicable for discerning between true believers and false believers.

Matthew 7:16-20 *You will know them by their fruits. Grapes are not gathered from thorn bushes nor figs from thistles, are they? So every good tree bears good fruit, but the bad tree bears bad fruit. A good tree cannot produce bad fruit, nor can a bad tree produce good fruit. Every tree that does not bear good fruit is cut down and thrown into the fire. So then, you will know them by their fruits.*

Now in some cases we cannot always be sure, because we cannot see into a person's heart. We should never judge people based on a few actions, but over time. And we should never give up on people, period. That is for God Himself to decide.

The tables above will also give us some insight into how we will be attacked to prevent the seed from growing into maturity. The very Word that brings life to us may be snatched away because we have made no time to grab it. In some cases our initial excitement about following the Word in a particular area may be met with ridicule or pessimism, which will cause us to lose this fervor, and our root being scorched dies, and our enthusiasm dies with it. In other cases, we solidly believe the Word in a certain area of our life, and begin to pursue it, but then we become busy with the things of this world. Slowly but surely, our convictions become buried and choked by other seemingly more important or pressing concerns, and our pursuit of the Word dies from suffocation. In some cases God

The Ezra 7:10 Plan *1st Love* DISCIPLE SKILL Quiet Time

Himself may be desperately trying to get through to us. But instead of making time to hear and understand what He is saying we allow other things to take away this time.

This in part may help to explain why there is variability in fruitfulness from one person to the next. Both our understanding and our obedience will determine our fruitfulness. We can be very obedient to the Word, but if we have read or studied very little of the Bible we will not produce as much fruit. Conversely, if we study and understand the Bible from cover to cover, and yet we pick and choose only what we want to obey, we will not bear as much fruit as possible.

We will explain this in mathematical terms. If complete understanding of the Bible on a scale of 1 to 10 equals a 10, and complete obedience on a scale of 1 to 10 equals a 10, then let us say fruitfulness is the *product* of understanding times obedience. Thus absolute understanding met with perfect obedience yields maximum fruitfulness (i.e., 10 x 10 = 100 QED). Using this example, and knowing that we are all not "perfect tens" in both categories, shows how we can have this variability in fruitfulness. All formulas aside, to produce fruit continuously, we simply must continue to increase our understanding of the Word of God, and continuously put it into action.

Now, this is obviously a bit simplistic; and yet, following Jesus is not really supposed to be complicated. One important additional way to become fruitful should be mentioned here. That is the way of faith.

There are times when we will not initially understand the Word or we will think that it may be impossible for us to obey a certain teaching. This is where faith comes in. We can obey the Word because the Word itself is trustworthy. It will never fail us. We can obey the Word because we know the Lord will only ask us to do something that He knows is possible, and is in our best interests. Each time we step out in faith, even when we do not understand or are fearful, the Lord will confirm that following His Word yields the best results. In this way we build our confidence in the Word, we build our faith in the Lord, and of course, we will bear much fruit.

The Ezra 7:10 Plan  DISCIPLE SKILL Quiet Time

As we get to know Christ, our desire will grow to be like Him in all ways, and will eventually cause us to bear much fruit. It is hoped we will heed the warnings in the *Parable of the Sower* and make sure as we spend time with the Lord and His Word, we seek to understand it fully, accept it, hold it fast, and joyfully put it into fruitful practice as His disciple and friend.

John 15:12-17 *This is My commandment, that you love one another, just as I have loved you. Greater love has no one than this, that one lay down his life for his friends. You are My friends if you do what I command you. No longer do I call you slaves, for the slave does not know what his master is doing; but I have called you friends, for all things that I have heard from My Father I have made known to you. You did not choose Me but I chose you, and appointed you that you would go and bear fruit, and that your fruit would remain, so that whatever you ask of the Father in My name He may give to you. This I command you, that you love one another.*

The Ezra 7:10 Plan — 1st Love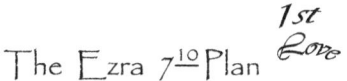

DISCIPLE SKILL Quiet Time

Our Focus

Every Day with God

So how do we spend time with God? We know how to spend time with our friends and family, yet to some of us, spending time with God seems so foreign and we find ourselves at a loss as to how this is done.

While there are many ways to do this, just as there are many ways to spend quality time with friends, perhaps it is best to focus on what we want to accomplish.

First, we want to know God. This is best accomplished by reading the Bible. But more than just reading, we want to focus on understanding the character and purposes of God. We should learn his commands for us, and the actions that He has taken on our behalf. But more importantly, we should try and understand *why* He commands us to do certain things, and *why* He acts in certain ways in certain circumstances. The Bible in some sense is like God's autobiography. The more we understand the why, the more we will really know the Lord; and we will begin to see His unmistakable fingerprints on our lives and the lives of others.

We will be able to discover what is true and false, what is prophecy and what is heresy, and what is sound doctrine and what is false doctrine. The best way to discern the genuine from the fake is to know the genuine so well that it is easy to spot any imitation.

It is comforting to know that the Bible says that God never changes. This is a true statement. God displays many moods in the Bible, but He is always consistent. For example, He does not display anger inappropriately, nor does He forgive indiscriminately.

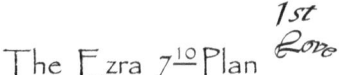

Knowing how God deals with others will help us discern how He is dealing with us.

Second, we want to know what He wants us to do as His disciple and as a child of God. As we begin to see who He is, and what He wants us to do in general, we will begin to discern what He wants us to do in particular. For example, we know that He wants us to pray, but perhaps He may want us to pray for a particular person, church or ministry. We know He wants us to work to pay for living expenses, but perhaps there is a particular job He wants us to do. We know He wants us to minister to others, but perhaps there is a particular ministry He wants us involved with. Also, included in telling us in particular what He wants us to do, we simply must be able to discern when God is telling us to avoid something.

To accomplish this, as we read the Bible we should always be asking ourselves if God is trying to tell us something about our current circumstances. God not only wants us to know Him, He wants to instruct us daily on what lies ahead that day, and perhaps even prepare us for events in the future.

Keeping our Focus — Sharpening our Focus

Probably the biggest reason people do not *hear* the Holy Spirit, is that they do not spend time with God on a consistent basis, and they do not spend time really meditating on what the Word is saying to them in particular. God is trying to speak to them through the Holy Spirit, but it is as though they are hearing only every third or fourth word, because they are not spending enough time with God to be able to discern anything.

One of the things we will discover as we spend consistent time with God is that we will see how God is dealing with us and our circumstances in a way that is unique to us. God does this for His children so that they can clearly recognize that it is the Lord's handiwork, and not just fate or luck or something else. He will affirm and confirm our prayers, answer our doubts, and ease our fears in a way that we will know that it is unmistakably from God. The Bible is very clear on

The Ezra 7:10 Plan *1st Love*   DISCIPLE SKILL Quiet Time

this. A heart that desires to understand God will understand God. Eyes that desire to see God, to see him act in their life and the lives of others, will see God act. Ears that long to hear that still small voice of God will hear, even amidst the noise of the world. When we seek him with all our heart we will find Him.

Although we touched on barriers to knowing God such as amusement and entertainment, there are other barriers that prevent us from properly understanding what God is trying to say to us. We ourselves can become a barrier to a close relationship with God if we lose the desire to bear fruit and lose our trust in Him. It all starts when we begin to go our own way. We must remember that although our Father wants to bless us materially, He is more interested that we bear spiritual fruit, and that we follow His ways.

Instead of spending consistent time with God discerning His will we may justify our actions and lack of fruit by saying things such as: *I am not as bad as this other person* (justifying our bad habit because it is not as bad as another's); or *this other person is making me this* way (meaning I do not have to take responsibility for my actions); or *I just cannot do what God is asking me to do* (meaning I don't trust or believe that God will help me grow in this area).

Another way that we subtly go astray is that we just do whatever we think is best and let God sort it out. We can start to think that God helps those who help themselves, which is not in the Bible, and reflects the thinking of someone who still wants to be in charge of his or her life. The Old Testament especially is full of examples of people who say they want to follow God's ways, but in reality they want what they desire or what makes them feel comfortable. These people try to justify their actions by using nice-sounding excuses, or by following what they think their image of God would say or do in a particular situation.

So how do we misinterpret what God is trying to say to us? Well, for example, God may be trying to get us to break a bad habit, but we do not see it that way, or we do not think we can do it. So instead of following a tougher course of action we may take the easy way out or do nothing.

A multitude of examples of this are in the Old Testament. His usual way of reminding us of needed changes in our life is through the Word, our daily Quiet Time, church, music, other believers, and sometimes circumstances. He does not delight in tripping people up to teach them, but He may use any method if He sees that we are starting to get complacent, and our mind, eyes and ears are starting to close.

One of the reasons David was a man after God's own heart was not that he was perfect. When David was challenged on a particular bad action or behavior, he did not make excuses, but fully agreed with God that he was in the wrong and willingly accepted his discipline. Fully agreeing with God about what is wrong, and turning away from our sinful actions, is the true definition of repentance. Just saying we are sorry does not necessarily mean we agree that what we did was wrong. Now God is not just trying to ping us for every little step we take off the straight and narrow. He gives us leeway to stray a little and then He will gently bring us back. It is hoped we will recognize this because we are in touch with Him on a daily basis with an open heart. Only when we seem to be developing a pattern of going our own way does He step up the discipline, just as a good father should.

To further this discussion let us look at the example of the Nation of Israel after they had been set free from their bondage in Egypt. That is symbolic of our being set free from the bondage of sin. Although God did promise them that they would be traveling to the Promised Land where they would experience material blessing, it was always predicated on following His ways as stated in the Law, the Books of Moses. The wilderness journey was a chance for each person to get to know God and His ways, and to develop a close relationship with his Lord. If we closely follow the journey, we will see that God was a very visible presence day and night. He desired a close relationship with His true children. His main goal was to teach them what it meant to be a child of God. But a great majority of the people cared only about the blessing part. They did not want to experience thirst or hunger or fear. They wanted all these things eliminated.

The Ezra 7:10 Plan *1st Love*   DISCIPLE SKILL Quiet Time

While God was trying to train up these children, the majority of the people wanted nothing of it. They completely missed what God was trying to accomplish for good in their lives. We should remember this before we start getting into a pattern where we are constantly asking God to bless us and answer our prayers so that we can do what *we* want instead of what our *Father* wants.

James 4:3 *You ask and do not receive, because you ask with wrong motives, so that you may spend it on your pleasures.*

Very subtly over time, we can begin to think that God is *our* resource who will give us what *we* want so that we can live how *we* want. God does desire to bless us, but He is more concerned that we bear spiritual fruit.

Before we start off on the wrong foot, it is best to realize that God wants us to bear fruit, such as love, joy, peace, patience, kindness, goodness, faithfulness, gentleness, and self-control. And for many of us who need work in these areas, one way to develop character is to experience adversity, in order to foster character growth. Thus, the next time we face the same adversity, we can more easily face it because of our more mature behavior and outlook. The following scenarios will give us some further insight into how God encourages and admonishes us to grow in His character, as we grow in our relationship with Him.

Let us start with the person who is just starting off on a new life in Christ. To encourage us to grow in a particular area the Lord will teach us through His Word, and other people, and as we take baby steps in the right direction He will most likely bless each correct step we take. He will continue this blessing as our actions turn into good habits. He may also bring people into our lives that exhibit very mature fruit that we admire so as to spur us on to be like Christ. That is just like the Lord to bring mentors our way to show us good visible examples. Daily Quiet Time helps us to recognize that this is what the Lord is doing for us!

Now what happens when we start developing bad character habits? Perhaps instead of being encouraged by other people, we try to find faults in them in order to justify why we do not listen to them. By overlooking even their good qualities we are missing God's messages to us through them. God may then try to show us where we are lacking in character by sending people into our lives that exhibit the same poor character qualities that we have. To those of us who are constantly angry, He may send angry people. For those of us who constantly criticize people, He may send people our way that do not encourage us in our good deeds, but will only criticize our failings. We may see the light and change our behavior. But conversely, instead of seeing ourselves in their actions, we may just criticize their poor behavior, not knowing that we act the same way. God will be creative and will never stop until we recognize our bad behavior and truly repent. This process may take awhile. That time frame is up to us.

And finally, what about those mature believers who are progressing well? Does God just leave them alone? He will bless their efforts of course, but God will continue to strengthen even their strengths. One key way is through adversity. God may place adversity or poor character examples in front of us to show us our bad sides, but He may also place adversity in our path (even if we are walking well) to make sure that we are still growing deeper in His character. He is exhorting us to be holy, simply because He is holy. One of the signs of a mature believer is that we do things for the Lord, less and less for the blessings that follow, but more and more just to please our Father. The Lord will allow us to experience circumstances that challenge our motives. If we follow God only when blessings follow, then our growth will eventually suffer. The Lord gently guides us into a more committed relationship and to a point where we are capable of withstanding just about anything, while still bearing much fruit. Again, daily Quiet Time is the only way we will continue to progress into an ever-deepening relationship with the Lord. And what a full and exciting life it will be! For example, while the lives of Moses, David and Paul ran the gamut of experiences, they would all agree that living for the Lord is the most fulfilling thing we can ever do.

We need to ask ourselves how often we beg God to give us more love, or more patience, or more kindness. This is what we need to focus on. Brother Lawrence (Nicholas Herman) reminds us of this in a book (*The Practice of the Presence of*

The Ezra 7:10 Plan 1st Love 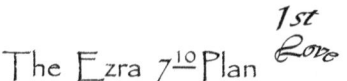 DISCIPLE SKILL Quiet Time

God: The Best Rule of Holy Life) containing several of his conversations and letters. Some excerpts follow:

That many do not advance in the Christian progress because they stick in penances, and particular exercises, while they neglect the love of God, which is the end...That there needed neither art nor science for going to God, but only a heart resolutely determined to apply itself to nothing but Him, or for His sake, and to love Him only. – from the Third Conversation

That we ought not to be weary of doing little things for the love of God, who regards not the greatness of the work, but the love with which it is performed. — from the Fourth Conversation

That the greater perfection a soul aspires after, the more dependent it is upon Divine Grace. — from the Fourth Conversation

God knoweth best what is needful for us, and all that He does is for our good. If we knew how much He loves us, we should be always ready to receive equally and with indifference from His hand the sweet and the bitter, all would please that came from Him. The sorest afflictions never appear intolerable, but when we see them in the wrong light. When we see them in the hand of God, who dispenses them when we know that it is our Father who abases and distresses us; our sufferings will lose their bitterness, and become even [a] matter of consolation.

Let all our employment be to know God; the more one knows Him, the more one desires to know Him. And as knowledge is commonly the measure of love, the deeper and more extensive our knowledge shall be, the greater will be our love; and if our love of God were great we should love Him equally in pains and pleasures.

Let us not amuse ourselves to seek or to love God for any sensible favours (how elevated soever) which He has or may do us. Such favours, though never so great, cannot bring us so near to God as faith does in one simple act. Let us seek

The Ezra 7:10 Plan 1st Love   DISCIPLE SKILL Quiet Time

Him often by faith. He is within us; seek Him not elsewhere. Are we not rude and deserve blame, if we leave Him alone, to busy ourselves about trifles, which do not please Him and perhaps offend Him? Tis to be feared these trifles will one day cost us dear.

Let us begin to be devoted to Him in good earnest. Let us cast everything besides out of our hearts; He would possess them alone. Beg this favour of Him. If we do what we can on our parts, we shall soon see that change wrought in us which we aspire after. – from the Fifteenth Letter, two days before his death at age 86 in the year 1691 AD.

To echo what Brother Lawrence says about God doing things for our good, consider someone who may be praying for a certain type of job, or looking for prestige or for a certain situation to change that God knows would actually be bad for him. The Lord will frustrate his plans until he realizes that the goal is not getting what he wants, but pressing on towards what he needs to be.

If our self-made plans will affect our growth as a believer negatively, then as a good father He will make sure those plans do not succeed. Sadly many of us are so wrapped up in our own plans that we have to experience failure after failure until we realize that we are acting like the Israelites in the desert. God does not want us to fail, but if failure is the only way He can get our attention, then He will allow us to fail. Our spiritual growth is the most important thing to God. He does not mind pruning some bad branches in order for us to experience optimum growth. We can avoid this constant pruning if we yield to His ways early on. We should not stubbornly insist on our own way or say we just cannot follow God's ways, because they are too hard for us or we are too afraid to trust Him. As Brother Lawrence says, *Let us begin to be devoted to Him in good earnest.*

Two great verses to pray every day are what David penned in Psalm 139:

Psalm 139:23, 24 *Search me, O God, and know my heart; Try me and know my anxious thoughts; And see if there be any hurtful way in me, And lead me in the everlasting way.*

The Ezra 7:10 Plan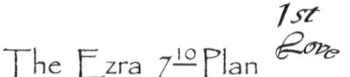

DISCIPLE SKILL Quiet Time

In summary: We want to know God, we want to know what He wants us to do as His disciple, and as we keep and sharpen our focus we want to reflect His character in what we do as a faithful child of our Father. Quiet Time helps us accomplish this.

Build Consistency with Goals and Structure

We can start off well if we set some solid goals. For example, we can plan for one week or one month that we will not miss our Quiet Time no matter what. Once we complete a week or month, we will be amazed at the difference, and it is hoped we will begin a lifelong habit that will transform our life forever as we see God as never before.

Ephesians 2:10 *For we are God's workmanship, created in Christ Jesus to do good works, which God prepared in advance for us to do.*

So now that we have set the time aside, what are some good practical things to do during our time with God? Here are a few ideas:

- Spend a minimum of 15 minutes and watch it grow to 30 minutes or longer
- Pick or make a time of the day that we know is most often free from distractions
- Use a Bible-reading plan (We may want to start in the New Testament, but we should try and read through the entire Bible every year)
- Write notes in our Bible as we read
- Keep a Quiet Time journal of thoughts
- Spend a few minutes after we read, meditating and praying about what we just read, reflecting on how it applies to us and to our particular circumstances

And throughout the day we may:

- Memorize a Scripture that we read that day
- Pray for others
- Be watchful for God to answer our prayers
- Tell another person about our time with God

Final thoughts on keeping our focus...

We need to resist the impulse of turning our Quiet Time into just something that is on our to-do list. Our time with God needs to be unhurried. As we read through selected portions of the Bible, we need to have the time to meditate on the Word, ask God questions, reflect on what it means, etc. We should not feel that we have to hurry up and read a few chapters of the Bible. Perhaps during our Quiet Time God will ask us to pray for certain people or to look up some Bible cross references. We may even feel moved to sing or play a song. We need to have the freedom (from tight time constraints) to go where God may be leading us. And let us not think that we need to limit ourselves to just one Quiet Time a day.

Why did we recommend (not require) 15 minutes? Well, for several reasons. Sadly, today we actually have well-meaning Christian authors who develop devotions for people on the go that only take five or six minutes of our time. We have other publications advertising quick and easy ways to get our devotion time in. This is sad really. Firstly, it is turning a special time into some type of Pharisaical regulation. Secondly, it implies that the process of spiritual growth can somehow be shortened. Lastly, it is an insult to the Lord of Glory that we would want to spend so little time with Him after all He has done for us. Remember, God has gone to great lengths for us, and we should be willing to go to great lengths for Him.

No, my friends, 15 minutes is by no means a lot of time. We can just ask ourselves that if getting to know God is priority one in our life, would 5 minutes a day really reflect that priority? For example, if exercising to get in shape was a priority, would spending 5 minutes a day exercising reflect that priority? I think we know the answer.

Put another way, if God called us or sent us an e-mail and said He would really like to meet with us every day for an hour, would we be there? Would we make the time? Oh I think we would! Let us start with 15 minutes and see how it grows from there. Your Father is really looking forward to it!

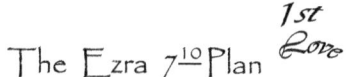

DISCIPLE SKILL Quiet Time

Our Field

Explaining God

Keep it Simple

This book has taught us much about Quiet Time, the benefits, the pitfalls to avoid, and how to put it into practice. But if we take an additional step and prepare a small teaching in order to instruct others we will help solidify this activity in our lives and in the lives of others. Preparing ourselves to teach others what we have learned is a great way to accomplish Christ's *Great Commission* found in Matthew 28:19, 20.

Go therefore and make disciples of all the nations, baptizing them in the name of the Father and the Son and the Holy Spirit, teaching them to observe all that I commanded you; and lo, I am with you always, even to the end of the age.

In order to explain anything first we must decide on the major points of emphasis. We should also pick our time frame. We should develop one-minute and perhaps three-minute versions to be prepared for those casual conversations. We need to be able to hit the high points without going into too much detail.

This book has been organized using easy-to-remember titles and sub-titles. Each title has two words, the first beginning with the letter "O" and the next with the letter "F." The sub-titles are equally easy to remember as the first word begins with the letter "E" and the last word begins with the letter "G."

Strung together the titles and sub-titles are as follows:

Our Father:	Experiencing God
Our Failures:	Extinguishing God
Our Fruit:	Ever-increasing in God
Our Focus:	Every Day with God
Our Field:	Explaining God

A possible outline of key points per section is included at the end of this discussion. We encourage everyone to develop individual outlines and key points as well. One easy way to pass on a particular teaching in just a few seconds is to memorize a few key points in each section. If the person we are talking to has more time or interest we can expand as he asks questions. By using easy-to-memorize titles and sub-titles, it makes it that much easier to recall the material.

By being familiar with all the key points of each section we can tailor our conversation about Quiet Time depending on the needs of the individual. We may have to deal with different issues related to Quiet Time. For example, someone may need to know how to start; another person may not be getting a lot out of his Quiet Time and may need some encouragement. Someone who is completely unfamiliar with Quiet Time may ask us to explain the whole concept. We may see others who are allowing the ways of the world to crowd out their time with God and we can warn them of the pitfalls they are heading into and remind them of the blessings of Quiet Time. Of course if we are developing a more formal teaching on the subject of Quiet Time we can use the full outline and go into each key point more systematically and in more detail.

So our assignment is to use the outline at the end of this section as a guide, but to develop our own outline in our own words. It is fine to use some of the outline if needed. It is best to make the outline with its key points *our own* so we can more readily share it in our own unique way.

The Ezra 7:10 Plan *1st Love*   DISCIPLE SKILL *Quiet Time*

Motivate — Encourage

We should make it one of our goals to share some aspect of Quiet Time with another person each and every week! People are motivated to spend time with God when they see and hear of others doing the same thing. We should share the highs and lows (keep it real) as the apostle Paul says:

Philippians 4:11-13 *Not that I speak from want, for I have learned to be content in whatever circumstances I am. I know how to get along with humble means, and I also know how to live in prosperity; in any and every circumstance I have learned the secret of being filled and going hungry, both of having abundance and suffering need. I can do all things through Him who strengthens me.*

Our part in equipping new disciples will have eternal results! The harvest is indeed plentiful but the laborers are so few.

Perhaps we should think as Brother Lawrence has said that our real employment is to know God (and make Him known). Many people view serving the Lord as something they do only if there is time left after they go to work, fulfill other obligations, spend time with friends and family, etc.

How would it be if we told others that we are employed by God? Now what would happen if this was our true mind set? What if all of our earthly work that we do for pay, all our possessions, all of our friends and family, all our free time, were simply part of and subservient to our heavenly employment? Think about it.

The outline follows.

The Ezra 7:10 Plan *1st Love*   DISCIPLE SKILL Quiet Time

Quiet Time Outline

Our Father: **Experiencing God**

Why Our Father is worth our time
- *He never gives up on people*
- *He cares about us*
- *The Lord cherishes communing with us*
- *God has gone to great lengths for us, we should go to great lengths with Him*
- *It is exciting to see how He leads us*
- *He is our source of total supply*

Our Failures: **Extinguishing God**

Distractions from spending time with God
- *Amusement*
- *Entertainment*

Our Fruit: **Ever-increasing in God**

Insights from the Parable of the Sower
- *A person controlled by the Holy Spirit will produce fruit*
- *We must make sure that our heart is receptive to the Word, so that it goes deep into our heart – Hard Soil*
- *The long haul cannot be fueled just by emotion, but by devotion – Rocky Soil*
- *We will not bear fruit if we allow the things of the world to choke us – Thorny Soil*
- *Keys to fruit bearing: Hear the Word, Hold the Word in an Honest Heart – Good Soil*

The Ezra 7:10 Plan *1st Love* DISCIPLE SKILL Quiet Time

Our Focus: Every Day with God

How to
- *Pick an unhurried time slot*
- *Spend a minimum of 15 minutes and watch it grow*
- *Pick or make a time of the day that we know is most often free from distractions*
- *Use a Bible-reading plan*
- *Write notes in our Bible as we read*
- *Keep a Quiet Time journal of thoughts*
- *Spend a few minutes after we read, meditating and praying about what we just read, reflecting on how it applies to us and to our particular circumstances*
- *Memorize a Scripture that we read that day*
- *Pray for others*
- *Be watchful for God to answer our prayers*
- *Tell another person about our time with God*

Bibliography

Aland, B., Aland, K., Black, M., Martini, C. M., Metzger, B. M., & Wikgren, A. (1993, c1979). *The Greek New Testament* (4th ed.). Federal Republic of Germany: United Bible Societies.

Herman, Nicholas (c. 1605-1691). The Practice of the Presence of God: The Best Rule of Holy Life. Public Domain.

Merriam-Webster, I. (1996, c1993). *Merriam-Webster's collegiate dictionary.* (10th ed.). Springfield, Mass., U.S.A.: Merriam-Webster.}

New American Standard Bible : 1995 update. 1995. LaHabra, CA: The Lockman Foundation.

Strong, J. (1996). *The exhaustive concordance of the Bible : Showing every word of the test of the common English version of the canonical books, and every occurence of each word in regular order.* (electronic ed.). Ontario: Woodside Bible Fellowship.

Swanson, J. (1997). Dictionary of Biblical Languages with Semantic Domains : Greek (New Testament) (electronic ed.). Oak Harbor: Logos Research Systems, Inc.

Ammo

Prayer & Petition

The Ezra 7:10 Plan *1st Love*

Prayer & Petition

> **AMMO**

The Ezra 7:10 ™ Plan includes a discussion on the full armor of God as mentioned in Ephesians 6:10-18. We have split these weapons of spiritual warfare into two groups: *Armor* and *Ammo* (ammunition).

It is obvious that armor is primarily defensive as it is worn to withstand attacks. However, within the description of the *Armor of God* a few offensive weapons (*Ammo*) are mentioned such as the *Sword of the Spirit* (Word of God). We have also included *Prayer and Petition*, and the *Gospel of Peace*, as examples of offensive weapons we can use to stay on the attack. In this section we will discuss the offensive weapon of *prayer and petition*.

Ephesians 6:18 *With all prayer and petition pray at all times in the Spirit, and with this in view, be on the alert with all perseverance and petition for all the saints,*

It may seem strange to separate petition from prayer, but since the Scriptures make the separation (both Old and New Testaments), we will discuss them individually as well. Although we will discuss these two words separately, it should be noted that *prayer,* when used by itself, normally includes the idea of *petition*. While we may not have thought of prayer as a weapon, after this discussion it is hoped that our eyes will be opened to the tremendous power (and privilege) that is available to us.

The Ezra 7¹⁰ Plan *1st Love*   AMMO Prayer & Petition

This privilege needs to be accessed correctly and used properly; otherwise it will be ineffectual and worthless to us.

Prayer & Petition contains five main sections: *Intimate, Inhibit, Infinite, In to it* and *Inform it*. First in *Intimate* we look at the many dimensions of prayer and petition. *Intimate* also discusses how prayer and petition can enhance our relationship with the Lord. *Inhibit* candidly talks about some common pitfalls and distractions that prevent us from praying as we should. *Infinite* discusses the amazing power that is available to us. In the next section *In to it*, we relay some very tangible ways to get started on our prayer and petition time. Finally, in the last section, *Inform it*, we talk about ways we can teach others to pray.

Remember when the disciples asked Jesus to teach them how to pray? As our prayer life increases people will notice and they will ask us about it. We need to be ready to teach, train, and raise up new prayer warriors.

Before we forge ahead we want to preface the upcoming sections with a word of admonition and encouragement. Praying effectively is not simply kneeling down and talking as some may think. There is some good in doing that. If that is all it takes, however, then Jesus would have communicated that to His disciples. In reality He gave them quite an outline of things to include in prayer, and things not to include in prayer.

In many ways learning to pray is similar to learning how to ride a bike or drive a car. For those who can do both, perhaps we think nothing of all the detailed preparations we go through before and during our voyage. In our mind we simply get on the bike and pedal. We just turn the key and start driving. Our driving is just second nature to us and we may be oblivious to the many things we pay attention to during our travels.

But let us recount our initial learning process for riding a bike or driving a car. All the seeming thousands of instructions! Sit up straight, keep your balance, don't just look down, keep your feet on the pedals, don't forget to use the brake, don't go too slowly, don't go too fast, watch out for that tree. And all the countless

The Ezra 7:10 Plan ~1st Love~ AMMO Prayer & Petition

attempts to ride ending with the bike on top of us, or worse, with us atop a thorn bush. All the while our well-meaning tutors (read: Dad or Mom) telling us how great we were doing even as we plowed into (over) yet another obstacle requiring even more bandages. And yet, a few painful days later we were well on our way to mastering it all. Now we think nothing of hopping on that bike and going for the ride of our lives.

   Such is the process of learning to pray, the right way. Initially as we read through these sections it may seem that there are a lot of things to do and things to avoid doing. But if we are patient and make it our purpose to learn, we will master prayer and thus pray like the Master.

   Remember, just as there are good drivers and bad drivers, there are also effective pray-ers and ineffective pray-ers. The secret is to patiently learn all the Bible says about prayer, and then to put it into practice.

   Many times the difference in skill level between two people is not necessarily in the amount of time they practice, but in how correctly they perform the exercise. Compare two athletes, two musicians, two surgeons, and two artists and perhaps the difference can be boiled down to which one not only did their homework, but did their exercises using the correct form. And while it is true, as we will learn, that the Holy Spirit does help us to pray, we must make sure that we are *in tune* with Him.

   When we learn anything new it is important to practice, but practice correctly. Bad habits early on can be hard to break. So it is with prayer. The good news is that this section on Prayer and Petition is designed to teach us what to do and what not to do. Although it may seem like a lot of information to digest, once we learn to pray the right way, it will all be second nature to us.

   If our prayer life seems lacking in the future we can always return and read again the truths contained in these pages. We can always improve our driving, and we can always improve our prayer life!

The Ezra 7:10 Plan 1st Love   AMMO Prayer & Petition

Intimate

Purposes of Prayer

Prayer has been defined as a conversation with God. This is a good definition and even the Greek will bear that out. The Greek verb *to pray* is προσεύχομαι (*proseuxōmai*). It is a combination of the preposition προσ (*pros*) and the verb εὔχομαι (*euxōmai*). The verb without *pros* is usually translated *to pray* or *to pray to God*. The prefix *pros* means *to* or *toward* and adds definiteness and a conscious direction to our prayers. Prayer is not just talking to ourselves, nor is it wishing or dreaming. Prayer is communication with God, as if He Himself were sitting right next to us. As we pour out our soul to Him in prayer, our relationship with Him will continue to deepen.

Why and how we converse with God will differ depending on our circumstances. Let us first look at different ways we can talk to God *without asking Him for something*.

What we do	What we mean
Cry, Sigh, Groan, Weep	I am sad and I want You to know it
Rejoice, Sing	I am happy and I want You to know it
Give Thanks	Thank You for what You have done
Worship, Praise, Adore, Magnify	Thank You for who You are
Confess, Repent	I am sorry, I performed poorly, I sinned

The Ezra 7:10 Plan *1st Love*   AMMO Prayer & Petition

The order of these actions was intentional in that the usual priority in our prayer life can be *me first*. After we tell the Lord about all our problems and ups and downs, we barely have time to thank, praise and just worship Him. Oh, and admitting that we blew it and sinned somehow is not usually high on our list. Before we get to the asking part of prayer (petition), let us spend some time dwelling on how to develop an intimacy in prayer that perhaps we have not experienced before.

Confession

One key to intimate prayer is to reverse the order of the above and start with confession first. This is very biblical in that to approach our Father at all, we must not be carrying any weight of sin with us. Now most people tend to skip reading the book of Leviticus, but that is a shame. This book more than most will drum in the principle that to approach a Holy God, albeit our Father, atonement must be received for any ongoing sinful thoughts or actions. We are wasting time if we have unconfessed sin on our hearts. Our prayers will not be heard.

Now some may be confused at this point. We may have thought that when we became believers all our sins were forgiven. That is true. When we accepted by faith God's plan of salvation for us we were sealed with the promised Holy Spirit as a sign of the everlasting covenant between us and our Father. We were officially adopted into His Family for all time. Although our entrance into Heaven is assured, the relationship we have with our Father is still based on walking by faith and obedience. Sin is the impediment to our faith and obedience, and thus to a close relationship with the Lord as Isaiah says.

Isaiah 59:2 *But your iniquities have made a separation between you and your God, And your sins have hidden His face from you so that He does not hear.*

We do not need to be perfect to approach God. We do need to have a clear conscience, or a *cleansed* conscience, because in spite of ourselves, we still do commit sin and need to ask for forgiveness. David says it best.

The Ezra 7:10 Plan — 1st  AMMO Prayer & Petition

Psalm 51:2, 3 Wash me thoroughly from my iniquity And cleanse me from my sin. For I know my transgressions, And my sin is ever before me.

Psalm 32:5 I acknowledged my sin to You, And my iniquity I did not hide; I said, "I will confess my transgressions to the Lord"; And You forgave the guilt of my sin.

We often struggle with calling sin a sin, but we must be honest with ourselves, and not just acknowledge sin, but continue to forsake it so that we can be open to God. The Lord knows we will never be perfect, but what He wants is that we submit ourselves to the goal of being perfected by Him. If we truly agree with God that what we have done is sinful and displeasing to Him, then as we move forward we should sin less and less. Confession and repentance basically involve agreeing that God's ways are best and involve turning away from following our own ways. The Lord rejoices at our progress. We do not need to compare ourselves with others. As long as we are moving in the right direction, the Lord will take care of the rest.

So as we approach God in prayer we first make sure our hearts are clean before Him. Sadly, many continually carry around the weight of unconfessed sin, and their relationship with God suffers. Remember, God does not demand instant perfection. He does require that we confess our sins to Him. So instead of hiding our past sins from the One who knows them anyway, we should run to the One who loves us unconditionally and is always ready to move us steadily on to perfection one step at a time. Our relationship with our Father will improve steadily as well! Keeping this in mind will keep us on our way to achieving a close intimate relationship with our God and Father through prayer.

Approaching God without sin (i.e., our sins have been forgiven and put away as far as east is from the west), gives us peace and confidence. But instead of just launching into a one-way dialogue, or firing off a bunch of requests, the best thing to do is to concentrate on the Lord first. Perhaps because we are so rushed for time, or maybe we have not been in the habit of worship, we seldom take the time to thank and praise our Father on a daily basis.

The Ezra 7:10 Plan *1st Love* AMMO Prayer & Petition

Worship

If we look at the people in the Bible who had a great relationship with the Lord, we will discover that praise for God was a regular part of their life. In the hustle and bustle of life our lives can become too *me* centered. To mimic those in the Bible who had a close relationship with God, we also need to mimic the time they invested with God. Spending time with God just praising and worshipping Him without thought to ourselves is not only personally uplifting, but faith building. It is interesting that by concentrating on God in praise and worship, we end up as the major beneficiary. But it makes sense in a way. We are magnifying God, and at the same time extolling the virtues of His counselor, the Holy Spirit who resides within us. So as we *lift up* the Lord, our Spirit, heart, soul, mind and strength are also lifted. What did Jesus say about worship?

John 4:23, 24 *But an hour is coming, and now is, when the true worshipers will worship the Father in spirit and truth; for such people the Father seeks to be His worshipers. God is spirit, and those who worship Him must worship in spirit and truth.*

Thanksgiving

The Lord does so much for us on a daily basis, and often we just do not take the time to show our appreciation. Unfortunately this bad habit of taking things for granted, or expecting things from God, can lead to downright ungratefulness. In severe cases it can lead to extreme bitterness. The Bible encourages us to be faithful in little so that we will be faithful in much. The same holds true with being thankful. Read the verses below and let us ponder how it is possible that nine of the ten people could be so ungrateful.

Luke 17:11-19 *While He was on the way to Jerusalem, He was passing between Samaria and Galilee. As He entered a village, ten leprous men who stood at a distance met Him; and they raised their voices, saying, "Jesus, Master, have mercy on us!" When He saw them, He said to them, "Go and show yourselves to the priests." And as they were going, they were cleansed. Now one of them, when he saw that he had been healed, turned*

The Ezra 7:10 Plan — 1st Love   AMMO Prayer & Petition

back, glorifying God with a loud voice, and he fell on his face at His feet, giving thanks to Him. And he was a Samaritan. Then Jesus answered and said, "Were there not ten cleansed? But the nine—where are they? Was no one found who returned to give glory to God, except this foreigner?" And He said to him, "Stand up and go; your faith has made you well."

Also, it is possible that we may be mad at God for some reason and do not want to thank Him or show appreciation for what He gives us. We may convince ourselves that He is mean, just like the people in the following story.

Numbers 11:4-9 *The rabble who were among them had greedy desires; and also the sons of Israel wept again and said, "Who will give us meat to eat? We remember the fish which we used to eat free in Egypt, the cucumbers and the melons and the leeks and the onions and the garlic, but now our appetite is gone. There is nothing at all to look at except this manna." Now the manna was like coriander seed, and its appearance like that of bdellium. The people would go about and gather it and grind it between two millstones or beat it in the mortar, and boil it in the pot and make cakes with it; and its taste was as the taste of cakes baked with oil. When the dew fell on the camp at night, the manna would fall with it.*

We may also compare our lives to others and our envy deceives us into thinking God is playing favorites, and unfairly blessing others above us. This will also foster an ungrateful attitude.

Matthew 20:8-16 *When evening came, the owner of the vineyard said to his foreman, 'Call the laborers and pay them their wages, beginning with the last group to the first.' When those hired about the eleventh hour came, each one received a denarius. When those hired first came, they thought that they would receive more; but each of them also received a denarius. When they received it, they grumbled at the landowner, saying, 'These last men have worked only one hour, and you have made them equal to us who have borne the burden and the scorching heat of the day.' But he answered and said to one of them, 'Friend, I am doing you no wrong; did you not agree with me for a denarius? Take what is yours and go, but I wish to give to this last man the same as to you. Is it not lawful for me to do what I wish with what is my own? Or is your eye envious because I am generous?' So the last shall be first, and the first last.*

The Ezra 7:10 Plan *1st Love*   AMMO **Prayer & Petition**

No, my friends, we need to show thanks in all things. No matter how small, no matter what our current feelings are, no matter that another's blessing may dwarf ours. Become a thankful person. Be known as a thankful person!

1 Thessalonians 5:18 *in everything give thanks; for this is God's will for you in Christ Jesus.*

So far we have seen that our intimacy in prayer depends on who we regard as the real center of our lives. We approach the Lord through confession, praise and thanks. We can almost visualize this as first being on our knees bowed down then up on our feet, with eyes, head and hands lifted up.

Again, reading Leviticus would open our eyes to this pattern. Are we pushing the Book of Leviticus? We think so. The Lord asked that we would receive atonement for any sin first, before we would offer any fellowship, votive, praise or thank offerings. Even the New Testament bears out this principle.

Matthew 5:23,24 *Therefore if you are presenting your offering at the altar, and there remember that your brother has something against you, leave your offering there before the altar and go; first be reconciled to your brother, and then come and present your offering.*

We will discuss more on the how to's of confession, praise and thanksgiving in the Section *In To It: The Plans for Prayer*. Now that we have properly approached the Lord of Glory and have provided Him with our sacrifices of praise,

Hebrews 13:15,16 *Through Him then, let us continually offer up a sacrifice of praise to God, that is, the fruit of lips that give thanks to His name. And do not neglect doing good and sharing, for with such sacrifices God is pleased.*

... He will say to us, "Now what will you have Me do for you?"

Petition

   The Lord encourages us to ask, seek and knock. Now if the Lord knows our needs and the needs of others, then why does He request that we ask Him to meet these needs? The answer is pretty obvious. He wants us to develop a habit of counting on Him for all our needs as well as the needs of others. Perhaps more importantly He wants us to recognize that He is the one who is providing for us. Our relationship with God can be cemented so close if we grasp this.

   The Old Testament is chock full of stories where people were completely oblivious to God's provision. How would you feel as a parent after faithfully providing for your children year after year, then suddenly your children start giving credit to someone or something else for your gifts? For some, not only did they discount God's acting on their behalf, but actually gave other gods the credit. Or even worse, they completely rejected God's way of provision and sought welfare totally apart from God. This actually happens repeatedly in many Bible stories.

   So how do we develop an ever-deepening relationship with God through petition and avoid the temptation to credit other things for what are really God's actions? How do we stand firm in faith instead of fear and patiently wait for God's provision? How do we recognize God's fingerprints on the gifts He gives us so freely?

   There are many verses all over the Bible we can go through to help us here, but before we inundate ourselves with too many verses let us look at a story. If we were to read the Bible from cover to cover every year, we will notice that one story will be constantly mentioned throughout most of the books of the Old Testament and in quite a few verses in the New Testament. That is the Exodus story.

   Let us recount just a small portion of the wilderness journey in Exodus and see if we can pick up a few good principles for properly, purposefully, patiently, persistently, petitioning the Lord, and for perceiving that He has provided to us

The Ezra 7:10 Plan *1st Love*  AMMO Prayer & Petition

His previously planned precious promises. Anyway, we digress. Let us briefly recount that classic journey from Egypt into the desert wilderness.

Let us look at the story knowing ahead of time that God will be trying to teach us the following about petition: God knows our needs and He alone will be meeting our needs; we can ask in faith and patience instead of fear; God uniquely creates situations of need where He can teach us about His faithfulness when we petition Him, and our motives in petition are important!

Even before the Israelites left Egypt they saw the awesome power of God's hand in the plagues against Pharaoh and his country. They should have realized that God was true to His word. As they left Egypt as promised, the Lord led them via a pillar of cloud by day and a pillar of fire by night. God's visible presence should have been a comfort to them, to remind them that He is near, just a prayer away. Also the Lord did two wonderful things for the people to show His utmost care for them, although they were completely unaware of it.

He did not lead them into the Promised Land the quick way following the coast through the land of the Philistines as Exodus 13:17 states,

Now when Pharaoh had let the people go, God did not lead them by the way of the land of the Philistines, even though it was near; for God said, "The people might change their minds when they see war, and return to Egypt."

He also led them on a course that enticed the Pharaoh to chase them so that ultimately Israel's most immediate concern would be erased. This clearly shows that although we may not understand the path we are on, we can be sure that God is aware of where we are and where we are headed. Unfortunately, many people on that trip did not see it that way.

Most folks who have read through the Bible recall the fact that the Israelites grumbled along their desert journey but it is amazing that many of them grumbled even before they crossed the Red Sea. If God has been faithful in the past to help us, He will be faithful in the future, even if we are in a different situation. The only way to build faith (and patience) and lessen fear is to remember each of God's faithfulnesses to us. Visualize this as stacking them (the faithfulnesses) one by one, like building the foundation of a house. If we are standing on His promises in our spiritual house, we will become stronger and stronger. We simply cannot adopt the attitude that God may fail us the next time. If we start thinking that way, we are constantly breaking the very foundation we are trying to build. We pray in faith, not in fear.

Of course God came through and parted the Red Sea and allowed the Israelites to go through. The Egyptian army was enticed and then trapped within the sea when God allowed the waters to flow back together. Thus not only were the Israelites freed from Egypt, but their enemies were destroyed so they would not have to worry about any attacks from them while they were in the desert.

So we can see that the Lord clearly orchestrated this escape for their good, but also to test their faith. Those who prayed steadfastly even though they were not sure why they were going the *long* way, were rewarded with a stronger faith and a closer relationship with God. The others probably grew angrier and were filled with more doubt because they started to think that this God did not know the best way to handle things. They probably figured that they were *lucky* to escape, and that if they had gone the *shorter* way they would have outrun Pharaoh and would have been in a much better position than they were in now. These same people probably continued to think that this God was weak because it took Him so long and so many plagues to get Pharaoh to agree to release them, and finally defeat him.

Then the Lord set up another test as He allowed them to go without finding water for three days. They came to a place they called Marah because the water they found there was bitter and undrinkable. Some of the people again grumbled at this. Moses petitioned the Lord and He showed him a tree and threw it into the waters and made the waters sweet and drinkable. Just finding drinkable water would have been nice; but it is interesting that the Lord shows them that even in the face of impending disaster (dying of thirst), he can provide a miracle (a tree,

The Ezra 7:10 Plan — 1st Love   AMMO Prayer & Petition

of all things, changes the chemical composition of the water, so that it goes from undrinkable to eminently drinkable, even sweet)!

Once again the grumblers lost a great opportunity to build their faith and relationship with the Lord. The others who placed their faith in God were rewarded with more confidence and patience in the Lord, not to mention an increase in admiration and thankfulness. They began to see that obstacles are opportunities to see God in action. We could go on, as this story contains many more examples. The principles are clear. So now let us answer the questions we asked previously.

So how do we develop an ever-deepening relationship with God through petition and avoid the temptation to credit other things for what are really God's actions? How do we stand firm in faith instead of fear and patiently wait for God's provision? How do we recognize God's fingerprints on the gifts He gives us so freely?

We need to go to God often in prayer and keep our spiritual eyes wide open to discern his answers. We need to keep in memory all the many times God has come through in the past to build our faith for the future. Moses wrote a song about crossing the Red Sea. He even wrote another song before they crossed over the Jordan. That is a really good way to remember things. To recognize God we need to spend time with Him every day and see how He works with us individually. God knows what moves us and what will stop us. If we spend time each day to reflect, we will begin to see the pattern, and recognize God's actions on our behalf. This is the key to discerning answers to our petitions and the key to drawing closer to God. Let us always keep our spiritual eyes wide open so that we can recognize His actions amidst the world we live in.

We will discuss more details on the "How To's" of Prayer and Petition in the sections entitled *Infinite* and *In to it*. But now let us discuss some common pitfalls to Prayer and Petition in the following section *Inhibit*.

The Ezra 7:10 Plan *1st Love* 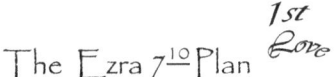 AMMO **Prayer & Petition**

Inhibit

Pitfalls to Prayer

Lack of True Repentance

Sin is clearly the biggest hindrance to prayer. The Old Testament especially is full of admonitions that state the Lord hears the righteous (those who have right standing with God), and does not even hear the prayers of those who are harboring sin.

But before we move on we need to talk about this a little more. First of all it is a tremendous blessing that God gave us a way to have our sins removed each day by our confession and through His intercession on our behalf. In the Old Testament the shedding of blood through the various sacrifices accomplished this until Christ came. We can learn something of God's view of confession, repentance and forgiveness from the Old Testament.

While God commanded a sacrifice for the remission of sins, He also stated on numerous occasions the same sentiments as described in Hosea 6:6,

For I delight in loyalty rather than sacrifice, And in the knowledge of God rather than burnt offerings.

Samuel also echoes these words in 1 Samuel 15:22,

Samuel said, "Has the Lord as much delight in burnt offerings and sacrifices As in obeying the voice of the Lord? Behold, to obey is better than sacrifice, And to heed than the fat of rams."

What can happen over time, especially for a particularly difficult sinful behavior, is that our confession becomes robotic, not heartfelt and almost ritualistic. What the Lord looks for when we sin is that we first call a sin a sin. This agreement with God over our action is what confession is all about. While the Lord will indeed forgive us when we confess our sins to Him, the next steps we take are equally important. The Lord hopes that we will also decide to forsake that sin. It may take a while to completely stop, but with God's help we will stumble less and less. That is what repentance is all about. We decide to turn away from the behavior.

Jeremiah 3:12-15 *Go and proclaim these words toward the north and say, 'Return, faithless Israel, declares the Lord; I will not look upon you in anger. For I am gracious, declares the Lord; I will not be angry forever. Only acknowledge your iniquity, That you have transgressed against the Lord your God And have scattered your favors to the strangers under every green tree, And you have not obeyed My voice,' declares the Lord. 'Return, O faithless sons,' declares the Lord; 'For I am a master to you, And I will take you one from a city and two from a family, And I will bring you to Zion. Then I will give you shepherds after My own heart, who will feed you on knowledge and understanding.'*

Another thing the Lord hopes we develop is an abhorrence of sin, in addition to our fleeing from it. Only then will the path to that particular sin become truly forsaken. This attitude toward sin takes time, but as we draw closer to the light of our lives, we find that darkness only destroys. What we truly want is a life lived in harmony with God.

So we see that forsaking sin is a process. Let us examine two spirals, one good, one very bad indeed: the bad one first.

The Ezra 7:10 Plan — 1st Love 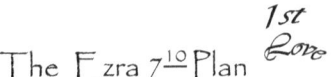   AMMO Prayer & Petition

The Unrepentant's downward spiral

Our Status	Downward Spiral	What we say	What is happening	What it leads to
Dusty	Confession without Repentance	We know we should do better, but...	We do not like sin's effect on us, but we do not hate the sin	Complacency
Rusty	Complacency without Repentance	We can justify it	Sin is not a sin, or is not that bad	Apathy
Cracked	Apathy without Repentance	It is too difficult to overcome	Sin is now beginning to control us	Deprivation
Broken	Deprivation without Repentance	We do not care	Physical, Financial, Personal Loss	Dire Consequences

Time does not permit a lengthy discussion (perhaps in another book), but please review the above carefully. The Bible has plenty of examples of people relying on God after repenting (turning away) to pull them out of this downward spiral.

Psalm 34:11-16a *Come, you children, listen to me; I will teach you the fear of the Lord. Who is the man who desires life And loves length of days that he may see good? Keep your tongue from evil And your lips from speaking deceit. Depart from evil and do good; Seek peace and pursue it. The eyes of the Lord are toward the righteous And His ears are open to their cry. The face of the Lord is against evildoers, ...*

This is such a great verse that Peter quotes from it in 1 Peter 3:10-12.

The Ezra 7:10 Plan 1st Love    AMMO Prayer & Petition

The Repentant's upward spiral

Our Status	Upward Spiral	What we say	What is happening	What it leads to
Clean	Confession with Repentance (Mind)	We know we should do better, and we plan for it.	We do not like sin's effect on us, therefore we plan to flee the sin	Avoidance of sin
Polished	Avoidance with Emotion (Soul, Heart)	We cannot stand the sin	Sin is so bad, that we begin to hate it, its effects on us and on others	Abhorrence of sin
Gold-plated	Abhorrence with Conviction (Strength)	God's mission is too important to allow sin to exist	God's mission is now beginning to control us	Abeyance of sin

To avoid the cycle of sin-repent-sin-repent, we need to plan ahead to avoid sin, and develop an actual hatred of sin. Romans chapter six says it well.

Romans 6:11-14 *Even so consider yourselves to be dead to sin, but alive to God in Christ Jesus. Therefore do not let sin reign in your mortal body so that you obey its lusts, and do not go on presenting the members of your body to sin as instruments of unrighteousness; but present yourselves to God as those alive from the dead, and your members as instruments of righteousness to God. For sin shall not be master over you, for you are not under law but under grace.*

Now that we have covered the primary pitfall to prayer, let us look at a couple more contained in one verse,

1 Peter 4:7 *The end of all things is near; therefore, be of sound judgment and sober spirit for the purpose of prayer.*

The Ezra 7:10 Plan — 1st Love  AMMO Prayer & Petition

Two things are mentioned in order that our prayers succeed: exercising *sound judgment* and being of *sober spirit*. Therefore if we lack these two things our prayers will become hindered.

Lack of Sound Judgment

In 1 Peter 4:7, the actual Greek word for *be of sound judgment* is written as σωφρονήσατε (*sōphronēsate*), and is in the imperative (i.e., it is a command) second person plural form. It can be translated as: *you (all) think sanely, sensibly, clearly, with self-control;* as well as, *be sober-minded.* The word itself contains the Greek for *mind,* or the part of the body believed to contain thoughts, judgments, etc. *Be of sound* or *clear mind* conveys the best meaning in 1 Peter 4:7. The idea is that we are focused and thinking seriously about what we are saying. We have a proper understanding of prayer, how to pray and what to pray for. Let us see if we can discover even more insight as to how we can develop sound judgment in our prayers. Read Matthew 6:5-7.

When you pray, you are not to be like the hypocrites; for they love to stand and pray in the synagogues and on the street corners so that they may be seen by men. Truly I say to you, they have their reward in full. But you, when you pray, go into your inner room, close your door and pray to your Father who is in secret, and your Father who sees what is done in secret will reward you. And when you are praying, do not use meaningless repetition as the Gentiles do, for they suppose that they will be heard for their many words.

To summarize these verses: Let us be genuine and not make an outward show of prayer to impress others; let us be focused and find a quiet place to pray uninterrupted; let us be sincere and avoid using empty words or repetitive phrases or spiritual jargon. We should examine our heart before we pray. We should pray *Your will* be done, not our will as James 4:3 says,

You ask and do not receive, because you ask with wrong motives, so that you may spend it on your pleasures.

The Ezra 7:10 Plan — 1st Love   AMMO Prayer & Petition

The book of 1 John relays the same sentiments as found in the Lord's Prayer as far as praying with respect to the Lord's will (and not our will).

1 John 5:14,15 *This is the confidence which we have before Him, that, if we ask anything according to His will, He hears us. And if we know that He hears us in whatever we ask, we know that we have the requests which we have asked from Him.*

Of course faith is a big factor in prayer as the Scripture says:

James 1:5,6 *But if any of you lacks wisdom, let him ask of God, who gives to all generously and without reproach, and it will be given to him. But he must ask in faith without any doubting, for the one who doubts is like the surf of the sea, driven and tossed by the wind.*

So how can we exercise sound judgment in prayer? Use the following list to remind you.

- ✓ Be righteous (no sin unconfessed)

- ✓ Be genuine (no showy display)

- ✓ Be focused (no wandering thoughts)

- ✓ Be honest (no wordy prayers)

- ✓ Be serious (no frivolous thoughts or wrong motives)

- ✓ Be trusting (no doubts)

- ✓ Be submissive (not your will, but His)

Let us move on to the next pitfall.

The Ezra 7:10 Plan    AMMO Prayer & Petition

Lack of a Sober Spirit

The other term, in the Greek, *be of sober spirit* written as νήψατε (*nēpsate*), is also in the imperative, second person plural form. It can be translated as, *you (all) be clear-headed, restrained, self-controlled,* as well as, *be sober-minded.* While it conveys a similar meaning to *sōphronēsate*, it has a slightly different emphasis. It is perhaps best translated as self-controlled. This term has to do with keeping external influences from negatively affecting us, thus affecting how we pray. The translation of *be sober*, or *be sober-minded* is a good picture in the sense that allowing ourselves to become *drunk* will negatively affect how we pray and what we pray for. But the word *sober* may be limiting in its application, so *self-controlled* is better, in that we need to keep our self controlled from many things, not just alcohol.

Let us look at a few other verses in the New Testament that employ the use of this term.

1 Thessalonians 5:6-8 *so then let us not sleep as others do, but let us be alert and sober. For those who sleep do their sleeping at night and those who get drunk get drunk at night. But since we are of the day, let us be sober, having put on the breastplate of faith and love, and as a helmet, the hope of salvation.*

2 Timothy 4:5 *But you, be sober in all things, endure hardship, do the work of an evangelist, fulfill your ministry.*

1 Peter 1:13 *Therefore, prepare your minds for action, keep sober in spirit, fix your hope completely on the grace to be brought to you at the revelation of Jesus Christ.*

1 Peter 5:8 *Be of sober spirit, be on the alert. Your adversary, the devil, prowls around like a roaring lion, seeking someone to devour.*

We can define being spiritually sober as allowing ourselves to be physically and emotionally controlled by the Holy Spirit. This is one big way the Holy Spirit helps us in prayer. Therefore, when we are not *sober* or we are *sleeping* we are allowing other things to control our behavior. When we do not yield to the Holy

The Ezra 7:10 Plan 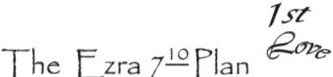   AMMO Prayer & Petition

Spirit, we are not taking up our cross, we are not denying ourselves, and we are not following Christ properly.

When we pray we must be controlled by the Spirit. If we are physically addicted to something it will negatively affect our prayer life. If we are emotionally controlled, by fear, anger, depression, envy, doubt, prejudice, etc., it will negatively affect our prayer life. If we are lured into the pursuit of the lust of the flesh, the lust of the eyes, and the pride of life, it will negatively affect our prayer life. All these unspiritual actions weaken our will, cause spiritual *drowsiness* and will lead to our being *inebriated* by worldliness, and will definitely affect how we pray and what we pray for.

From the above verses let us list by inference what will be lacking in our spiritual lives if we are asleep or not sober:

- ✓ We will forget to arm ourselves with faith, hope and love.

- ✓ We will not be able to endure hardships nor complete our ministry.

- ✓ We will not be prepared for action or we will rely on our own strength instead of God's grace.

- ✓ We will be more easily tricked and deceived by the devil and his ways.

We will be performing the opposite of Luke 9:23,

And He was saying to them all, "If anyone wishes to come after Me, he must deny himself, and take up his cross daily and follow Me,"

It is thus extremely important that we are self-controlled as we approach the Lord in prayer. Otherwise, our thoughts, motives and desires will be negatively affected and our prayers will become ineffectual (i.e., worthless).

The Ezra 7:10 Plan 1st Love    AMMO Prayer & Petition

Now for the good news. Assuming we are approaching the Lord wearing a white robe of righteousness (i.e., sins forgiven), with praise and thanksgiving, with a sound mind and a sober spirit, we can expect heaven itself to be hushed as the Lord waits to hear what we have to say.

Hold on to something — we are now going to talk about the infinite possibilities in prayer!

The Ezra 7:10 Plan 1st Love    AMMO Prayer & Petition

Infinite

Possibilities in Prayer

The Ultimate Guide: The Lord's Prayer

There are infinite possibilities and infinite power in prayer. The key to unlocking this potential is in the understanding of what we have been authorized to pray.

Perhaps the best guide to telling us how and what we should pray is found in what has been termed the *Lord's Prayer*. This is not an actual prayer, but more of a guide on how to pray. It is found in a couple of places in the New Testament, in Matthew 6:9-13 and Luke 11:2-4. Let us look at Matthew's version in detail.

Matthew 6:9-13 *Pray, then, in this way: 'Our Father who is in heaven, Hallowed be Your name. Your kingdom come. Your will be done, On earth as it is in heaven. Give us this day our daily bread. And forgive us our debts, as we also have forgiven our debtors. And do not lead us into temptation, but deliver us from evil.'*

As we further study this, remember that this guide is from the Master. This is what He wanted us to follow. Knowing the original Greek of this passage definitely adds insight to this prayer guide. We shall break this passage down thought by thought. We will move through this quickly and provide more discussion later.

The opening sentence in the original Greek could be more literally translated as:

Our Father, the one who is in heaven, let your name be honored as holy, let your kingdom come, let your will be done on earth in the same way as it is performed in heaven.

75

Next we are instructed to ask for our daily bread. Again the Greek can be more literally translated as, *Give to us today what bread we need.*

Next we are told to ask for forgiveness for our debts (sins). In the Greek we find, *and dismiss our debts as we also have dismissed our debtors.* The last few words, *as we also have dismissed our debtors*, is clearly a reminder that we need to be gracious and forgive others. If we are harboring bitterness towards others, which is a sin, it will be hard for us to have a close relationship with God. He expects us to forgive others as He forgives us.

Next an often misunderstood line, but clear in the Greek, *and may You not have cause to subject us to a trial.* Basically what we are praying for is spiritual readiness. We are telling the Lord that since we are equipping ourselves with the *Armor of God* each day (for example) and are ready for battle (we hope), we have no need for testing, since we are actively engaged in fighting the good fight. The Lord may still send a test our way, but if we are truly denying ourselves and taking up His cross, the test will only serve to give us more confidence as we pass it with flying colors. If we are not battle ready, the Lord's *trial* will show us our deficiencies.

Finally ending with, *rather rescue us away from evil* or *rather rescue us away from the Evil One* (since in the original Greek there is an article in front of the word evil (i.e., *the* evil one), possibly denoting Satan (as in Matthew 13:19)).

Now let us see this more rigorous translation all together now:

Our Father, the one who is in heaven, let your name be honored as holy, let your kingdom come, let your will be done on earth in the same way as it is performed in heaven. Give to us today what bread we need. And dismiss our debts as we also have dismissed our debtors. And may You not have cause to subject us to a trial, rather rescue us away from evil.

Note that the Lord's Prayer is the perfect template as we pray for ourselves but also as we pray for others. We may pray that we advance the Kingdom of God, but

The Ezra 7:10 Plan *1st Love*   AMMO **Prayer & Petition**

we can also pray that God would use our friends in mighty ways. We can pray for our daily necessities, spiritual readiness and rescue and the same for others.

The broad categories of prayer from the *Lord's Prayer* may be stated as follows:

- ✓ Truly Honoring God as Holy   *Worship*
- ✓ Establishing God's Kingdom   *Sound Judgment*
- ✓ Doing God's Will   *Sound Mind*
- ✓ Daily Necessities   *Thanksgiving*
- ✓ Forgiveness   *Confession*
- ✓ Spiritual Readiness   *Self Control*
- ✓ Spiritual Rescue   *Sober Spirit*

It is very interesting that the previous topics that we have discussed (shown in italics above) seem to line up well with the Lord's Prayer categories. So, does the *Lord's Prayer* outline the complete scope of what we are allowed to pray? A great homework assignment would be to fit verses in the Bible that command us to do or pray for something under the above categories. In this way we can see that the *Lord's Prayer* (LP) really does cover everything we have been authorized to pray. We have selected a handful of verses and placed them in the proper categories as an example. Perhaps some verses will fit into more than one category.

LP category: Truly Honoring God as Holy

1 Timothy 2:8 *Therefore I want the men in every place to pray, lifting up holy hands, without wrath and dissension.*

Acts 16:25 *But about midnight Paul and Silas were praying and singing hymns of praise to God, and the prisoners were listening to them;*

1 Samuel 2:1 *Then Hannah prayed and said, "My heart exults in the Lord; My horn is exalted in the Lord, My mouth speaks boldly against my enemies, Because I rejoice in Your salvation."*

The Ezra 7:10 Plan — 1st Love   AMMO Prayer & Petition

LP category: *Establishing God's Kingdom*

1 Thessalonians 3:10 *as we night and day keep praying most earnestly that we may see your face, and may complete what is lacking in your faith?*

Jeremiah 29:7 *Seek the welfare of the city where I have sent you into exile, and pray to the LORD on its behalf; for in its welfare you will have welfare.*

Nehemiah 2:4, 5 *Then the king said to me, "What would you request?" So I prayed to the God of heaven. I said to the king, "If it please the king, and if your servant has found favor before you, send me to Judah, to the city of my fathers' tombs, that I may rebuild it."*

Judges 1:1 *Now it came about after the death of Joshua that the sons of Israel inquired of the Lord, saying, "Who shall go up first for us against the Canaanites, to fight against them?"*

LP category: *Doing God's Will*

James 5:17 *Elijah was a man with a nature like ours, and he prayed earnestly that it would not rain, and it did not rain on the earth for three years and six months.*

Acts 1:24 *And they prayed and said, "You, Lord, who know the hearts of all men, show which one of these two You have chosen"*

Matthew 26:42 *He went away again a second time and prayed, saying, "My Father, if this cannot pass away unless I drink it, Your will be done."*

The Ezra 7:10 Plan — 1st Love   AMMO Prayer & Petition

LP category: *Daily Necessities*

Matthew 22:17 *Tell us then, what do You think? Is it lawful to give a poll-tax to Caesar, or not?*

Isaiah 30:23 *Then He will give you rain for the seed which you will sow in the ground, and bread from the yield of the ground, and it will be rich and plenteous; on that day your livestock will graze in a roomy pasture.*

Exodus 16:29 *See, the LORD has given you the sabbath; therefore He gives you bread for two days on the sixth day. Remain every man in his place; let no man go out of his place on the seventh day.*

LP category: *Forgiveness*

Acts 8:22 *Therefore repent of this wickedness of yours, and pray the Lord that, if possible, the intention of your heart may be forgiven you.*

Matthew 5:44 *But I say to you, love your enemies and pray for those who persecute you,*

LP category: *Spiritual Readiness*

Philippians 1:9 *And this I pray, that your love may abound still more and more in real knowledge and all discernment,*

Mark 14:38 *Keep watching and praying that you may not come into temptation; the spirit is willing, but the flesh is weak.*

Nehemiah 4:14 *When I saw their fear, I rose and spoke to the nobles, the officials and the rest of the people: "Do not be afraid of them; remember the Lord who is great and awesome, and fight for your brothers, your sons, your daughters, your wives and your houses."*

The Ezra 7:10 Plan — 1st Love

AMMO *Prayer & Petition*

LP category: *Spiritual Rescue*

Luke 22:32 *but I have prayed for you, that your faith may not fail; and you, when once you have turned again, strengthen your brothers.*

Jonah 2:1, 2 *Then Jonah prayed to the Lord his God from the stomach of the fish, and he said, "I called out of my distress to the Lord, And He answered me. I cried for help from the depth of Sheol; You heard my voice."*

Genesis 32:11 *Deliver me, I pray, from the hand of my brother, from the hand of Esau; for I fear him, that he will come and attack me and the mothers with the children.*

The *Lord's Prayer* really is our *Mission Statement* and our list of spiritual objectives (purposes) rolled into one. Not only is it the great sieve through which we must pour our prayers, but indeed our life's objectives need to mirror those of the *Lord's Prayer* as well.

Most successful churches (and businesses for that matter) all have a clearly stated mission with a list of goals or objectives that they rally everyone behind. Every project, plan or action taken must be sifted through the mission statement or master plan to make sure that it achieves the correct objective. If it does not it should not be pursued. The plan can also be used to spot ineffective activity. Perhaps an action was started incorrectly, and after further examination it was found lacking. That activity would then be cut.

So it is with prayer. We must use the *Lord's Prayer* to guide us to pray for what truly is in our *Mission Statement* from the Lord. Also we must remember that the *Lord's Prayer* is not a buffet of different offerings. Everything in the *Lord's Prayer* should be included in our prayer time on a regular basis. We cannot just pick and choose to complete the objectives that may be easy for us. We will mature in our prayers and in our prayer time only when we pray through all of the *Lord's Prayer* objectives.

The Ezra 7:10 Plan *1st Love*   AMMO Prayer & Petition

At least two things will happen when we do this. We will become very strong in the Lord, full of faith, and fully faithful. The other is even more wonderful. We will begin to see into the very heart of our Father God. By faithfully praying for the dearest things on God's heart, we will develop a mind set on doing God's will all the time. The distinction between what is and what is not God's will become easier to recognize. No longer will we hope we are in God's will; we will *know* we are in God's will. It will be second nature. It will be that our spiritual nature has now taken control over the fleshly nature. We can now ride that bike with skill and full confidence.

This takes time. But to mature in prayer the right way, we must pray through all of the Lord's objectives regularly. If we practice this incorrectly at the very beginning of our prayer life it can lead to bad habits and confusion later in our prayer life. We can become discouraged and stop praying. Prayer will achieve its intended results if performed properly.

Notice the focus of prayer is really not on us but on honoring God, and seeking to do His will as a citizen of the kingdom of God. When we pray using the *Lord's Prayer* as our guide it also helps us achieve what Jesus calls the two greatest commandments. These two commandments are (one) loving God with everything that we are: heart, soul, mind, and strength, and (two) loving our neighbor as ourselves. So we have a tremendous opportunity through prayer to honor God, serve God, and help others, and ourselves in the process.

Perhaps there are some nagging questions such as, "I know that the *Lord's Prayer* is the perfect guide but how do I know if what I am praying for really fits into one of the categories?" For example, what one may consider a daily necessity, another may consider a luxury. Some may think they have forgiven someone, and yet in reality they still harbor bitterness. Some may think that they are establishing God's Kingdom by praying for a multi-million dollar church building. Some may think that all adversity in their life is not from God but rather from some other source. Yes, there will be confusion at times. How do we keep this confusion to a minimum? Quite simply actually: what does the Word of God say?

81

The Ezra 7:10 Plan 1st Love    AMMO Prayer & Petition

James 1:5,6 But if any of you lacks wisdom, let him ask of God, who gives to all generously and without reproach, and it will be given to him. But he must ask in faith without any doubting, for the one who doubts is like the surf of the sea, driven and tossed by the wind.

1 John 5:14,15 This is the confidence which we have before Him, that, if we ask anything according to His will, He hears us. And if we know that He hears us in whatever we ask, we know that we have the requests which we have asked from Him.

Luke 18:1 Now He was telling them a parable to show that at all times they ought to pray and not to lose heart,

If we are unsure, then we ask God for guidance. Our confidence in prayer comes from knowing that God has authorized what we are praying. So we pray, pray, and pray even more. To develop this wisdom in praying we must consistently spend time with God, spend time in His Word and spend time praying.

It may surprise us but some of the most well-known Christians in America that have suffered through various scandals have all admitted to the same problem: they simply did not spend time with God every day. Some admitted that they had not even read through the entire Bible. While it may have appeared that their ministries were growing, in fact they were building their own kingdoms and not God's. Why do we bring this up? Because it is easy to become discouraged when we see Christians we view as really spiritual *get it so wrong*. But if we go back to the basics, we can see where they made their mistakes.

One thing we should try and keep in mind as we pray. We should be careful about praying so specifically for something that we may miss how the Lord is trying to answer our true need and not our specific request. For example, we may think that the answer to our situation may be a new car, or a new job, or a new boss, or a new church. We may think we need a wife or a husband. We may think we need more play time, less stress, etc. Our mind could be so locked on one specific answer to prayer that it may miss how the Lord is actually meeting our needs. His way will actually be better, just not the way we see it. Remember, we

The Ezra 7:10 Plan 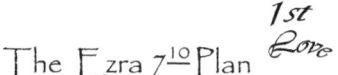   AMMO Prayer & Petition

1st Love

should be of a sound mind and of a sober mind, and not let our own way of thinking limit how God meets our needs.

Proverbs 3:5,6 *Trust in the Lord with all your heart And do not lean on your own understanding. In all your ways acknowledge Him, And He will make your paths straight.*

   Praying in the will of God is not a difficult thing to grasp; rather, it is a difficult thing to be *grasped by*. Many people end letters and e-mails with various phrases such as, *in Christ, in His Service, in His grip, in His grace*, but are they really living that way? If we do not spend time with God, time in prayer and time in His Service every single day, it is doubtful if we have become *gripped by God*. Our confusion in prayer may be coming from the simple fact that we do not have a *firm grip on the plow*. We have not *taken up our cross daily* (maybe weekly, maybe monthly, maybe yearly). Once we set our hearts to live each day for the Lord, amazingly this cloud of confusion starts to clear. What could not be grasped before seems almost black and white now. Prayer is a mighty weapon in the right hands, and in the right heart.

Genesis 32:28 *He said, "Your name shall no longer be Jacob, but Israel; for you have striven with God and with men and have prevailed."*

James 5:16 ...*The effective prayer of a righteous man can accomplish much.*

As Jacob wrestled in prayer, so must we.

Let us move on to some practical ways to pray.

The Ezra 7¹⁰ Plan *1st Love*   AMMO Prayer & Petition

In to it

Plans for Prayer

Fix the Time and Place

Perhaps the best place to look for a plan for prayer should be the Scriptures. We first must choose a time and place. With that in mind let us review the following verses:

Matthew 6:6 *But you, when you pray, go into your inner room, close your door and pray to your Father who is in secret, and your Father who sees what is done in secret will reward you.*

Mark 1:35 *In the early morning, while it was still dark, Jesus got up, left the house, and went away to a secluded place, and was praying there.*

There are many more verses on this same theme. From just these two verses we can see that it is very important to schedule a time for prayer, and to pick a place for prayer that is free from distractions.

We need to find this time and place so that we can become habitual in our prayers. We may have to give up some wordly pleasure in the process, but so much the better, as we are pruning ourselves so that we can bear more fruit. Perhaps we do not need to give up anything per se, but rather we can work more diligently each day to free up some time for prayer. Instead of taking an hour to do something perhaps we can finish it in thirty or forty-five minutes.

In addition to our consistent time in prayer each day, we can supplement it with time throughout the day. If we find ourselves driving, riding, exercising, waiting or with a few free minutes to spare, we can commune with God during those times as well. Perhaps we will not be able to pray audibly, but we can still pray

The Ezra 7:10 Plan    AMMO Prayer & Petition

such that God will hear us. The Holy Spirit can hear our *inward* prayers and convey them to the Lord.

Provide Structure

How do we know what to pray? We should use the *Lord's Prayer* as a guide as we have already discussed. There are also some other tried-and-true simpler acronyms that others have used.

A doration   **J** esus
C onfession   **O** thers
T hanksgiving   **Y** ou
S upplication

Perhaps we can think of an acronym for the *Lord's Prayer*? The following are some attempts.

Declare	*Truly Honoring God*
Disciple	*God's Kingdom*
Do	*Doing God's Will*
Daily	*Daily Necessities*
Debts	*Forgiveness*
Diligent	*Spiritual Readiness*
Deliverance	*Spiritual Rescue*

Reveal	*Truly Honoring God*
Reach Out	*God's Kingdom*
Run the Race	*Doing God's Will*
Re-supply	*Daily Necessities*
Reconcile	*Forgiveness*
Readiness	*Spiritual Readiness*
Rescue	*Spiritual Rescue*

The Ezra 7:10 Plan — 1st Love    AMMO Prayer & Petition

P roclaim	*Truly Honoring God*
R each Out	*God's Kingdom*
A lways in his will	*Doing God's Will*
Y our food	*Daily Necessities*
E rase sin	*Forgiveness*
R eady always	*Spiritual Readiness*
S ave me	*Spiritual Rescue*
W orship	*Truly Honoring God*
A dvance	*God's Kingdom*
R ight path	*Doing God's Will*
R e-supply	*Daily Necessities*
I nnocent	*Forgiveness*
O n guard	*Spiritual Readiness*
R escue	*Spiritual Rescue*

These are just some examples. The idea is to pray thoroughly and thoughtfully. That is the key to a life of individual effectual prayer.

As we pray through the *Lord's Prayer* the Lord will bring things to our mind to pray. As we continue we will find it necessary to write things down and keep a prayer list. We can use this list to record His many answers. This will give us confidence.

Some may argue that if we keep a Quiet Time journal and a Prayer list, we are needlessly complicating things. Not true. In fact a close reading throughout the entire Bible clearly shows that God expressly asked His followers to constantly set up memorials in writing (song), and literally in stone, marking God's answers, victories, reminders and prophecies. The prophets were asked to do all kinds of things to show people God's message as a visible reminder. God wants us to record the present, so that as it fades into the past, our future will become clear, as we remind ourselves of His messages to us. Do not be deceived into thinking that recording our life with God is a needless chore. That is what the deceiver would like us to think. We may start with just a few things on our list. That will grow.

Before we talk about group prayer, one additional word should be mentioned here about praying for people's needs. From Jesus' great prayer detailed in the Gospel of John chapter seventeen, it is clear that God will give us specific people to pray for. Jesus clearly stated who He was praying for and who He was not praying for. We should not just grab a list of dozens of names and start praying. While that may seem to be a spiritual thing to do, in fact, it may not be what God wants us to do. God raised up prophets for very specific areas of ministry. So it is with our prayer ministry. He needs His prayer warriors to fight the right battles. He does not need Jonahs who go their own way and do their own thing. He does not want us to go south when He wants us to go north. If we are open to the Lord in this area and wait for His direction, He will clearly show us the who, what and where.

One final word of admonition here: it has become a disturbing trend in some churches that most of the items on a given prayer list are devoted to only a few things that are mentioned within the *Lord's Prayer*. A close examination of the prayers in the Bible would show that the vast majority of the prayers in the Bible have to do with advancing God's kingdom, and performing His will and helping others to do the same. How often do people stand up and say, *Pray for me that I would share the Gospel boldly where I work*. How often do we see requests for personal discipline, for more love, etc. As the Lord leads, we need to find out the real spiritual needs of people (in a sensitive way of course) and be open to pray for those. We have to be careful that our prayer time is not just an activity that we can *check off our list*. Prayer is a God-directed ministry that we should be excited about and actively participating in.

The Ezra 7:10 Plan 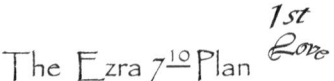   AMMO Prayer & Petition

Group Prayer

Now some may ask about corporate prayer (prayer in groups). This is also encouraged in the Scriptures. Let us review some verses on this topic:

1 Timothy 2:8 *Therefore I want the men in every place to pray, lifting up holy hands, without wrath and dissension.*

James 5:14 *Is anyone among you sick? Then he must call for the elders of the church and they are to pray over him, anointing him with oil in the name of the Lord;*

Acts 16:25 *But about midnight Paul and Silas were praying and singing hymns of praise to God, and the prisoners were listening to them;*

2 Chronicles 6:34 *When Your people go out to battle against their enemies, by whatever way You shall send them, and they pray to You...*

When we pray in groups we may be doing so as part of a church or a specific group within the church. We may be praising God, praying for specific people, works or ministries. The above verses bear this out. The topical context of the verse in 1 Timothy is eliminating dissensions and developing unity. One of the ways to do this is through group prayer. The specific people referenced in the prayer requests of I Timothy chapter two included: *all men, for kings and all who are in authority*. James encourages the leaders of a church to collective prayer for a sick member. These are great reasons for corporate prayer. It unifies the leadership and encourages individual members of the body of Christ. The verse in Acts shows how group prayer can encourage the people praying while they are experiencing difficult times. Group prayer can also serve as a witness and lead others to Christ. Finally, the verse in Chronicles shows an example of praying together when the body of Christ, or a group within the body, sets out to accomplish a particular mission. We can clearly see elements of the *Lord's Prayer* in these prayers.

The Ezra 7:10 Plan — 1st Love   AMMO Prayer & Petition

Yes, group prayer has its place. But we must remember that the group is composed of individuals. And our strength in prayer as a group grows as each individual grows. Thus each of us needs to develop a strong prayer life, and that will help to ensure that the church as a whole will have a strong prayer life.

The Ezra 7:10 Plan  1st Love AMMO Prayer & Petition

Inform it

Passing on Prayer

Motivation

There are many ways to instruct others how to pray and we shall go into a few of them. Before we discuss those perhaps it is best to talk about motivating them to pray first.

As we have said elsewhere in this narrative, praying effectively is not something you master as much as it masters you. Those who have matured in their prayer life know that prayer is not something they do, but something they have become. They do not simply pray here and there; rather, prayer is so woven into their life that not to pray is not to breathe.

One of the best ways to motivate others to immerse themselves into a life of prayer is by getting them to read writings of noted prayer warriors. We have so many to choose from: George Mueller, Charles Spurgeon, Jonathan Edwards, John Wesley, Andrew Murray, Brother Lawrence, John Calvin, St. Augustine and Thomas à Kempis, to name just a very few.

More recently, Edward McKendree Bounds' (1835-1913) series on prayer has served to motivate countless thousands to pray. Although apprenticed as an attorney and admitted to the bar, Bounds felt called to the ministry in his early twenties. He was ordained by his denomination in 1859, and was named pastor of the Monticello, Missouri, Methodist Church. Instead of practicing law, however, He became a chaplain in the Confederate States Army (3rd Missouri Infantry CSA). Bounds was a chaplain in the Confederate States Army during the American Civil War. He was captured by the Union Army in Franklin, Tennessee, and later released. (It is one thing to pray in the comfort of a home or church, but try it on the battlefield. Read his biography, *E. M. Bounds* by Darrel D. King, for even more motivation.) After his release, he strove to build up the spiritual state of Franklin by starting weekly prayer sessions. Bounds was an associate editor of the official Methodist newspaper, *The Christian Advocate*, and compiled numerous books on the subject of prayer (most were published after his death).

The following quote is by Claude Chilton, Jr., in the foreword to Bounds' book *Necessity of Prayer*.

"Edward McKendree Bounds did not merely pray well that he might write well about prayer. He prayed because the needs of the world were upon him. He prayed, for long years, upon subjects which the easy-going Christian rarely gives a thought, and for objects which men of less thought and faith are always ready to call impossible. From his solitary prayer vigils, year by year, there arose teaching equaled by few men in modern Christian history. He wrote transcendently about prayer, because he was himself, transcendent in its practice. As breathing is a physical reality to us so prayer was a reality for Bounds. He took the command, 'Pray without ceasing' almost as literally as animate nature takes the law of the reflex nervous system, which controls our breathing." E.M. Bounds books include: *Power Through Prayer, Purpose in Prayer, Prayer and Praying Men, Possibilities of Prayer, The Reality of Prayer, The Necessity of Prayer,* and *The Weapon of Prayer.*

We should collect a few books on noted prayer warriors that we can hand out to motivate others to a life of prayer.

Of course our own disciplined prayer life and answers to prayer that we can share will also highly motivate others. We should not underestimate this. People are motivated by seeing that we are as fervent about prayer today as we were last year or even ten years ago. They will be even more motivated by observing that what we pray, and how we live, yields results that bring glory to God. Faithful prayer, and faithful lives, will generate enthusiasm. We can count on it. We will be asked, *teach me how to pray as you pray.*

The Ezra 7:10 Plan 1st Love  AMMO Prayer & Petition

Structure

While our prayer disciples are reading the books we give them for motivation, we can add structure to their prayer time. While this time does not always need to follow a rigid framework, some structure is necessary to make sure we follow through with good prayer habits. Remember if we practice wrong, we pray wrong and our prayer life may become aimless and powerless.

At this point we can pass on a good, easily remembered acronym such as those provided in the previous section to provide structure. Or as we have said we can make up our own to pass on. And certainly we will want them to record their prayers and the answers. There are many ways to do this, especially today with many more options (digital devices) to record our prayers.

Encouragement

Finally a good way to pass on prayer, is to pray with the person you are discipling. Pray with them in a variety of settings. Pray with them in church, pray at work, and say grace over a meal with them. Sharing answers to prayer also provides much encouragement as we stated earlier.

When it appears that God is not answering our prayers we can revisit the *Pitfalls* section and make sure we are on the right track. Perhaps all that may be needed on our part is patience.

So collectively we provide the motivation, the structure, and the encouragement. What a wonderful thing to pass on — truly more valuable than gold.

The Ezra 7:10 Plan *1st Love* AMMO **Prayer & Petition**

To all those future prayer warriors out there,

Prayer is not something we do that is a separate activity such as playing a sport or engaging in a hobby. And it is certainly not something we just do while at church. It is our very life. It is who we are. We are children of God and we talk to our Father all the time and every day. It is no chore.

Prayer is the asking, seeking and knocking that opens the door to the most exciting life imaginable.

Bibliography

Aland, K., Black, M., Martini, C. M., Metzger, B. M., Robinson, M., & Wikgren, A. (1993; 2006). *The Greek New Testament, Fourth Revised Edition (Interlinear with Morphology)*. Deutsche Bibelgesellschaft.

Bounds, E.M. (2004). The Complete Works of E. M. Bounds on Prayer: Experience the Wonders of God through Prayer, Grand Rapids, Mich.: Baker Books.

Calvin, J. (1997). *Institutes of the Christian religion*. Bellingham, WA: Logos Research Systems, Inc.

Doulos, Geoseff (2011). The Ezra 7:10 Plan, Book 1 – First Love: *A Heart to Understand*. Front Royal: Ezra 710 publications.

Galli, M., & Olsen, T. (2000). *131 Christians everyone should know*. Nashville, TN: Broadman & Holman Publishers.

King, Darrel (1998). *E. M. Bounds*, Grand Rapids, Mich.: Bethany House Publishers.

Kittel, G., Friedrich, G., & Bromiley, G. W. (1995, c1985). Theological dictionary of the New Testament. Translation of: Theologisches Worterbuch zum Neuen Testament. (243, 284). Grand Rapids, Mich.: W.B. Eerdmans.

Louw, J. P., & Nida, E. A. (1996, c1989). *Greek-English lexicon of the New Testament : Based on semantic domains* (electronic ed. of the 2nd edition.) (1:408). New York: United Bible societies

New American Standard Bible : 1995 update. 1995. LaHabra, CA: The Lockman Foundation.

Spurgeon, C. H. (2006). *Morning and evening : Daily readings* (Complete and unabridged; New modern edition.). Peabody, MA: Hendrickson Publishers.

Strong, J. (1996). The exhaustive concordance of the Bible: (electronic ed.). Ontario: Woodside Bible Fellowship.

Thomas à Kempis. (1996). *The Imitation of Christ*. Oak Harbor, WA: Logos Research Systems.

Wuest, K. S. (1997, c1984). Wuest's word studies from the Greek New Testament : For the English reader. Grand Rapids: Eerdmans.

Armor

What You Wear

Belt, Breastplate and Helmet

The Ezra 7:10 Plan *1st Love*

What You Wear
Belt, Breastplate and Helmet

ARMOR

In this section we will be examining some of the *Armor of God* as mentioned in the Book of Ephesians chapter six.

Ephesians 6:14,17a *Stand firm therefore, having girded your loins with truth, and having put on the breastplate of righteousness, ...and take the helmet of salvation...*

These particular pieces of the *Armor of God* were to be worn as protection and thus they are defensive weapons *against the rulers, against the powers, against the world forces of this darkness,* and *against the spiritual forces of wickedness in the heavenly places* (Ephesians 6:12).

We will discuss each piece separately. We will look into the spiritual aspect of the armor as well as the symbolism of the actual armor itself. It may surprise some but the *Armor of God* is also mentioned in the Old Testament. We will provide a look at some of those verses as well.

The Bible says to take up and put on the full *Armor of God*. It is important that we do not forget to wear all of our armor. We can bet the enemy will attack us first where there is no armor. We do not want to become a casualty of war so easily because we have so poorly equipped ourselves for the battle.

The Ezra 7:10 Plan — 1st Love 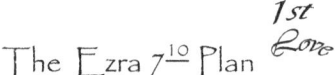 ARMOR   What You Wear

Belt

Before we discuss the symbolism of the belt that helps us *gird our loins with truth,* we need to understand the intended meaning behind the word *truth* in this verse. There are at least two basic translations of this verse, depending on our version of the Bible. One mentions *girding our loins with truth,* the other mentions *fastening the belt of truth around our waist.* In either case the word *truth* in this verse is not to be used as a synonym for the Word of God. Verse seventeen of Ephesians chapter six mentions the *sword of the Spirit* as the Word of God, so it is clear that the word *truth* in this verse stands for something different.

The phrase *with truth* in the Greek is written as, ἐν ἀληθείᾳ (*en alētheia*). The Greek word *alētheia* is normally translated as *truth,* but depending on what preposition is used before it and the context of the sentence, the meaning can change slightly. The expression, *en alētheia* (the preposition in this case being *en,* often translated as *in*), is used in other New Testament books. Some of the phrases include: *walking in truth, whom I love in truth, teach the way of God in truth,* and *in truth and love.* The sense here is that *truth* equates to that which is faithful, genuine, sincere and without any deceit.

Isaiah 11:5 states in part, *...And faithfulness the belt about His waist.* The Greek translation of the Old Testament (*The Septuagint*), translates *faithfulness* as our word *alētheia.* The Hebrew word for faithfulness in Isaiah 11:5 is, אֱמוּנָה (*ʾĕmûnā(h)*). The word is translated variously as *faithfulness, trustworthiness, steadiness, dependability, security* and *truth.*

So the belt we wear signifies that we are faithful, genuine and true. Now that we have that cleared up we can talk about the great symbolism of the belt.

The belt was no mere adornment of the soldier, but an essential part of his equipment. The belt passed around the loins (waist, hips and abdomen) and by the end of the breastplate. It was used to keep other parts of the armor and clothing in place. If so equipped the belt could also hold a sword. The belt once secured also provided the soldier freedom of movement.

By using the belt the soldier was indicating that he was preparing for a battle. If he did not intend to see fighting then there would be no need to use a belt. The spiritual symbolism behind *girding our loins with truth* means that we fully intend on participating in spiritual battle: unencumbered, faithfully, sincerely, truly and to the very best of our ability.

How sad for some who have taken themselves out of the battle and have loosened their belts. Some perhaps have thrown them away, or some have forgotten where they have put their *belt of truth*. Unfortunately these weekend warriors seem to have convinced themselves that they can fight their battles without the need for a belt. They have overindulged their appetite for worldly pleasures and the *belt of truth* became much too uncomfortable to wear. It was so much easier just to take it off, for it was too tight on their belly. And without the *belt of truth* on to remind them of just how bloated they had become they were free to indulge themselves even more.

It is never too late to get into shape spiritually or physically. Perhaps we need to start exercising on a regular basis before we feel comfortable wearing the belt. That is fine. We should not allow ourselves to be deceived into thinking that it is too late for us. We need to prepare for the battle. The life that is saved may be our own. We will then be ready to be of service to others as we follow the Lord's command.

Homework follows!

The Ezra 7:10 Plan 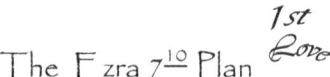   ARMOR   What You Wear

What You Wear Homework
Explain how the **Belt of Truth** is supposed to be used. Support your teaching with a few verses.

Verses

The Belt of Truth

The Ezra 7:10 Plan 1st Love  ARMOR   What You Wear

Breastplate of Righteousness

Before we discuss the symbolism of the *breastplate* we need to understand the intended meaning behind the word *righteousness* in this verse. There is a basic agreement among popular translations for this term in Ephesians. All use *breastplate* and all use *righteousness*. The Old Testament references this *breastplate* in Isaiah. Isaiah 59:17 states in part, *He put on righteousness like a breastplate...* The majority of popular translations use the terms *breastplate* and *righteousness* for this verse in Isaiah.

Righteousness implies a correct relationship to the will of God and a right standing with God. It does not imply that we have reached perfection. Right standing with God occurs only if we are not carrying around the weight of any unconfessed sin. We are righteous because He has wiped our slate clean following our confession and repentance of sin. We cannot expect victory if we are not in the will of God and thus do not have right standing in God's sight. We cannot expect victory if we desire to follow our own will instead of the Lord's will.

An example of this is found in the Book of Numbers. It was such a bad example that Moses reiterated the story in the Book of Deuteronomy. This story takes place right after the twelve spies bring back their report of the Promised Land. This occurred towards the end of the second year of their wilderness journey. Only Joshua and Caleb were positive in affirming that the people should go into the land. The other ten convinced the people that it would be impossible to defeat the people living in the Promised Land. Because of their rebellion the Lord said that the grumblers twenty years and older would not enter the Promised Land and the rest of the congregation would have to wait until forty years of wandering in the desert had elapsed. The ten rebellious spies died by a plague. The grumblers, although they were supposedly sorry that they sinned, were not willing to accept wandering around in the desert for thirty-eight more years. Thus they planned on going ahead with entering into the Promised Land without the blessing of God. The rest of the story and the re-cap in Deuteronomy follows:

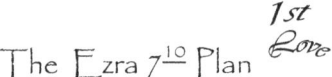

The Ezra 7:10 Plan — 1st Love   ARMOR   What You Wear

Numbers 14:41-45 *But Moses said, "Why then are you transgressing the commandment of the Lord, when it will not succeed? Do not go up, or you will be struck down before your enemies, for the Lord is not among you. For the Amalekites and the Canaanites will be there in front of you, and you will fall by the sword, inasmuch as you have turned back from following the Lord. And the Lord will not be with you." But they went up heedlessly to the ridge of the hill country; neither the ark of the covenant of the Lord nor Moses left the camp. Then the Amalekites and the Canaanites who lived in that hill country came down, and struck them and beat them down as far as Hormah.*

Deuteronomy 1:42-45 *And the Lord said to me, "Say to them, Do not go up nor fight, for I am not among you; otherwise you will be defeated before your enemies." So I spoke to you, but you would not listen. Instead you rebelled against the command of the Lord, and acted presumptuously and went up into the hill country. The Amorites who lived in that hill country came out against you and chased you as bees do, and crushed you from Seir to Hormah. Then you returned and wept before the Lord; but the Lord did not listen to your voice nor give ear to you.*

To reiterate: We cannot expect victory if we desire to follow our own will instead of the Lord's will. When we wear this breastplate it signifies that we fully intend on following God's will and not our own.

The breastplate as used as a piece of armor was made of metal plates or chains, and covered the body from the neck to the waist, both front and back. It is interesting to note that the Greek word for *breastplate*, θώραξ, is basically our English word *thorax*. In Job 29:14 and Isaiah 61:10 righteousness is mentioned as being wrapped around the person as a piece of clothing or as a robe.

The breastplate protects the body against wounds that would prove fatal or extremely disabling. It protects us against anything that might slip past our shield or our sword. And of course the key organ that the breastplate protects is the heart. From a spiritual standpoint, our righteousness is a protective covering preventing us from going outside the will of God and being susceptible to attack, as recounted in the previous Old Testament story. Going into battle without making sure of our right standing in the will of God would be foolish. Putting on the breastplate also means we are battle savvy, knowing that it is smart to protect vulnerable areas. It means that we are not overconfident, thinking that we are too spiritual to be defeated.

1Corinthians 10:12 *Therefore let him who thinks he stands take heed that he does not fall.*

Finally, there are three individuals who so distinguished themselves for their righteousness that they are mentioned together. Perhaps one day we will be mentioned with the *Big Three of Righteousness*. Who are they? The answer is found in Ezekiel 14:12 – 20. (Hint: the first letters of their names are N, D and J, respectively). What can we learn from their lives about righteousness? What do we have to do to have our name included with these warriors!?

Homework follows!

The Ezra 7:10 Plan 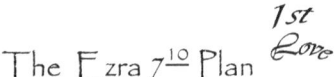 1st Love

ARMOR   What You Wear

What You Wear Homework
Explain how the **Breastplate of Righteousness** is supposed to be used. Support your teaching with a few verses.

Verses

The Breastplate of Righteousness

Belt, Breastplate and Helmet

The Ezra 7:10 Plan — 1st Love 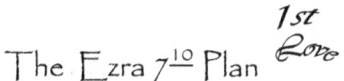   ARMOR   What You Wear

Helmet of Salvation

Before we discuss the symbolism of the *helmet* we need to understand the intended meaning behind the word *salvation* in this verse. There is a basic agreement among popular translations for this term in Ephesians. All use *helmet* and all use *salvation*. The Old Testament references this *helmet* in Isaiah. Isaiah 59:17 states in part, *...And a helmet of salvation on His head...* The majority of popular translations use the terms *helmet* and *salvation* for this verse in Isaiah.

Salvation in this verse means *to be saved, to be born again, to have deliverance from the guilt and penalty of sin*, etc. Our salvation is the key to our existence as a child of God. A hit in this area could take us out of the battle for a long time. If we begin to have doubts about our salvation it will be impossible to be successful in spiritual warfare. The enemy knows this and will try his best to throw many deceptions, doubts and detours our way. He will try to replace our *good soil* with *hard, rocky, thorny soil* that may stop us in our tracks. We cannot lose our salvation if it is genuine, but the accuser will try his best to make us doubt the legitimacy of our salvation. We can counter this by the Word of God as in the following verses:

John 3:16 *For God so loved the world, that He gave His only begotten Son, that whoever believes in Him shall not perish, but have eternal life.*

John 5:24 *Truly, truly, I say to you, he who hears My word, and believes Him who sent Me, has eternal life, and does not come into judgment, but has passed out of death into life.*

Romans 10:10 *for with the heart a person believes, resulting in righteousness, and with the mouth he confesses, resulting in salvation.*

Ephesians 1:13 *In Him, you also, after listening to the message of truth, the gospel of your salvation—having also believed, you were sealed in Him with the Holy Spirit of promise,*

The Greek for *helmet* is περικεφαλαία *(perikephalaia)*. It is a compound word being formed by the prefix περι *(peri, meaning about, concerning, around)* and κεφαλή *(kephalē, meaning head)*. Thus the meaning behind the word *helmet* in the Greek is literally that which is *around the head*. The helmet protects the head, and by extension the brain.

The brain contains all of our thoughts, intellect and will. If our brain is damaged, we will not be able to function correctly. How we think and order our actions with respect to our salvation is crucial if we want to serve the Lord with all our heart, soul, mind and strength. When we put on the *helmet of salvation* we protect our salvation, a most precious possession. When we put our helmet on we are battle savvy. We know the schemes of the devil and we are protecting ourselves from his devices. We do not question our salvation. We have crossed the Red Sea and will not look back. Our hand is on the plow and we will not quit. Our eyes are fixed on Jesus the author and finisher of our faith. All that from just putting on a helmet!

The following table provides a summary of the *Armor of God* that we have studied. In reality the soldier would put on the breastplate before the belt, and the helmet after the belt. Thus we have ordered the table accordingly. We have not forgotten about the shoes, the sword and the shield. They will be covered in another publication. Homework follows after the table!

Summary of the Armor of God

Equipment	Protects	Function	What it Says About Me	Action
Breastplate	Heart	Major source of upper body protection	I am ready to do God's will. I do not turn to the left or right.	Ready
Belt	Abdomen	Holds everything together securely, increases mobility	I am ready to fight. I am genuine. I am trustworthy.	Set
Helmet	Brain	Protects the head	I am ready to move forward. I do not look back. I am confident in His grace and in the plans He has for me.	Go

The Ezra 7:10 Plan — 1st Love

ARMOR   What You Wear

What You Wear Homework

Explain how the **Helmet of Salvation** is supposed to be used. Support your teaching with a few verses.

Verses

The Helmet of Salvation

Study

Context is the Key

Looking at the Forest

The Ezra 7:10 Plan — 1st Love

Context is the Key
Looking at the Forest

STUDY

Making good observations is a key part of studying the Scriptures. Many interesting thought-provoking and encouraging insights can be found by meditating thoroughly on the Word. We need to observe the Word itself closely but we must not lose sight of the context(s) in which the Word is placed. Many false doctrines have been developed because Biblical teaching has been taken out of its context. In fact, many false doctrines can be easily recognized by knowing the context of the verses that false teachers use to twist to their own means. In this section we will learn how to examine the Scriptures properly in light of their grammatical, geographical, cultural, historical and biographical contexts.

Making good observations starts with prayer, asking the Lord to open His Word to us.

Psalm 119:18 *Open my eyes that I may see wonderful things in your law.*

Before we begin let us briefly look at a few of the basic rules of Biblical interpretation. These will help us whether we are looking at the big picture or we are examining the smallest jot or tittle.

STUDY   Context is the Key

Rules Of Interpretation

We shall look at four very important *rules* of Biblical interpretation that do need to be clearly understood.

- ✓ The first rule is that *Scripture best interprets Scripture.*

Therefore, a definitive conclusion about a particular subject, teaching or doctrine should not be made unless it can be supported by other Scriptures. If the Scriptures are silent or not definitive about a particular topic, please resist the temptation to pour a meaning into a verse that is not there.

- ✓ The second rule is that *when the common sense of Scripture makes common sense we should seek no other sense.*

In other words, interpret every word in its usual literal meaning unless it is clear from the context that another meaning is required. When we encounter symbolisms, allegories, parables, clearly figurative language, etc., it is obvious that a literal interpretation cannot be used.

- ✓ The third rule is that we should *interpret difficult verses on a particular topic using clearly understood verses on the same topic.*

If many verses seem to indicate the same truth about a particular subject, but one verse seems to be unclear, the unclear verse needs to be interpreted in light of the clear verses.

Looking at the Forest

The Ezra 7:10 Plan — 1st Love   STUDY   Context is the Key

- ✓ The fourth rule is that *personal experience or tradition do not define the Scriptures or justify doctrine.*

For example, if someone told you that after confessing Jesus Christ as Savior and Lord you must leap up and down in the Spirit, because that is what they experienced, this would be erroneous since it is not supported in the Scriptures as something that *must* happen. Also as an example, if you have been taught that it is a sin to play all card games because it is part of a church's traditional teachings, this definition of sin would not match the Biblical definition because it is not explicitly backed up by Scripture, only tradition.

Let us move on to study how we can more accurately interpret Scripture in light of its grammatical, geographical, cultural, historical and biographical contexts.

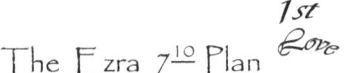

Grammatical Context

Probably the most important part of the study of a particular verse or passage, besides a thorough review of the verse or passage itself, is knowing its grammatical context. This book defines the grammatical context as:

that portion of a narrative that precedes and/or follows a specific word, verse or passage, usually influencing its meaning or effect

For example, if a set of verses is being studied, the entire paragraph that contains these verses should be read. In some instances the entire chapter or chapters should be read. Some verses can be fully understood only by reading the broader context of the entire book of the Bible. Although this is rare, reading an entire book of the Bible to discern the context of a few verses may be necessary, especially for verses that may affect major theological doctrines.

The following questions are provided to get us started in discerning how the grammatical context affects the interpretation of a particular verse.

> ➤ *Is there something mentioned before and/or after the passage under review, that can help in the understanding of the passage itself?*

> ➤ *What is the main topic or theme being addressed?*

> ➤ *Is the writer talking in generalities or trying to address a specific issue?*

> ➤ *If you see the word "therefore," find out what it is there for.*

The following are specific examples of how discerning the grammatical context can actually change or refine the interpretation of individual verses.

The Ezra 7:10 Plan — 1st Row   STUDY   Context is the Key

Grammatical Context Example: Matthew 6:33

Matthew 6:33 *But seek first His kingdom and His righteousness, and all these things will be added to you.*

For this first example we will use the previous questions to see how we might better understand this verse. We have included the following verses from Matthew 6:19-34 with verse numbers included for easy reference:

19 Do not store up for yourselves treasures on earth, where moth and rust destroy, and where thieves break in and steal. 20 But store up for yourselves treasures in heaven, where neither moth nor rust destroys, and where thieves do not break in or steal; 21 for where your treasure is, there your heart will be also. 22 The eye is the lamp of the body; so then if your eye is clear, your whole body will be full of light. 23 But if your eye is bad, your whole body will be full of darkness. If then the light that is in you is darkness, how great is the darkness! 24 No one can serve two masters; for either he will hate the one and love the other, or he will be devoted to one and despise the other. You cannot serve God and wealth.

25 For this reason I say to you, do not be worried about your life, as to what you will eat or what you will drink; nor for your body, as to what you will put on. Is not life more than food, and the body more than clothing? 26 Look at the birds of the air, that they do not sow, nor reap nor gather into barns, and yet your heavenly Father feeds them. Are you not worth much more than they? 27 And who of you by being worried can add a single hour to his life? 28 And why are you worried about clothing? Observe how the lilies of the field grow; they do not toil nor do they spin, 29 yet I say to you that not even Solomon in all his glory clothed himself like one of these. But if God so clothes the grass of the field, which is alive today and tomorrow is thrown into the furnace, will He not much more clothe you? You of little faith! 31 "Do not worry then, saying, 'What will we eat?' or 'What will we drink?' or 'What will we wear for clothing?' 32 For the Gentiles eagerly seek all these things; for your heavenly Father knows that you need all these things. 33 But seek first His kingdom and His righteousness, and all these things will be added to you. 34 So do not worry about tomorrow; for tomorrow will care for itself. Each day has enough trouble of its own.

Looking at the Forest

> *Is there something mentioned before and/or after the passage under review that can help in the understanding of the passage itself?*

On first glance at this verse we might ask ourselves, what are the *these things* that this verse is talking about? If we were to read the preceding verses starting with verse twenty-five, we would see that *these things* refer specifically to food, drink and clothing. We would also gain additional insight into why verse thirty-three starts out with *But seek first*. Verse thirty-two says that *the Gentiles eagerly seek all these things* (i.e., they seek them as a first priority in their lives). The verse also states that our Father knows that we need these things. In contrast to the Gentiles (a generic term for unbelievers) then, we are exhorted to seek God's kingdom and His righteousness first, instead of seeking food, drink and clothing first.

> *What is the main topic or theme being addressed?*

The main topic being addressed may be best discovered by reading verses nineteen through twenty-four. These verses directly precede verse twenty-five which begins the paragraph that contains our study verse (Matthew 6:33). Verse twenty-five starts off as *For this reason* (*Therefore* in the King James Version), which refers back to previous statements (Matthew 6:19-24). Verse twenty-four says we cannot serve two masters, God and wealth. The theme here is that we cannot have two number-one priorities in our life. We can have one or the other but not both.

So we see clearly that we should not make the pursuit of our material welfare a higher priority than seeking His kingdom and righteousness. We can expect that if we pursue His kingdom and His righteousness as the first priority in our life then all our material needs will be provided.

> *Is the writer talking in generalities or trying to address a specific issue?*

Although very specific items are mentioned, food, drink, and clothing, these are also representative of general physical needs. The kingdom of God and His righteousness are broad in definition. Entire books have been devoted to these subjects. Suffice to say for this study that the kingdom of God and His righteousness have to do with devoting our life to His service. Additional insight into the meaning of *the kingdom of God and His righteousness* can be found by reading the two chapters five and six in full. Especially valuable is Matthew 5:1-20. This should come as no surprise, since chapters five, six and seven of Matthew contain the *Sermon on the Mount*. Since this is basically in the form of one long sermon it would make sense that we read the whole sermon in order to understand fully the context of any verse(s) within the sermon.

> *If you see the word "therefore," find out what it is there for.*

We have already discussed the *therefore* in verse twenty-five. Looking at verse thirty-four we note that it starts with *so*, a word similar in meaning to *therefore*. Verse thirty-four sums up the whole paragraph by advising us not to worry about tomorrow. Thus we do not worry about tomorrow or the future as to whether or not we will have *these things* because God says He will provide them as we seek Him first.

Therefore, by examining the context we can clarify some potential false teaching! God does not promise to simply provide us with everything we want, but only the necessities of life. In no way does the Bible instruct us to command God to make us perfectly healthy, wealthy, and wise in the world's eyes. Although we still have to earn a living and make enough money to obtain *these things*, we are not to be consumed with nor worry about this pursuit as the main goal of our life. In fact, the seeking after *the kingdom of God and His righteousness* is to be the highest priority of our life. This priority is for all believers. It is not just for the exclusive realm of those in full time, professional Christian work. Thus we can eliminate this worry and concentrate on serving and bearing fruit for God. Remember in the *Parable of the Sower*, how the thorns choked the seeds. What were the thorns symbolic of?

Matthew 13:22 *And the one on whom seed was sown among the thorns, this is the man who hears the word, and the worry of the world and the deceitfulness of wealth choke the word, and it becomes unfruitful.*

The Ezra 7:10 Plan 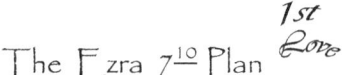 STUDY Context is the Key

Hmm...worry and wealth. This is just what Jesus was talking about in Matthew 6:19-34, wealth as our master and worry consuming our life. The choice is ours. It is very clear that the worrisome pursuit of *these things* and the deceitfulness of wealth will only choke us and make us afraid of the future. The single-minded pursuit of *the kingdom of God and His righteousness* will lead to peace, confidence and the bearing of much fruit for God.

The Ezra 7:10 Plan — 1st Love   STUDY   Context is the Key

Grammatical Context Example: Matthew 18:19

Matthew 18:19 *Again I say to you, that if two of you agree on earth about anything that they may ask, it shall be done for them by My Father who is in heaven.*

On first glance we may ask ourselves, does this verse really mean *anything* and why does it mention the fact that two people have to be in agreement? We do not have to look too far before this verse (Matthew 18:15-18) to see that a number of things come to light. We have included the following verses from Matthew 18:15-20 with verse numbers included for easy reference:

15 If your brother sins, go and show him his fault in private; if he listens to you, you have won your brother. 16 But if he does not listen to you, take one or two more with you, so that by the mouth of two or three witnesses every fact may be confirmed. 17 If he refuses to listen to them, tell it to the church; and if he refuses to listen even to the church, let him be to you as a Gentile and a tax collector. 18 Truly I say to you, whatever you bind on earth shall have been bound in heaven; and whatever you loose on earth shall have been loosed in heaven. 19 Again I say to you, that if two of you agree on earth about anything that they may ask, it shall be done for them by My Father who is in heaven. 20 For where two or three have gathered together in My name, I am there in their midst.

The main theme of Matthew 18:15-20 is the disciplining of a brother (that sins) in order to restore fellowship and reconcile him to the body of believers. The number two initially comes up from verse sixteen, where it talks about bringing one or two others along, so that every fact (about the sin) may be established by the testimony of two or three witnesses. (Note that this practice was commanded in the Old Testament — see Deuteronomy 19:15).

Jesus in these passages is saying that the *anything* in verse nineteen really refers to anything related to the *treatment* of the sinning brother. In other words, if, with the input from two or three witnesses, we *bind* him to discipline or punishment, or *loose* him to forgiveness, then the Holy Spirit will have already given approval to the treatment. The sense here is that the Holy Spirit is truly the one who communicated the correct treatment to us and we simply followed His lead.

Looking at the Forest

It should be noted that verse eighteen in some translations (such as the KJV and RSV) is stated as, ... *whatever you bind on earth will be bound in heaven, and whatever you loose on earth will be loosed in heaven.* This makes it appear that *the Lord* in *heaven* waits for our action before He begins His. The Greek verb tense for the words *will be bound* and *will be loosed* is not the future tense, but rather the perfect tense. A more precise rendering as indicated in the NASB version (others versions such as the NIV (in the footnotes) and the NET Bible also agree with the NASB) used in this book, is *shall have been bound* and *shall have been loosed*. In other words the Lord in *heaven* acted first and then our actions followed being in perfect agreement. This is extremely important in the sense that people do not have the power to indiscriminately bind or loose as they see fit. Only if the Lord agrees will the binding or loosing be allowed.

Note that both the discipline (*binding*) and forgiveness (*loosing*) have the common goal of reconciliation and restoration. It is interesting to note in the previous set of verses (grammatical context) in Matthew 18:10-14 (part of the same conversation), that Jesus had just told the disciples about the *Parable of the Lost Sheep*. We remember this as the story where a man who owns one hundred sheep discovers that one has wandered off. He takes the time and trouble to stop everything that he is doing to make sure that this lost sheep is restored to the flock. What is the goal? It is the same as our study passage, reconciliation and restoration.

Even more insight may be found by reading the very beginning (further grammatical context) of Jesus' discussion with his disciples (Matthew 18:1-9), which precedes the *Parable of the Lost Sheep*. Jesus answers a question posed by the disciples about who is the greatest in the kingdom of heaven. His answer was mind boggling. He related entering the kingdom of heaven, being the greatest in the kingdom of heaven, and having fellowship with Jesus — with children. Jesus said, to be like them, be as humble as they are, and to treat other children with respect. Jesus went on to say that the disciples should do everything, even going to extremes to deal with sin if necessary (i.e., cutting off hands/feet and plucking out eyes) in their own lives, so that these children would not be tempted to sin by our example or actions. Just before Jesus relates the story of the *Parable of the Lost Sheep*, He says to, *see that you do not despise one of these little ones, for I say to you that their angels in heaven continually see the face of My Father who is in heaven.*

Therefore, if you put our study verse (Matthew 18:19), together with its immediate context (Matthew 18:15-20), with the broader context of the *Parable of the Lost Sheep* (Matthew 18:10-14), with the broadest context of how this conversation got started (Matthew 18:1-9), we make an amazing discovery. Jesus is telling the disciples that the greatest in the kingdom is he who is concerned with the least in the world. We should be so concerned about their (the least in the world) welfare and not leading them astray that we are willing to serve them, go to great lengths to find them if they are lost, be a blameless example in front of them, and have the courage to confront their sin and restore them to fellowship. Keep in mind, all of this trouble is for a person who would be considered a child, the least in the world.

So perhaps now we see that our study verse, Matthew 18:19, is not some kind of magical formula where two people can simply agree on anything they want to satisfy their wants and desires. False teachers have twisted this verse for their own use in what really amounts to a *name-it and claim-it Gospel of Greed*.

In reality, this passage is amidst one of the most challenging sections in the entire Bible concerning how we are to live as believers. This section teaches us that we should be doing everything we possibly can to find and restore the wayward believer, and to rid our lives of every sin that could cause people to be led astray.

Looking at the Forest

The Ezra 7¹⁰ Plan 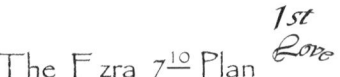 STUDY   Context is the Key

The following sentences summarize two different interpretations of this verse. See if you can determine which statement is based on the *Without Context* interpretation (place an X in the box) and the one based on the *With Context* interpretation (place a ✓ in the box).

☐ *God is my resource. I tell Him what He needs to provide so that I can do what I want.*

☐ *God is my source. He tells me what I need to receive so that I can do what He wants.*

Now that we know the correct interpretation, we should ask ourselves which of the two statements more closely resembles how we currently lead our life.

Homework follows!

The Ezra 7:10 Plan — 1st Love

STUDY Context is the Key

Grammatical Homework

Pick one or more verses below (or another one). First record any insights observed by looking only at the verse itself. Then, read the grammatical context (before and after) and record any additional insights gained.

Lev 26:9	Prov 3:18	Isa 58:5	Lam 3:22,23	Mal 2:16
Jos 24:19	Jon 2:9	Jer 29:11	Neh 8:10	Mal 4:6

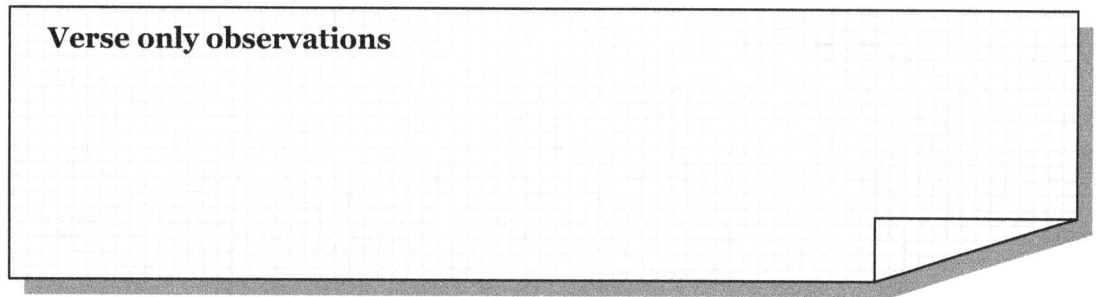

Verse only observations

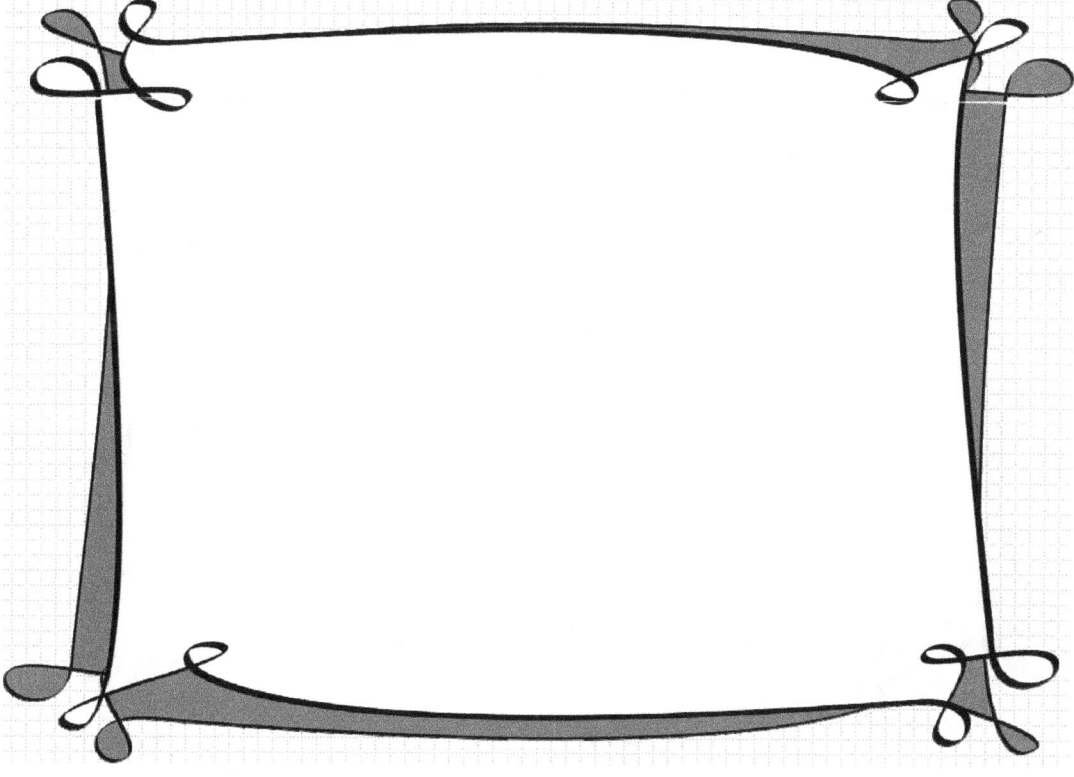

Full grammatical context observations

Looking at the Forest

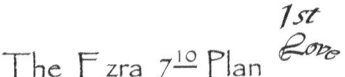

The Ezra 7:10 Plan — 1st Love   STUDY   Context is the Key

Grammatical Homework continued...

Pick one or more verses below (or another one). First record any insights observed by looking only at the verse itself. Then, read the grammatical context (before and after) and record any additional insights gained.

Mt 11:30	Lu 1:37	Jn 1:35	Jn 10:30	1Cor 10:13
Mk 14:36	Lu 18:27	Jn 3:30	1Cor 9:19	Rev 3:20

Verse only observations

Full grammatical context observations

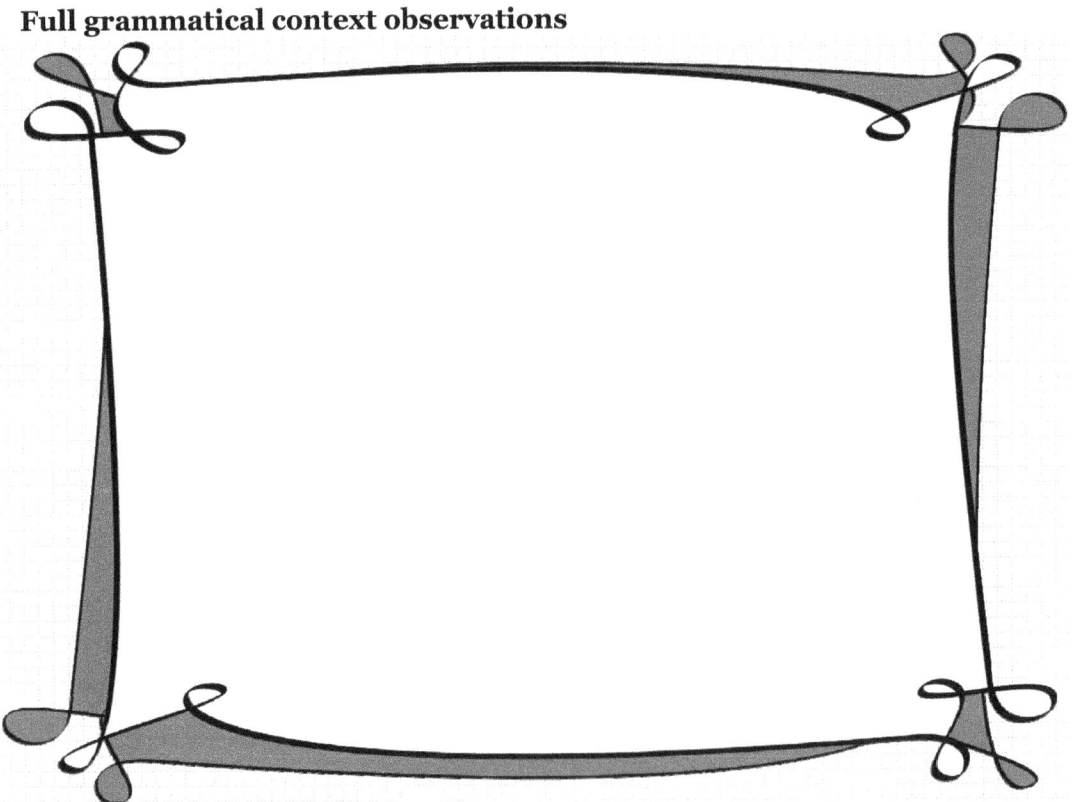

The Ezra 7:10 Plan 1st Love STUDY Context is the Key

Geographical Context

Although knowing the geographical context of a verse or passage may not be essential for interpreting its meaning, it can enhance the meaning of a passage and bring to light other insights that may not be so apparent.

This book defines the geographical context as:

The physical characteristics of the land, travel ways, climate, community locations and boundaries

When reading a passage that contains the names of mountains, streams, countries, cities, etc., the following questions may get us started in discerning how the geographical context affects the interpretation of a particular verse.

- ➢ *Where are these physical features located?*

- ➢ *What are the dimensions (i.e., how tall is the mountain, how far apart are the cities, what is the size of the town, how big is the body of water, etc.)?*

- ➢ *Does knowledge of the physical features(s) add additional insight into the passage?*

To find this information a good Bible Atlas or set of Bible maps of the Holy Land is required. Many study Bibles have a good set of maps towards the back, or interspersed throughout.

Geographical Context Example: Elijah's Victory and Retreat

The following is an example of how knowing the geographical context can enhance our understanding of a passage of Scripture. The passage we will be reviewing is found in 1Kings 18:16 - 19:18. This passage is too long to print here. We can read this ahead of time, or leave our Bibles open to this passage.

The Ezra 7¹⁰ Plan — 1st Love   STUDY   Context is the Key

In this passage several things happen. Elijah the prophet challenges the 450 prophets of Baal and 400 prophets of Asherah to a contest to see whose sacrifice would be accepted. Elijah says, *The God who answers by fire, He is God.* All Israel is summoned to meet at Mount Carmel to observe this. After almost a full day of futility the prophets of Baal and Asherah fail. Elijah's sacrifice is the only one accepted and the false prophets are then killed in the Kishon Valley. Elijah then prays for rain seven times, each time asking his servant to *look toward the sea* for a sign of rain. The seventh time a cloud appears and rain is imminent. Elijah dispatches his servant to tell Israel's King Ahab about the impending storm, telling the king, *Prepare your chariot and go down, so that the heavy shower does not stop you.* In the meantime Elijah, on foot *with the hand of the Lord,* actually gets to Jezreel before Ahab. Elijah then finds out that Jezebel, King Ahab's wife, wants him killed for killing the prophets of Baal and Asherah. So Elijah, afraid for his life, runs to Beersheba in Judah, leaves his servant there, and travels another day south into the wilderness. Then after being fed by angels, he travels another forty days and forty nights to Horeb, the mountain of God. God speaks to him there and gives him some tasks to do, one of which involves going to the wilderness of Damascus.

This story is amazing in itself without knowing the locations of the towns and cities and mountains. This sequence of events is nothing short of miraculous if the geographical context is researched.

First of all it is interesting to note that all Israel is summoned to Mount Carmel, which is not centrally located within Israel. (Note at this time that David and Solomon's united kingdom had been split up into the ten northern tribes, named Israel, and the two southern tribes, named Judah). Mount Carmel is located in northwest Israel right next to the Mediterranean Sea, as part of a small ridge of mountains. However, it was close (twenty-six miles) to King Ahab's palace at Jezreel. The Kishon Valley where the false prophets were killed is just north of this range (basically at the bottom of the mountain to the north).

So we see that the people did not have to go far to kill the prophets of Baal and Asherah. They just had to descend the mountain on the north side which emptied out into the Kishon Valley. The sea that the servant looked toward and could most

Looking at the Forest

definitely see was in fact the Mediterranean Sea. To beat King Ahab to Jezreel Elijah had to run twenty-six miles! A marathon! Knowing that Elijah ran ahead of Ahab to Jezreel in the power of the Lord would not seem such a big event unless you know that he also ran faster than a chariot for twenty-six miles. Even if he did not beat the chariot (which he did), running twenty-six miles by itself takes amazing feet, *and is an amazing feat*. But keep in mind, right before he ran twenty-six miles, he had climbed to the top of Mount Carmel, spent all day watching the false prophets make fools of themselves, seen God send fire down from heaven to accept his sacrifice, climbed down the mountain to kill the false prophets, and then climbed back up on the mountain to pray for rain (a full day's work in anyone's book). And then he ran a marathon after that!

To flee from Jezebel Elijah fled to Beersheba in Judah, a distance of ninety-seven miles (based on a good Bible map). Add on a day's journey into the desert (about twenty miles), and you have a total journey from Mount Carmel to the desert of 143 (26+97+20) miles. Elijah was running or walking fast most of the way! It is no wonder that in 1 Kings 19:7, the angel says to Elijah, *Arise, eat, because the journey is too great for you.* The angel said this after Elijah had traveled a day's journey south of Beersheba, but before he started his journey to Mount Horeb. The journey to Mount Horeb was another 175 miles, so that the total journey from Mount Carmel to Mount Horeb was 318 miles. It is very interesting to note just how far Elijah goes in this *Jonah-esque* retreat. Remember in the past how God had wanted Jonah to go East (to Nineveh), but Jonah went West (towards Tarshish)? In this episode God eventually wants Elijah to go north, but Elijah proceeds south! He starts in northern Israel, travels to another country altogether (Judah), then precedes to travel to the southernmost town in this other country (Beersheba), then a day's travel still south of that town, out of that country into the desert, and then for forty days and forty nights, 175 miles south (again) into the wilderness to Mount Horeb (another name for the area around Mount Sinai). This is the same mountain on which Moses received the Ten Commandments. Note that the journey to Mount Horeb from Beersheba is only about a ten-day trip. So Elijah after being fed by the angels and no longer running in fear, had slowed his pace considerably (a ten-day trip in forty days), as his fear turned to discouragement, then to despair.

Looking at the Forest

The Ezra 7^10 Plan 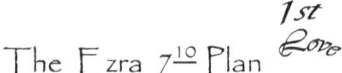   STUDY   Context is the Key

Keeping all of this exhaustive traveling in mind, coupled with death threats, it is no wonder Elijah wanted to give up. He was emotionally, spiritually and physically fatigued. 1 Kings 19:4 ... *It is enough now ... take my life...* and 1 Kings 19:10,14 ...*I alone am left...*

Knowing the exact number of miles Elijah traveled in a relatively short time gives us additional insight into how his fatigued state altered his spiritual outlook on things.

Note that once he was refreshed in the Lord, the daunting task of returning the way he came (including traveling through Jezreel and possibly facing Ahab and Jezebel again), all the way to the wilderness of Damascus, a distance of close to 400 miles, no longer frightened Elijah. He boldly undertook these tasks that God gave him.

Find a good Bible Atlas, Bible Handbook or Bible Encyclopedia and complete the following homework.

The Ezra 7:10 Plan — 1st Love   STUDY   Context is the Key

Geographical Homework

Pick one or more questions and find and record the information requested.

What Old Testament cities were near to Nazareth? What OT tribe would Nazareth be a part of? John 2:1 - Find the distance from Nazareth to Cana.	To build Solomon's Temple and to rebuild the Temple during Ezra's time, wood came from Tyre and Sidon. Chart the route the wood might have taken (see 1Kings 5:8,9 and Ezra 3:7).
Find the area of the Decapolis and list its major cities. What U.S. metropolitan areas compare in size to it?	Judges 18 – Find the town that the tribe of Dan conquered. How was it isolated (vs27,28)? What is the distance from Dan to Beersheba?

Looking at the Forest

The Ezra 7:10 Plan 1st Love   STUDY   Context is the Key

Geographical Homework continued …

Pick one or more questions and find and record the information requested.

1Sam 7:15-17 – Samuel had an annual *preaching* circuit. How long was this loop of cities in miles?	Gen 14:13-24 – How far did Abraham travel rescuing Lot and chasing the enemy?	How far did Joseph travel to check on his brothers (Hebron to Dothan)?
To buy grain Jacob's sons traveled to Egypt. What was this distance (Hebron to the land of Goshen)?	Superimpose the boundaries of Israel in the time of King David onto a U.S. State.	How far was Mary's trip from Nazareth to Bethlehem? Using a topographic map look at the elevation profile of this trip. List insights.

Looking at the Forest

The Ezra 7:10 Plan — 1st Love   STUDY   Context is the Key

Cultural Context

The culture and customs of a particular group of people, country or era can be vastly different from our own. In many instances Scriptures containing references to ancient cultural practices and customs may seem strange unless we understand some of the ways people lived in those days.

This book defines the cultural context as:

A way of doing or saying things, or using certain objects that may be unique to a particular country or stage of civilization and different from our own

The following questions are provided to get us started in discerning how the cultural context affects the interpretation of a particular verse.

- ➢ *What is the modern day equivalent of this object, saying or practice?*

- ➢ *Does knowing how this object, expression or action was viewed in its own time and culture affect the meaning of the passage today?*

The following are examples of how knowing the cultural context can enhance our understanding of a passage of Scripture.

Cultural Context Example: A Sabbath Day's Journey

Acts 1:12 *Then they returned to Jerusalem from the mount called Olivet, which is near Jerusalem, a Sabbath day's journey away.*

We might ask ourselves what constitutes *a Sabbath day's journey*? The appropriate resource we should use would be a book on manners and customs in Biblical times or perhaps a Bible dictionary. Looking up a *Sabbath day's journey* we discover that it was the maximum distance a Jew could travel on the Sabbath day

Looking at the Forest   131

without it being considered unlawful. Supposedly the rabbis who made up this law based it on Exodus 16:29.

Exodus 16:29 *See, the LORD has given you the sabbath; therefore He gives you bread for two days on the sixth day. Remain every man in his place; let no man go out of his place on the seventh day.*

The distance according to the rabbis that one could go out or travel on the Sabbath was limited to about 3/4 mile (Note that some books indicate this distance as less than two miles). We now know that Mount Olivet was around a mile away from Jerusalem, a fact that we can confirm using a map of the Holy Land.

Cultural Context Example: Eating Your Neighbor's Grain

Matthew 12:1,2 *At that time Jesus went through the grainfields on the Sabbath, and His disciples became hungry and began to pick the heads of grain and eat. But when the Pharisees saw this, they said to Him, "Look, Your disciples do what is not lawful to do on a Sabbath."*

We might ask ourselves if this is stealing another man's property. By consulting the proper resource book or perhaps checking out a Scripture cross reference in a study Bible we may be led to the following verse in Deuteronomy.

Deuteronomy 23:25 *When you enter your neighbor's standing grain, then you may pluck the heads with your hand, but you shall not wield a sickle in your neighbor's standing grain.*

Therefore, it was perfectly lawful for persons when hungry to help themselves to as much grain as they needed that day. They were not allowed to use a harvesting tool but only gather what their hands could pick. It is interesting to note that the Pharisees did not complain about the grain being plucked, but rather that it was done on the Sabbath. Their traditions (not the Scriptures) forbid this *work* on the Sabbath. Jesus answers them very clearly.

The Ezra 7:10 Plan — 1st Love   STUDY   Context is the Key

Matthew 12:7 *But if you had known what this means, 'I desire compassion, and not a sacrifice,' you would not have condemned the innocent.*

Cultural Context Example: Corban

Mark 7:11-13 *but you say, 'If a man says to his father or his mother, whatever I have that would help you is Corban (that is to say, given to God),' you no longer permit him to do anything for his father or his mother; thus invalidating the word of God by your tradition which you have handed down; and you do many things such as that.*

What does it mean to say something is *Corban* and why does Jesus say that this tradition nullifies the Word of God?

The Corban was an offering of any kind consecrated to God. It was right to make such offerings because God had commanded them but the Pharisees had so twisted this doctrine by their additional instructions (tradition) that it could override other commands of God contained in the Scriptures. For example, God commanded that parents should be honored, but if their son should say, *My property or money is Corban,* it released him from helping his parents. The son could still use it for his own purposes or give it to whom he pleased, but not to those to whom he said *it is Corban*. No wonder Jesus was upset with the Pharisees. In case a parent or a needy neighbor came to ask for help, this tradition of Corban effectively got the person out of obeying the following Scriptures:

Exodus 20:12 *Honor your father and your mother, that your days may be prolonged in the land which the LORD your God gives you.*

Deuteronomy 15:7,8 *If there is a poor man with you, one of your brothers, in any of your towns in your land which the LORD your God is giving you, you shall not harden your heart, nor close your hand from your poor brother; but you shall freely open your hand to him, and shall generously lend him sufficient for his need in whatever he lacks.*

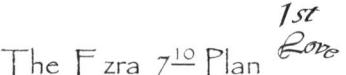

STUDY Context is the Key

Deuteronomy 15:10,11 *You shall generously give to him, and your heart shall not be grieved when you give to him, because for this thing the LORD your God will bless you in all your work and in all your undertakings. For the poor will never cease to be in the land; therefore I command you, saying, 'You shall freely open your hand to your brother, to your needy and poor in your land.'*

Homework follows.

On the following pages we will be looking up cultural references within a verse of the Bible. Using the appropriate Biblical resource book such as a Bible Handbook, a book on manners and customs in Biblical times, or a Bible Encyclopedia, record the information requested and any new insights about the verse in the space provided.

The Ezra 7:10 Plan — 1st Love   STUDY   Context is the Key

Cultural Homework

Pick one or more questions and find and record the information requested.

Ezek 21:21 -Three divination methods are mentioned here. Research each one.	Isa 46:1 - Who is Bel? Who is Nebo?	Ex 38:24-26, Jos 7:20,21 , 1King 10:14, 2King 5:23, 1Chron 22:14 – What was the weight and value of a talent / shekel? What insight does this add?
Acts 14:12 - Who were Zeus and Hermes?	Gen 37:34, Judges 11:35, 2Sam 3:31 – Why were the clothes torn and sackcloth worn? What is sackcloth?	

Looking at the Forest   135

The Ezra 7:10 Plan *1st Love* STUDY Context is the Key

Cultural Homework continued ...

Pick one or more questions and find and record the information requested.

Mt 23:5 – What is a phylactery? What is a tassel (hem, fringe, border)? Why was it wrong to make them so noticeable? What OT verses commanded the use of these?	
Lev 5:11, Ruth 2:17, 1Sam 17:17 – How much is an ephah?	Explain the differences between threshing, winnowing and sifting. How have they been used symbolically in Scripture (Isa 41:14-16, Jer 15:7, Lu 3:17, Lu 22:31)?

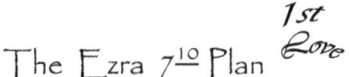

STUDY　Context is the Key

Historical Context

When we read the Scriptures we may have a tendency to develop tunnel vision to a certain extent and only view the events as they relate to the person or area mentioned in the passage of Scripture. For example, if the event occurs in Jerusalem we do not necessarily think about events occurring simultaneously in Bethlehem. If the passage is talking about the Israelites, we may not wonder what the Egyptians were doing at the same time. If the passage talks about King Herod, we may not wonder which Roman Caesar was in power. If the passage is talking about Elijah do we know what other Biblical prophets were around as contemporaries? If the passage talks about a certain King of Israel, do we know who was the corresponding King of Judah? And more importantly, do we have an idea what year it is? Are we familiar with the chronology of the Bible? It should come as no surprise by now if we have read the Bible at least once from cover to cover that it is not arranged in exact chronological order. In fact, chapters within some books of the Bible are not even arranged in the proper time sequence. Although we are not advocating obtaining a Ph. D. in ancient history, a proper understanding of world events including their proper sequence in time will lead to a fuller understanding of Scripture. Understanding this global view will also illustrate that God is in complete control and that all of His purposes and plans have and will continue to be accomplished.

This book defines the historical context as:

Personalities, places and events occurring at the same time or era that is referred to by the verse or passage

The following questions are provided to get us started in discerning how the historical context affects the interpretation of a particular verse.

Looking at the Forest

- What year is this?

- Who is in power that may affect this area?

- Who are the major Biblical personalities living at this time?

- Has any great world event just happened or is about to take place?

Many study Bibles list much of this type of information at the beginning of each book, so that the reader understands the historical setting of the book. Before a passage of Scripture is studied within a book of the Bible this overview of history should be reviewed. The following is an example of how knowing the historical context can enhance your understanding of a passage of Scripture.

Historical Context Example: King Herod and John the Baptist

Mark 6:17-28 17 For Herod himself had sent and had John arrested and bound in prison on account of Herodias, the wife of his brother Philip, because he had married her. 18 For John had been saying to Herod, "It is not lawful for you to have your brother's wife." 19 Herodias had a grudge against him and wanted to put him to death and could not do so; 20 for Herod was afraid of John, knowing that he was a righteous and holy man, and he kept him safe. And when he heard him, he was very perplexed; but he used to enjoy listening to him. 21 A strategic day came when Herod on his birthday gave a banquet for his lords and military commanders and the leading men of Galilee; 22 and when the daughter of Herodias herself came in and danced, she pleased Herod and his dinner guests; and the king said to the girl, "Ask me for whatever you want and I will give it to you." 23 And he swore to her, "Whatever you ask of me, I will give it to you; up to half of my kingdom." 24 And she went out and said to her mother, "What shall I ask for?" And she said, "The head of John the Baptist." 25 Immediately she came in a hurry to the king and asked, saying, "I want you to give me at once the head of John the Baptist on a platter." 26 And although the king was very sorry, yet because of his oaths and because of his dinner guests, he was unwilling to refuse her. 27 Immediately the king sent an executioner and commanded him to bring back his head. And he went and had him beheaded in the prison, 28 and brought his head on a platter, and gave it to the girl; and the girl gave it to her mother.

The Ezra 7:10 Plan *1st Love* STUDY Context is the Key

This passage recounts John the Baptist's imprisonment and subsequent beheading at the orders of King Herod. Several questions related to the historical context could be asked about this passage:

- *Was this King Herod the same king that tried to kill the baby Jesus?*
- *What were the limits of his Kingdom?*
- *Was he a Roman King or a Jewish King?*
- *Was his brother Philip also a king or a ruler?*

Although not specifically related to the historical context, we may also ask these questions.

- *Where in the Old Testament Law did it forbid marrying your brother's wife?*
- *Why would Herod fear John the Baptist and want to protect him?*

Looking at any number of historical reference books we discover that there were many Herods that existed before and after the life of Christ. We have included a family tree in order to make sense of the following narrative. It can be quite confusing to follow the many plots and intrigues in this family unless you understand how each person is related to the other.

Note that the actual date of the birth of Jesus may vary somewhat based on the Biblical resource used. We have assumed that the birth of Jesus occurred around 6-5 B.C. He was probably less than 2 years old when Joseph took Him and Mary to Egypt (based on Herod trying to kill all boys two years and younger in Bethlehem). Since it appears that Joseph brought his family back shortly after the death of Herod (4 B.C.) Jesus was probably around one to three years old (4-3 B.C.) when Joseph brought his family to Nazareth.

Looking at the Forest

The Ezra 7:10 Plan   1st Love   STUDY   Context is the Key

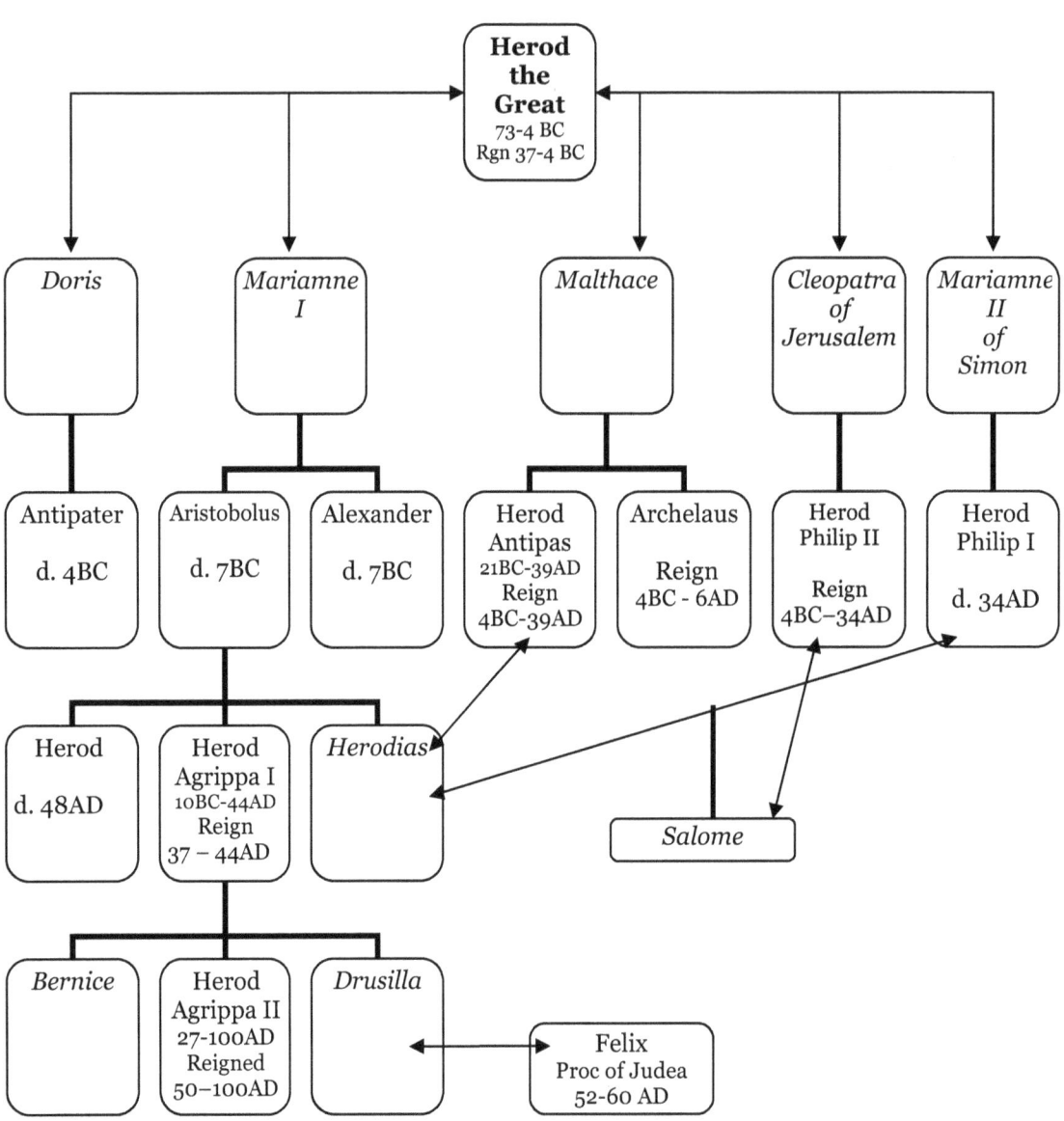

Looking at the Forest

The Ezra 7:10 Plan 1st Love   STUDY   Context is the Key

The King Herod mentioned in the above passage was Herod Antipas, who was not the same Herod who tried to kill the baby Jesus. That Herod was Herod the Great, who was the father of Herod Antipas and the father or grandfather of many other Biblical personalities.

Originally the succession to Herod the Great's (King of Judea) throne included Herod the Great's first three sons: Antipater (mother: Doris), and Alexander and Aristobulus (mother: Mariamne I). Antipater in trying to eliminate any competition tried to kill or imprison his two brothers. However, Alexander and Aristobulus were killed at Sebaste after being convicted of plotting to kill their father Herod the Great. Antipater, who was impatiently waiting to receive his father's kingdom, then plotted to overthrow his own father. He sent poison to Pheroras (Herod's brother) so that he would kill Herod. Antipater, Pheroras and his wife, and Herod's wife at that time (Mariamne II: mother of the Philip(I) mentioned in our study passage), were in on the plot. Pheroras however, became ill and Herod so kindly treated his brother Pheroras (he eventually died of his illness), that Pheroras decided not to go through with the poisoning. However, Herod the Great found out about the plot and divorced Mariamne II, and blotted out Philip's(I) name from his will.

This was especially devastating to Philip(I) since only his brother Antipater was in front of him in succession to receive Herod the Great's kingdom. Philip(I) had already married Herodias who was actually his niece, being the daughter of his half-brother Aristobulus (mentioned above). They had a daughter whose name was Salome who was the one that asked for John the Baptists's head on a platter as mentioned in our study passage. Antipater, was later tried and convicted of the plot to kill his father and was killed. Herod the Great then amended his will appointing Archelaus, now his eldest son (who was currently King of Cappodocia) as his successor, Antipas (The Herod in our passage above) as Tetrarch of Galilee and Perea, and Philip II (mother: Cleopatra of Jerusalem) was appointed Tetrarch of Trachonitis and neighboring territories.

It should be noted that Malthace, a Samaritan woman, was the mother of both Archelaus and Antipas, making them both non-Jews, and thus not popular with the Jews in Judea.

Looking at the Forest

Archelaus went to Rome to secure his kingship after the death of Herod the Great, but was followed by Antipas who thought he was the rightful heir to the throne. Meanwhile trouble broke out in Jerusalem which was subsequently quieted by the Roman army. A delegation of fifty Jews arrived at Rome this time to ask for the elimination of royal authority in Judea and was supported by some 8,000 Jews in Rome. Caesar then decided to appoint Archelaus not as king, but as Ethnarch of Judea, Idumea and Samaria, promising to make him king should he prove deserving. Antipas received Galilee and Perea, while Philip II obtained Batanea, Trachonitis, Auranitis and Panias. Ten years later (A.D. 6), Archelaus was banished to Vienne, a city in Gaul (what is now France), for extreme cruelty to the Jews. He also married his deceased brother's (Alexander, mentioned above) wife Glaphyra, which was against the Old Testament Law, since she was not childless.

As a side note, it is very interesting that Joseph on his way back from Egypt after the death of Herod the Great, avoids living in the area of Archelaus' rule because of his horrible reputation. Joseph resides in the friendlier confines of Galilee (Nazareth) ruled by Herod Antipas.

Matthew 2:22 *But when he heard that Archelaus was reigning over Judea in place of his father Herod, he was afraid to go there. Then after being warned by God in a dream, he left for the regions of Galilee,*

Meanwhile, Herod Antipas had attained a high place among the friends of Tiberius (who had succeeded Caesar Augustus who died in A.D. 14). Valerius Gratus, who was the Roman Procurator of Judea from A.D. 15 to 26, appointed Joseph Caiaphas to the office of high priest. Gratus retired and was replaced by Pontius Pilate.

Antipas first married the daughter of King Aretas (King of Arabia Petraea). Before Philip I died, his brother Antipas married his wife Herodias. It is not clear if Antipas divorced his first wife or if Philip I also divorced Herodias. In any scenario it was clearly against the Old Testament Law as John the Baptist proclaimed. When Antipas married Herodias, King Aretas eventually invaded Herod Antipas' territory, defeating him with great losses. This was done after the death of John the Baptist.

Many believed this defeat was God's judgment on Antipas for having killed John the Baptist. Some time later, Herodias urged Antipas to go to Rome (Caligula was then Emperor) to gain the official title of King, but emissaries of Herod Agrippa I (Herodias' brother — sibling rivalry?!) opposed him and Antipas and Herodias were banished to Lugdunum in 39 A.D. (what is now Lyon, France) and Antipas died a year later. His territory was then given to Herod Agrippa I.

It should be noted that this Herod Antipas was the Herod that examined Jesus who had been sent to him by Pontius Pilate. Also, Antipas founded the City of Tiberias.

Note that the prohibition against marrying your brother's wife is clearly stated in the Old Testament in Leviticus 18:16. The only time a brother could marry his brother's wife was listed in Deuteronomy 25:5-10, the law of the kinsman redeemer. Divorcing someone for just any reason was strictly forbidden. It was permitted only in very specific circumstances as the following passage in Matthew illustrates.

Matthew 19:3-9 *Some Pharisees came to Jesus, testing Him and asking, "Is it lawful for a man to divorce his wife for any reason at all?" And He answered and said, "Have you not read that He who created them from the beginning made them male and female, and said, 'For this reason a man shall leave his father and mother and be joined to his wife, and the two shall become one flesh'? "So they are no longer two, but one flesh. What therefore God has joined together, let no man separate." They said to Him, "Why then did Moses command to give her a certificate of divorce and send her away?" He said to them, "Because of your hardness of heart Moses permitted you to divorce your wives; but from the beginning it has not been this way. And I say to you, whoever divorces his wife, except for immorality, and marries another woman commits adultery."*

Why would Herod Antipas want to protect John the Baptist? First of all he had John arrested because he feared that so many people were following this great preacher that he might be organizing a revolt against him. Second, killing a man so greatly loved by the people might stir them up to revolt. And finally, as the passage says, he actually enjoyed listening to John the Baptist speak. However, while John was imprisoned within the fortress at Machaerus, on the eastern shore of the Dead

Sea, he was beheaded because of the foolish promise Antipas made to the dancing Salome, the daughter of Herodias as mentioned in our study passage.

It is thus extremely interesting to note why this same Antipas did not perceive Jesus Christ himself as a big enough threat to his kingdom to have him arrested. Knowing that Antipas could have had him imprisoned was probably one of the reasons that Jesus Christ tried as much as possible to keep his outward ministry as low key as possible, until the very end. He went from town to town, rather than have huge assemblies which would create suspicion. Even when he spoke to large crowds he would disperse the crowds as quickly as possible.

Homework follows.

The Ezra 7:10 Plan — 1st Love

STUDY   Context is the Key

Historical Homework

Pick one or more assignments/questions and find and record the information requested.

List the Israelite king's reigns who reigned during the life of King Asa of Judah.	Record the time period of Jonah's and Nahum's preaching to Nineveh. What nation were they preaching to?	Micah 1:1 - What was the time period of Micah's ministry?
2Chr 35:18,19 - How many years was it between Josiah's reign and the days of Samuel?	Rev 16:13-16 - Where is Armageddon? What does it mean? What previous events happened there? (Judges 5:19; Judges 7:1-25; 1Sam 31:1-13; 2Kings 9:27, 2Chron 35:22)	List the reigns of the Roman emperors of the first century.

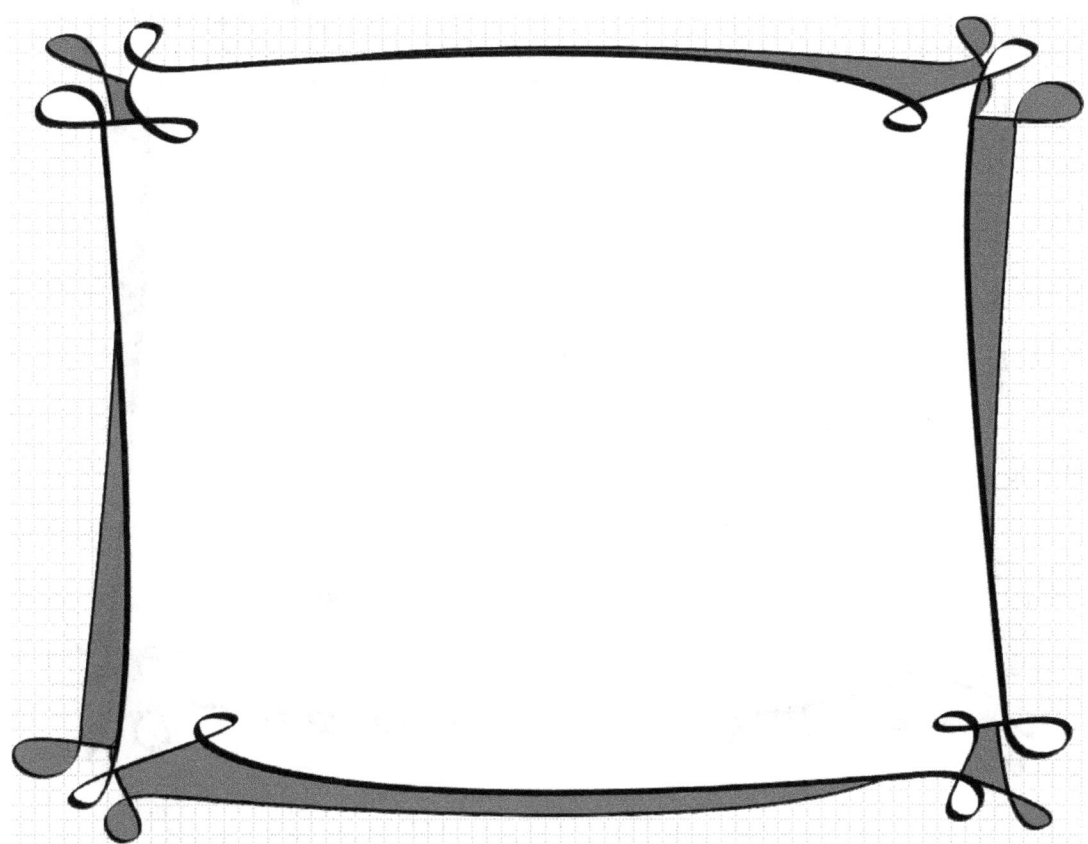

Looking at the Forest

The Ezra 7:10 Plan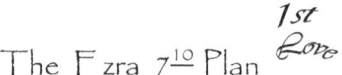

STUDY Context is the Key

Historical Homework continued ...

Pick one or more assignments/questions and find and record the information requested.

What was the time period in the days of Ruth, of Esther?	What nation ruled the land where Joseph was in prison showing favor to the Hebrews? What nation ruled later and was mean to the Hebrews?	Isa 28:21 – What happened at Mt Perazim? What happened in the valley of Gibeon?
How old was Jacob when he met Rachel?	What prophets helped Ezra and Nehemiah rebuild the temple and walls?	What Kings of Judah spanned the ministry of Jeremiah?

Looking at the Forest

The Ezra 7:10 Plan — 1st Love   STUDY   Context is the Key

Biographical Context

This context will not usually affect the Biblical interpretation of a verse or passage. In fact, this contextual study does not present itself as often as the rest of the contexts we have studied.

This book defines the biographical context as:

The life history of a personality

It is possible to gain additional insight into the Scriptures by having a thorough knowledge of the life of the people that are mentioned in the Bible. Knowing what an individual has already experienced or not experienced may affect how we relate to a particular passage of Scripture. We will look at a passage in the Book of Timothy.

Biographical Context Example: The Apostle Paul at the Writing of 2 Timothy

2 Timothy 4:7 *I have fought the good fight, I have finished the course, I have kept the faith;*

If we knew little about the Apostle Paul's life, we might not realize to what tremendous depths Paul fought and ran (sometimes literally) to keep his faith. It should be noted that 2 Timothy was the last book written by Paul and he wrote it just a few years before his death. A cursory review of his life up to this point reveals that for the sake of his faith in Christ Paul was: imprisoned several times, flogged severely (five times with thirty-nine lashes, three times with rods), often exposed to death, stoned once, shipwrecked three times, and one time spent a night and a day drifting on the open sea. He was constantly in danger of being robbed or killed by the Jews, Gentiles and false brothers, he often went without sleep or food, and he had been cold and without sufficient clothing. Included with all these physical calamities, he felt the daily pressure of trying to make sure that all of these new churches that were being started were growing and not being led astray. Most of us in our entire life may not experience one-tenth of the degree of suffering that Paul

Looking at the Forest

went through. Can we say as Paul did, *...I am well content with weaknesses, with insults, with distresses ... for when I am weak, then I am strong.*

Knowing Paul's background gives us a little more insight into what a *good fight* is, and what it means to *finish the course*. It lets us know what will possibly take place during the *fight*, and what obstacles there may be to *finish the course*. It also gives us some insight as to what probably was going through Paul's mind as he wrote these words!

Another important thing to keep in mind is what period of a person's life is this passage referring to, their early life or later life? When we read about a person in Scripture we may have a tendency to think about that person in only one phase of his or her life. A modern day example would be to think of Elvis Presley as always young and slim, or of the Beatles as a group still in their early twenties. Certain snapshots of peoples' lives may permanently cloud our overall impression of them. We may forever judge them by one episode instead of viewing their life in total. A modern-day example of this would certainly apply to impressions of ex-Presidents such as John Kennedy, Richard Nixon or Jimmy Carter, where single episodes of their lives were so dramatic that other major events in their lives may be completely forgotten.

Also as people age they may change in their commitment to serving the Lord. As we age we may grow stronger in our resolve to follow and serve the Lord or we may slowly lose this resolve. Thus many of our actions in our early years are different from those as we age. We can clearly see this in the lives of King David and his son King Solomon. It is also very apparent in many of the Kings of Judah and Israel. We should observe the actions of Biblical personalities but also try and remember at what age these actions occurred. This gives us additional insight as to why these actions may have taken place. The Bible is full of life lessons that we can apply to our life. The more we fully understand the context of these lessons, the more we can benefit.

Homework follows.

The Ezra 7:10 Plan *1st Love*   STUDY   Context is the Key

Biographical Homework

Pick one or more questions and find and record the information requested.

How has the Apostle John changed over the years? Compare Mk 3:17, Lu 9:54, 1Jn 2:1, and 3Jn 4.	Matt 23:35 - Who was Zechariah and why is he listed?
Heb 11:32 - Who was Jephthah?	Jude 1:9 - Who is the archangel Michael?

The Ezra 7¹⁰ Plan 1st Love   STUDY   Context is the Key

Biographical Homework continued ...

Pick one or more questions and find and record the information requested.

How has Solomon changed over the years? Compare 1Kg 3:6-9, 1Kg 6:1,38 - 7:1, Prov 1:7, 1Kg 9:1-13, 1Kg 10:14-29, 1Kg 11:1-13, 1Kg 11:28-40, Book of Ecclesiastes, and Eccl 12:13,14.
How did Saul change over the years? Compare the following: 1Sam9:2-21, 1Sam10:18-27, 1Sam 11:5-15, 1Sam 13:11-14, 1Sam 14:24, 1Sam15:10-31, 1Sam 17:11, 1Sam 18:6-17, 1Sam 22:7-18, 1Sam 28:3-25, and 1Sam 31:1-5.

Practice

Making Good Applications

Exercising the Truth

The Ezra 7^{10} Plan — 1st Love

PRACTICE

Making Good Applications
Exercising the Truth

Application can be defined as *the act of putting to use or purpose, close attention, or persistent effort.* Probably the most important part of our study of the Scriptures is making personal applications. In other words, based on what we have studied, what does God want *me* to do? If we have no plans to obey what God is sharing with us, why should we study or read the Bible at all? Even before we begin to study the Bible, our attitude needs to be one of humility and reverence as a child to a father, or as a student to a teacher.

Some people simply decide which parts of the Scriptures they want to follow and then forget or ignore the rest. Perhaps they follow the *easy* Scriptures but ignore the commands that are *hard* to follow. A common reason for people being turned off about Christianity is that they see too much hypocrisy in the church. This, of course, certainly does not give them a legitimate excuse for not turning to Christ, but we are supposed to be drawing others to Christ not turning them away.

A person growing in knowledge and application of the Scriptures is described in the Bible by one word, salt. Salt makes us thirsty. Likewise, a growing Christian's life should make those around thirsty for what this person has in his or her life. Notice we said a growing Christian.

The Ezra 7:10 Plan 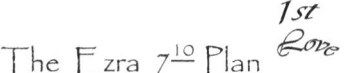 1st Love   PRACTICE   Making Good Applications

The apostle Paul never admitted that he was perfect but he did say,

Philippians 3:12 *Not that I have already obtained it or have already become perfect, but I press on so that I may lay hold of that for which also I was laid hold of by Christ Jesus.*

People will remember our progress more than they will remember the times we stumble, that is, assuming we continue to progress. It is clear that growth takes *practice* as Hebrews states,

Hebrews 5:14 *But solid food is for the mature, who because of practice have their senses trained to discern good and evil.*

It is also clear that growth takes *perseverance* as James states,

James 1:22-25 *but prove yourselves doers of the word, and not merely hearers who delude themselves. For if anyone is a hearer of the word and not a doer, he is like a man who looks at his natural face in a mirror; for once he has looked at himself and gone away, he has immediately forgotten what kind of person he was. But one who looks intently at the perfect law, the law of liberty, and abides by it, not having become a forgetful hearer but an effectual doer, this man will be blessed in what he does.*

A believer is like an uncut diamond. The more this diamond is cut and polished, the more it becomes a thing of beauty to be admired. The Lord is cutting and polishing us as we follow His Word. By following the Word, God will make our lives abundant and a blessing to others. Some of the effects of His polishing are described in Galatians.

Galatians 5:22,23 *But the fruit of the Spirit is love, joy, peace, patience, kindness, goodness, faithfulness, gentleness, self-control; against such things there is no law.*

The Ezra 7:10 Plan *1st Love*   PRACTICE   Making Good Applications

Types Of Applications

An application does not necessarily have to be in the form of an outward action. There are at least three ways we can *do* something that will help us become more Christ-like, and they can be grouped into the following categories:

- *Knowledge*

- *Attitude*

- *Action*

Knowledge

A knowledge application would include remembering the key points of what we have studied, including committing to memory what God may have been speaking to us in particular about. All too often the initial spiritual battle is won and lost here simply because we do not remember what we have learned. How many times have we heard sermons or gone to Sunday school classes and only a few days or weeks later we have no clue what the sermon or lesson was on, let alone remember anything about it.

As we study the Scriptures we should ask ourselves if there is anything we need to really commit to memory: a verse, truth, promise, warning, doctrine, or a new thought about God. We should write it down and memorize it. We can put it in writing and then post it on the refrigerator or any other place that we frequent. We do not want to stay in spiritual kindergarten forever as Hebrews says,

Hebrews 5:12-14 *For though by this time you ought to be teachers, you have need again for someone to teach you the elementary principles of the oracles of God, and you have come to need milk and not solid food. For everyone who partakes only of milk is not accustomed to the word of righteousness, for he is an infant. But solid food is for the mature, who because of practice have their senses trained to discern good and evil.*

Exercising the Truth

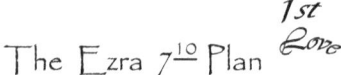

PRACTICE Making Good Applications

Attitude

Another type of application we can make is to change our attitude. Sometimes to enact real change in our actions we have to change the way we think. Attitude adjustments may be required before we are even able to start doing something we should. We may need to change the way we view God or other people. We may be making decisions or taking actions based solely on fear, guilt, anger or compulsion. Our attitude will need to change before we can begin to act correctly. Perhaps we are doing good deeds but we are doing them grudgingly. Our application may not affect the amount or frequency of doing certain deeds, but we will commit to doing them in the right frame of mind. Why is attitude so important? If we do things with the wrong attitude long enough, we may eventually lose heart and completely stop. Doing the right things in the right way will lead to maturity. We should take a quick attitude inventory as we study the Scriptures.

Philippians 2:3-8 *Do nothing from selfishness or empty conceit, but with humility of mind regard one another as more important than yourselves; do not merely look out for your own personal interests, but also for the interests of others. Have this attitude in yourselves which was also in Christ Jesus, who, although He existed in the form of God, did not regard equality with God a thing to be grasped, but emptied Himself, taking the form of a bond-servant, and being made in the likeness of men. Being found in appearance as a man, He humbled Himself by becoming obedient to the point of death, even death on a cross.*

Action

When we think about making an application from the Scriptures we probably think in terms of actions and activities. We should ask ourselves if there is any action that would help us to follow the Scriptures more closely or to exhibit more Christ-like behavior. Our action application can be to start a new course or even to stop some bad habits.

The Ezra 7:10 Plan — 1st Love

PRACTICE   Making Good Applications

Guidelines for Making Good Applications

Making good applications that will actually make a difference in our lives requires some effort on our part. We should pray and ask the Lord for help. The hardest part about making applications is being honest with ourselves. Too often we can go for a quick fix, while the Lord has some long-term solutions in mind. If our heart's desire is to follow in Christ's footsteps, then let us take the time to make sure the shoes fit. The process of becoming like Christ and maturing as His disciple takes time. It will take longer if we are not honest in assessing our faults. Unless we admit that we need correction, we will continue to stumble along. So pray first.

Once we have agreed with God on what area(s) needs correction, we need to be as specific as possible in planning our next steps. If we know that we need to work on a particular area in our life, but we do not put pen to paper, we will most likely forget to work on it. If we specify a particular task or person it will be easier to commit to action than some vague thought of, *I need to do better in this area.* So be specific.

We also need to set a goal for ourselves that is reasonable, measurable and achievable for the short term, without being too easy. While we hope that corrections we make will last for a lifetime, it is important that we give ourselves a short-term goal to get off to a good start. The goal needs to push us forward without discouraging us. So set a goal.

- ➢ *Pray First*
- ➢ *Be Specific*
- ➢ *Set a Goal*

We have included some real-life examples to illustrate how to make good applications and how to avoid making bad ones.

Exercising the Truth

The Ezra 7:10 Plan 1st Love   PRACTICE   Making Good Applications

Example Applications

<u>Action</u>

Bad: *I need to pray more.*

Good: *I will start a prayer list including needs of my friends. I will pray from 6:45 a.m. to about 7:00 a.m. I will pray on Mondays, Wednesdays and Fridays. I will do it for two weeks and see if I need to make any changes after that.*

<u>Knowledge / Attitude</u>

Bad: *I should pray even if I do not feel like it.*

Good: *I need to remember that it does not matter where or how I feel when I pray. God always honors faithful prayer. I will memorize James 5:16 to remind me, by this Sunday. I will write the verse on a card and stick it in my wallet and review it once a day until I have it down cold.*

<u>Action</u>

Bad: *I need to show more love to others.*

Good: *I have come up with a list of ways to love those around me. For the next month I will do the dishes three times a week, talk to my pastor to encourage him at least once a week, start to support a child through a Missionary Society, write one encouraging letter to my child every month, and volunteer to clean the office refrigerator even though I do not even use it.*

The Ezra 7:10 Plan — 1st Love   PRACTICE   Making Good Applications

Attitude

Bad: *Not being so grumpy all the time*

Good: *I will take the initiative to ask how others are doing (and be sincere in asking and listening). I will ask my wife, my children and my co-workers each day this week. On the weekend I will see if this has helped me not be so self-absorbed.*

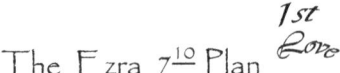

PRACTICE   Making Good Applications

Making Good Applications Homework

Using a recent Bible study or based on something you read in the Bible this week, develop good knowledge, and/or attitude, and/or action applications.

Teach

Developing Questions

Preaching the Word

The Ezra 7:10 Plan *1st Love*

Developing Questions
Preaching the Word

TEACH

Our objective in this section is to learn how to ask discovery, understanding, and application questions that cause us to dig deeper into the Scriptures. Learning how to develop these questions will also prepare us to lead Bible studies. We will explain each type of question and then using a verse from Scripture we will provide examples of good questions that will help us gain further insight and understanding.

Discovery Questions

Discovery questions are designed to flush out basic observations. These questions find out the *who, what, when* and *where* of the passage. Most of the time the Scriptures are clear on these points, but there are times when additional digging is required. We should always ask ourselves discovery questions to make sure that we understand these basic facts and can communicate them clearly in leading a Bible study.

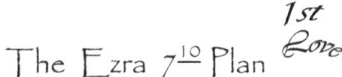

TEACH   Developing Questions

Understanding Questions

Understanding questions are designed to find out what something means. These questions are designed to draw out the *why* and the *how*. The answers to these questions usually reveal the deeper meaning and significance behind the words or deeds mentioned in the Bible. Starting a question with one of these words (*why* or *how*) will usually prevent one-word answers from a Bible study group. The group will have to reflect on the question before answering, instead of just saying yes or no.

Application Questions

Application questions deal with how a verse or passage applies to our life. Is there any promise, warning, doctrine or new thought about God we should remember? Do we need to change our attitude? Is there any action that would help us follow this teaching? Is this an area that God has been convicting (convincing) us of lately?

The following is a good summary of these three types of questions:

- **Discovery:**   *What does it say?*

- **Understanding:**   *What does it mean?*

- **Application:**   *What should I do?*

Asking questions as we study the Bible will give us deeper insights. If there is a question we cannot answer initially, we should use the appropriate Bible resource books and try to dig out the answer ourselves. We can double-check our answer with our pastor, Bible study leader, or from a more mature Christian friend who is knowledgeable about the Bible. This is part of the learning process. It is always better to try and discover the meaning of a verse on our own first. This gives us practice. We may be surprised after a few weeks how well we are doing.

The Ezra 7:10 Plan — 1st Love

TEACH — Developing Questions

An excellent way to get practice developing these questions, discovering the answers and checking our interpretation is to find out what passage our pastor is preaching on ahead of time. We can do our own study of the same passage during the week and on Sunday we can check our answers while we listen to the sermon!

The following are examples of discovery, understanding and application questions that can be asked while we study a verse from the Bible and can be used in leading a Bible study. Sometimes the answers we find with our initial questions lead to further questions, as we shall see in the following example. We will study the following passage:

2Corinthians 2:11 *so that no advantage would be taken of us by Satan, for we are not ignorant of his schemes.*

Possible Discovery Questions:

- ❖ *Who is Satan?*
- ❖ *What advantage would Satan have over us?*
- ❖ *What are his schemes?*
- ❖ *What does the "so" refer back to?*

Who is Satan? If we open just about any Bible dictionary we will find him described in many ways. Instead of going into a detailed review of all the Scriptures surrounding Satan (which we could do if we had more time), let us simply look at the names given to Satan. We can learn much about him just from this exercise.

He is called: adversary, accuser, roaring lion, tempter, and the evil one, and he is associated with anti-Christ. From these terms it is clear that he is not on our side and in fact is against us. His modus operandi is to trick us into doing things that go contrary to what God wants us to do. He is not only against God, but tries to take the place of God by providing an enticing counterfeit spiritual system. Note that the prefix *anti* in front of anti-Christ, in the Greek, means *against* or *instead of*. Satan is trying both to destroy the children of God outright and to lure them away from God by counterfeit religious systems. One of the ways that he tries to destroy

The Ezra 7:10 Plan 1st Love   TEACH   Developing Questions

believers is to make them feel as if they are worthless and cannot be forgiven when they sin. That is why he is called the accuser of the brethren. He hopes this will discourage them and prevent them from having a strong relationship with the Lord. He wants believers to feel so bad about themselves that they do not look to the Lord for forgiveness, they stop going to church, they stop reading the Bible, etc. What he plans to do is no secret.

What kind of advantage would Satan have over us? Any time Satan can make us doubt God's Word or make us think that God cannot forgive us he has an advantage over us. He is preventing us from growing confident in God's Word and in our relationship with Him. He is trying to take out spiritual soldiers one by one and put them out of commission. True believers cannot lose their salvation, but they can lose their saltiness and shine.

Matthew 5:13-16 *You are the salt of the earth; but if the salt has become tasteless, how can it be made salty again? It is no longer good for anything, except to be thrown out and trampled under foot by men. You are the light of the world. A city set on a hill cannot be hidden; nor does anyone light a lamp and put it under a basket, but on the lampstand, and it gives light to all who are in the house. Let your light shine before men in such a way that they may see your good works, and glorify your Father who is in heaven.*

What are his schemes? We discussed a few of them when we looked at the names for Satan. These names revealed his character and his schemes. He tries to trick us into believing that God's Word is not trustworthy, just as he did with Eve in the Garden of Eden. He tries to twist Scripture to trick us into doing his bidding just as he tried with Jesus in the wilderness. He tries to make us doubt God's care and protection for us just as he did when King David commissioned his census of warriors available in Israel. And we are sure he was right there when Peter denied Christ three times. Satan tried to sift him like wheat and make Peter feel that he had no right to be called the *Rock,* or even an apostle, or even a Christian.

What does the "so" refer back to? The word *so* is like the word *therefore.* It tells us that the writer is summing things up from the previous narrative. To find out what he was talking about we need to look back a few verses, in this case back to the beginning of Second Corinthians chapter two, which follows.

The Ezra 7:10 Plan 1st Love   TEACH Developing Questions

2Corinthians 2:1-11 *But I determined this for my own sake, that I would not come to you in sorrow again. For if I cause you sorrow, who then makes me glad but the one whom I made sorrowful? This is the very thing I wrote you, so that when I came, I would not have sorrow from those who ought to make me rejoice; having confidence in you all that my joy would be the joy of you all. For out of much affliction and anguish of heart I wrote to you with many tears; not so that you would be made sorrowful, but that you might know the love which I have especially for you. But if any has caused sorrow, he has caused sorrow not to me, but in some degree—in order not to say too much—to all of you. Sufficient for such a one is this punishment which was inflicted by the majority, so that on the contrary you should rather forgive and comfort him, otherwise such a one might be overwhelmed by excessive sorrow. Wherefore I urge you to reaffirm your love for him. For to this end also I wrote, so that I might put you to the test, whether you are obedient in all things. But one whom you forgive anything, I forgive also; for indeed what I have forgiven, if I have forgiven anything, I did it for your sakes in the presence of Christ, so that no advantage would be taken of us by Satan, for we are not ignorant of his schemes.*

    The passage is discussing the discipline of someone in the church that Paul had previously written about. Paul states that the punishment inflicted on this individual was sufficient to cause true sorrow, and now this person should be forgiven and comforted. They are to reaffirm their love for him. Paul goes on to say that he forgives this person. After this, our study verse appears. So the *so* is referring back to the forgiving of a penitent brother in the church. In this verse, Paul does not want the repentant brother to feel ostracized from the church and fall under the condemnation (scheme) of Satan. He makes it clear that the brother is to be reaffirmed in love. Otherwise Satan would gain an advantage by keeping the brother discouraged and away from fellowship.

Preaching the Word

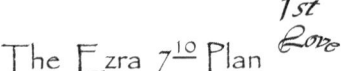

Possible Understanding Questions:

- *How does Satan get the advantage over us?*
- *Why would we ever be ignorant of his schemes?*

Based on what we have looked at so far in answering our discovery questions, *how is it possible that Satan gains the advantage over us?* It is clear that Satan uses deception and the placing of doubts about God's Word to fool us. He plays on emotions and tries to make people feel bad about their mistakes and feel unworthy to reach out for forgiveness. He can also gain the advantage if we are not properly schooled in the Word of God. If we have a poor or inconsistent relationship with God, Satan can more easily tempt us to walk away from following the Lord. One thing to remember about temptation: *we cannot be tempted by something that we cannot be tempted by.* Seems obvious yet, if we meditate on that fact we will realize why Jesus passed Satan's *tests* in the wilderness.

Why would we ever be ignorant of his schemes? This question is a good one. Is it possible to know that something is wrong and yet still do it? Sure it is. In the same way, perhaps it is not that we are ignorant of Satan's schemes; it is that subtly over time we become unaware that we are in fact falling into one of his traps. We will provide a good example for this based on the episode we just reviewed from chapter two of Second Corinthians.

Is it barely possible that two people in a given church would not get along? Now what if person *A,* who was having a hard time getting along with person *B,* heard or saw person *B* doing something uncharitable. Person *A* could go up to person *B* and say something like, *I cannot believe that you can go to church on Sundays and read your Bible and act like that!* Or Person *A* could get on the phone and tell five people how poorly person *B* acted, thus possibly alienating person B from these five people. This is doing Satan's job for him. What is needed is prayer and patience to allow the person to repent in an atmosphere that is filled with forgiveness and assurance. The sin is not tolerated, but it is not broadcasted either. Neither is the person to be lambasted. We must be careful or we may be an unwitting accomplice in Satan's schemes. Note that if the person arrogantly continues in their sinful ways despite our initial patience and perhaps private admonitions, then proper church discipline should be administered.

Possible Application Questions:

- ❖ Have I been *extra* unfriendly to another believer that I have a hard time getting along with?

- ❖ Do I repeat another person's failings even after I supposedly forgave him or her?

These questions are self-explanatory. There are more we could come up with. The idea is to search our hearts and see if the Lord is asking us to learn something from the text, think a certain way, or do something based on the passage we just studied.

As we can see, even one verse can offer a lot of opportunities for questions, as well as answers. We need to practice asking ourselves these questions as we study the Scriptures (and find the answers!). We will then also be able to lead a Bible study by asking these same questions. Homework follows!

The Ezra 7:10 Plan 1st Love

TEACH   Developing Questions

Developing Questions Homework

Pick a verse or passage to study and develop at least two questions each for Discovery, Understanding and Application. Provide suggested answers as well.

Verse or Passage

Questions

The Ezra 7:10 Plan *1st Love*   TEACH Developing Questions

Developing Questions Homework continued...

Pick a verse or passage to study and develop at least two questions each for Discovery, Understanding and Application. Provide suggested answers as well.

Verse or Passage

Questions

Preaching the Word

Discovery

God's Love for Me

The Ezra 7$\underline{10}$ Plan ^{1st Love}

God's Love for Me

Why this study

In the following pages we will be diving into a detailed study of selected verses of the *love* chapter (thirteen) of the Book of First Corinthians. While plenty of research will be provided, this will be our chance to do some Biblical digging, critical thinking, and summarizing of our thoughts about God's love for us.

There is the impression in some circles that the Lord was a God of judgment in the Old Testament but a God of love in the New Testament. A great study would actually be on judgment in the Old Testament. If we properly discern who receives judgment and why, and how the Lord spares the rest, we will discover that judgment is simply another characteristic of love. And of course, if we hone in on Jesus' life, we will see the same *Old Testament* judgment displayed in the New Testament. This comes as no surprise since the Lord never changes and His love never fails.

Bravery — Discovery

The Ezra 7:10 Plan — 1st Love   DISCOVERY   God's Love for Me

We can approach this study with excitement because of that fact. We are not studying about a God who is arbitrary and capricious about how He deals with His creation. Many misconceptions about the Lord exist because people do not read the Bible regularly. They remember bits and pieces while never actually having read the Bible through from cover to cover on a continual basis. One phrase that Jesus mentions more than once in the New Testament when dealing with doubters is, *have you not read…*

If we had a thousand-piece puzzle and put it together using only 250 pieces, we would not have a good idea of the true picture in front of us. We could speculate all we want, but until we have all the pieces placed in their proper context our opinions most likely would be in error.

The fact is that the Old Testament contains so many instances of God's love that to conclude otherwise would simply be wrong, to put it bluntly. That is why for the Bible study that follows, many of the examples of God's love have been taken from the Old Testament. It is our hope that this study will serve a two-fold purpose. For those of us new to faith in the Lord Jesus Christ, it will be our chance to be awestruck at the height, depth and breadth of the love God has for us. It is truly breathtaking. For those who have been believers for a while (maybe a long while), this is our chance to remember and embrace again the fullness of God's love for us. When we discover how much God loves us, we will begin to love others in the same way. God's love for us becomes a platform from which we feel safe and secure enough to open our hearts to love others.

For young and old, this will firmly establish and strengthen our spiritual foundation. We will begin to build up our spiritual temple as we see God as never before. We will continue to make more and more room for His Spirit to fill us and strengthen us to serve.

The Ezra 7:10 Plan — 1st Love

DISCOVERY   God's Love for Me

What the study covers

The Bible study covers the following aspects of love in detail:

Is patient	Is kind	Is not jealous	Does not brag	Is not arrogant
Does not act unbecomingly	Does not seek its own	Is not provoked	Does not take into account a wrong suffered	Does not rejoice in unrighteousness
Rejoices with the truth	Bears	Believes	Hopes	Endures
Never fails				

For each of the above characteristics some background material has been provided, including famous quotes and stories as well as a comic strip. We will then look up an Old Testament example of this characteristic. From there, we will record our thoughts on that passage, recall instances of how the Lord has displayed this action in our life, and really think about how specifically we can pattern our life after this Godly characteristic.

We should make sure before we make these applications that we pray first, be as specific as possible, and set a goal that is attainable. These applications can take the form of knowledge (remembering something we learned), attitude (a new way of thinking), and action (either starting or stopping an action as warranted).

177

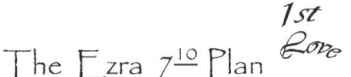

Finally we will have some space to prepare a little teaching on what we have just learned so we can easily pass it on to others. Here we can put some thoughts down that will help us remember how to explain this aspect of love to others. We can create an acronym or an illustration and/or memorize a key verse that summarizes the meaning, or memorize a parable or story that brings out the meaning. Of course, sharing from personal experience is always a good teacher. Keep it simple. This exercise of creating teaching points will force us to digest more thoroughly all the material that we have learned. Note that this teaching may be revised over time, and feel free to circle back to this Bible study many times. Our teaching may also make for a good devotion to share with others. There is an extra credit section that follows our teaching points that is designed to stimulate our thinking even more.

Suggested Schedule

Try and finish a Bible study on two characteristics of love each week. This will total eight weeks. Note that there are two more optional (but highly recommended) homework assignments in the final section titled *Encore*. They should be completed during what would be week nine.

Some Final Thoughts Before We Begin the Study

While it is true that the Lord brings people into our lives to encourage us and to display for us in person His many qualities, it is also true that we live in a world that displays every form of ungodliness. This tends to affect us negatively and makes it hard to see God's love shining through. Many people face issues of fear, doubt and low self-esteem, and find it hard to comprehend how much the Lord loves them. Now one answer for this may be to surround ourselves with godly people as much as possible. But this is not possible to achieve every hour of the day.

There is something more we must do: To experience the fullness of God's love, we need first and foremost to draw upon God's love for us directly from the Lord Himself. People fail, and people will let us down, but God will never let us down.

The Ezra 7:10 Plan — 1st Love

DISCOVERY — God's Love for Me

Remember that. The Lord designed His people to function as a body, as a team, but our main source of inspiration individually should always be from the Lord Himself. We need to view correctly how God sees us. We need to combat the lies and deception we are being fed with the truth about the love God has for us. And that is what this study is all about. We will see God as never before. We will, perhaps for the first time in our life, realize how much we are truly treasured by the Lord.

When we fully grasp the depth of love that the King of Kings and Lord of Lords has for us as His children, it is truly humbling, and yet at the same time empowering. Once we see how much we are loved, the fog will lift. We will then clearly see the goal — and what a lofty goal. Jesus sets the bar for us and communicates in no uncertain terms our goal: simply put, perfection. Ouch! Just when we were feeling so comfortable!

The next big step in fully comprehending God's love for us is when we begin to live it out. This step is when we dare to exhibit His love to all people and not just to people who will love us back. This is where many — so many — fail to experience the richness of His love. Remember when Jesus clarified what it meant to *love your neighbor as yourself*? Remember when He introduced a new commandment *Love others as I have loved you?* This was not really new but it put a simple yet profound perspective on loving others.

His is a selfless love, not desiring anything in return. He is also saying *do what I do*. The great thing about this is that we are not just adhering to rules and regulations, but we are imitating a person who has gone before us and left us many examples to follow. Examples abound in the Old Testament as well. Let us read His view of perfection as stated in Matthew chapter five.

Matthew 5:43-48 *You have heard that it was said, "You shall love your neighbor and hate your enemy." But I say to you, love your enemies and pray for those who persecute you, so that you may be sons of your Father who is in heaven; for He causes His sun to rise on the evil and the good, and sends rain on the righteous and the unrighteous. For if you love those who love you, what reward do you have? Do not even*

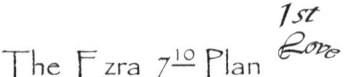

the tax collectors do the same? If you greet only your brothers, what more are you doing than others? Do not even the Gentiles do the same?" Therefore you are to be perfect, as your heavenly Father is perfect.

Also take a look at First John chapter four (paragraph breaks are author's for emphasis).

1 John 4: 7-21 *Beloved, let us love one another, for love is from God; and everyone who loves is born of God and knows God.*

The one who does not love does not know God, for God is love. By this the love of God was manifested in us that God has sent His only begotten Son into the world so that we might live through Him. In this is love, not that we loved God, but that He loved us and sent His Son to be the propitiation for our sins.

Beloved, if God so loved us, we also ought to love one another. No one has seen God at any time; if we love one another, God abides in us, and His love is perfected in us. By this we know that we abide in Him and He in us, because He has given us of His Spirit. We have seen and testify that the Father has sent the Son to be the Savior of the world. Whoever confesses that Jesus is the Son of God, God abides in him, and he in God. We have come to know and have believed the love which God has for us.

God is love, and the one who abides in love abides in God, and God abides in him. By this, love is perfected with us, so that we may have confidence in the day of judgment; because as He is, so also are we in this world.

There is no fear in love; but perfect love casts out fear, because fear involves punishment, and the one who fears is not perfected in love.

We love, because He first loved us. If someone says, "I love God," and hates his brother, he is a liar; for the one who does not love his brother whom he has seen, cannot love God whom he has not seen.

And this commandment we have from Him, that the one who loves God should love his brother also.

The Ezra 7¹⁰ Plan *1st Love*   DISCOVERY   God's Love for Me

And finally the goal of this study could not be stated any better than in Ephesians chapter three.

Ephesians 3:14-19 *For this reason I bow my knees before the Father, from whom every family in heaven and on earth derives its name, that He would grant you, according to the riches of His glory, to be strengthened with power through His Spirit in the inner man, so that Christ may dwell in your hearts through faith; and that you, being rooted and grounded in love, may be able to comprehend with all the saints what is the breadth and length and height and depth, and to know the love of Christ which surpasses knowledge, that you may be filled up to all the fullness of God.*

It is interesting to note that the apostle Paul is writing this to the church at Ephesus, expressing his hope for them to experience the depths of God's love, and yet dozens of years later another apostle, John, writes to a church in the Book of Revelation admonishing them because they have lost their first love. Guess what church it was.

'Nuff said — now we need to start putting those puzzle pieces together!

Note that many of the quotes in the following sections can be found in an excellent resource, the *Encyclopedia of 7700 illustrations: A treasury of illustrations, anecdotes, facts and quotations for pastors, teachers and Christian workers*, by Tan, P. L. (1996, c1979). Garland TX: Bible Communications.

CHARACTERISTIC OF LOVE

Discussion

Biblical patience includes the idea of long-suffering or being long-tempered (as opposed to being short-tempered). In fact, the Greek word translated as *being patient* (verb) or *patience* (noun) includes the concept *long* within the word itself. The verb in Greek is μακροθυμέω (*makrothumeō*). It is a compound of two words: μακρός (*macros*) meaning *long* or *long-lasting*, or for distances, *a long way away*; and θυμόω (*thumoō*) meaning *to become angry, to become incensed with wrath*. So literally translated, exhibiting patience means you take a very long time before you become angry. Instead of having a short fuse, you have a very long fuse. It is identical in the Hebrew, where the Hebrew word for *long* is usually paired with another word such as *anger*, denoting that God is *slow* (or *long*) *to anger*. It is interesting to note that the Greek translation of the Old Testament (*The Septuagint*, usually denoted as *LXX*) most often translates the Hebrew expression *slow to anger* with the Greek *makrothumeō*. Also note that patience is a fruit of the Spirit as detailed in Galatians 5:22.

Biblical patience is something we exercise. In our study verse, the words *is patient* are actually used as a verb in the original Greek. The more literal translation would be *love is being patient*. Perhaps one way to think of how to practice patience would be to think of what makes us angry. Does this mean that practicing patience means never being angry? Good point. So how do we know when it is acceptable to be angry or when patience should be displayed? What is God's view of patience? How does God want us to practice patience?

The Ezra 7:10 Plan 1st Love 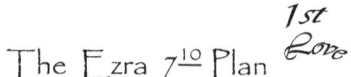   DISCOVERY   God's Love for Me

By looking up verses that contain patience or patient we can get a good idea of God's view of things. We could do an exhaustive study of this topic if we used a thesaurus to look up similar words, such as long-suffering, forgiving, lenient, etc.

Here are just a few to read.

God's Patience Toward Us	
2 Peter 3:9 *The Lord is not slow about His promise, as some count slowness, but is patient toward you, not wishing for any to perish but for all to come to repentance.*	Romans 2:4 *Or do you think lightly of the riches of His kindness and tolerance and patience, not knowing that the kindness of God leads you to repentance?*

God Requests Our Patience	
Psalm 37:7 *Rest in the Lord and wait patiently for Him...*	Hebrews 6:12 *so that you will not be sluggish, but imitators of those who through faith and patience inherit the promises.*

Examples of Our Patience Toward Others	
2 Timothy 4:2 *preach the word; be ready in season and out of season; reprove, rebuke, exhort, with great patience and instruction.*	
1 Thessalonians 5:14 *We urge you, brethren, admonish the unruly, encourage the fainthearted, help the weak, be patient with everyone.*	James 5:10 *As an example, brethren, of suffering and patience, take the prophets who spoke in the name of the Lord.*

By reading the verses above we may reach a few conclusions about patience. To discover God's perspective on patience we must discover His goal for all the qualities of love. It is clear from the verses above that He is patient when He sees into the very heart of people. He can see that there is still room for change, for repentance, for turning their life around towards His way, which is the goal. Even from the cross Jesus saw into the hearts of His accusers and could discern that they really did not know what they were doing, and perhaps there was still hope for them. That is why He asked the Father to forgive them. This is the very reason we need to display patience even toward our *enemies*. (We can, however, safely discount the Hitler and Nero-types out there.) This may be easier when we know the people we see, such as our friends and family. However, we all know that certain people try our patience more than others. Perhaps the Lord has placed these people in our path to help lengthen our *long* in our ability to display long-suffering.

Patience is thus a key ingredient in being able to work well with people. People who have little patience tend also to be those who are insensitive and unreasonable. Patience is needed as we work with co-workers, children, students, and disciples. We need to give people time to learn things and tailor our expectations according to the person. Patience is not easily upset when someone makes a mistake. We should not expect the exact same progress from everyone. God treats us as individuals. We should not be so quick to give up or give out on others. Remember, if we are quick to anger, we may also be slow to realize the potential in others. Conversely if we are slow to anger, we may be quick to see that progress is indeed being made. We should strive for the latter.

Proverbs 19:11 *A man's discretion makes him slow to anger, And it is his glory to overlook a transgression.*

The Lord exhibits anger when people resolutely decide to go their own way. In these situations, warnings, admonitions, and even rebukes may be warranted to open people's eyes to their sinful ways. That is tough love. We need to exhibit patience even when we admonish others. We should not fly off the handle or say something we will regret. Thus we exhibit patience in dealing with slow learners and those who are clearly going down the wrong path. Now remember how long it may have taken us to repent and place our faith in the Lord. The Lord had to wait for us patiently all that time. Recall Moses' first encounter with the Lord at the burning bush. Despite Moses' own reservations about his shortcomings, God saw into his heart and knew he was the man for the job. The Lord started to become angry when it appeared that Moses was going to resolutely turn down the offer, but Moses was so assured by God's continual encouragement and exhortation that he accepted the task. His worries about his own inabilities were overcome by God's assurance that his own weaknesses would be replaced with God's strengths. We need to keep this in mind when we interact with others, especially those of us who are parents, ministry leaders, teachers, coaches, etc. We should keep Moses in mind when we are waiting for the promises of God. We can be patient because we know that the Lord desires His best for us.

Our patience and sensitivity toward others and our patience in following the Lord will help us remove any barriers that may prevent us from having good relationships. Perhaps that is why patience is mentioned first in this list and why it is a key fruit of the Spirit.

Finally, let us view patience as it is needed for different relational groups. Some of the people we interact with on a daily basis may be placed into three very broad categories, each with its own challenges. One group includes all the people who are in an authoritative position over us. This would include the Lord Himself, but also includes church leaders; employers; federal, state and local government, etc. Another group includes those that we exhibit authority over, such as children, employees, various groups in the church, etc. The third group represents those personal challenges. These are people we have a hard time dealing with for a variety of reasons. Each group tries our patience in different ways. Those in authority may challenge our pride, as we may disagree with the way they do things. Those we lead and/or teach may challenge our authority or become discipline problems. Or perhaps we think they are not progressing as fast as we think they should. Those hard-to-get-along-with people perhaps challenge us the most to love whom we think may be unlovable. Think about these situations. Does anyone come to mind? Perhaps the Lord is reminding us to be patient with certain people in the same way as the Lord has been patient with us.

We will all go through experiences in which we find it hard to practice patience, perhaps even being patient with the Lord Himself. It is these times in which our patience has room for growth. We should not say that we will never be able to be patient with or work with someone. The Lord will help us increase our capacity for patience and sensitivity. It may take some time, but do not lock the door on patience. Sadly, once we decide that we will limit our patience or who we want to associate or deal with, our spiritual life in general will begin to suffer. We can just hear the Lord saying: *It's great that you love folks who love you back or you get along with easily. Now what about those who you do not even want to be around? What about those who you think won't amount to anything? I want you to work with them and be patient with them too. I do not want you to just be in a holy huddle, or stay in click groups all your life.*

One day we might wake up and feel that we have more enemies than friends. If we are patient with them while we seek guidance from the Lord, our entire perspective may change.

Perhaps these final words will also inspire us to gain more patience!

Quotes

John and Charles Wesley were blessed with a patient mother. At one time her husband said, "I marvel at your patience! You have told that child the same thing twenty times!" Susanna Wesley looked fondly at the child. She said, "Had I spoken the matter only nineteen times, I should have lost all my labor."
— *Choice Gleanings*

A man is a hero, not because he is braver than anyone else, but because he is brave for ten minutes longer. — *Emerson*

Two Christians were driving through an area where the road was being widened. At the end of the repair zone, a sign informed travelers, "Construction Ended. Thank You for Your Patience." "I think that would make an appropriate epitaph for my life," said one of the Christians.

The Ezra 7:10 Plan — 1st Love   DISCOVERY   God's Love for Me

XOgesis

KJ: "My mom says I have a short tempter. Does that mean I can't reach others to tempt them?"

Naz: "Knowing you it probably means you have no patience. Your mom no doubt said you have a short temper."

KJ: "Hey are you calling me names, why I oughta…"

Naz: "See what I mean, you get angry easily, you have a short temper."

KJ: "I can't help it. I'm short. Maybe when I grow taller I'll have a longer temper?!"

Naz: "Let's hope so. In the meantime, I guess we'll have to be patient with you, Shorty!"

From KJ & Friends ™ © 2010 by G Doulos

DISCOVERY God's Love for Me

OLD TESTAMENT EXAMPLES [Gen 18:16-33] [Book of Jonah]

Describe how the LORD displays **Patience** in these passages.

Describe how the LORD has been **Patient** with you and/or someone that you know.

The Ezra 7:10 Plan 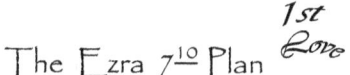   DISCOVERY   God's Love for Me

List a way you will be **Patient** this week. Prepare a concise teaching on **Patience**.

My Application:

My Lesson Plan

Extra Credit – Pick any of the 10 commandments and think about how being ***Patient*** will help you fulfill the commandment.

DISCOVERY God's Love for Me

CHARACTERISTIC OF LOVE

Kind

Discussion

Biblical kindness includes the idea that we are bringing some benefit to another person. When we have been treated with kindness, our life has benefited in some way, big or small. In fact, *Merriam-Webster's* dictionary defines benefit as *an act of kindness*. The word *benefit* from the Latin (*bene factum*) literally means *to do good*.

The word for *to be kind* or *kindness* in the Hebrew has a very interesting etymology. The verb *to be kind* in the Hebrew is חָסַד, (chasad) and the verb, *to be reproached* or *ashamed* share the exact same spelling. The same holds true for the noun forms (i.e., kindness and shame). They both come from a root word that means *eager zeal* or *desire* according to *The Enhanced Brown-Driver-Briggs Hebrew and English Lexicon*. So if our zeal is for good it leads to acts of kindness and if our zeal is morally destitute it leads to shame and reproach. Also, in the Greek, the words *is kind* in 1 Corinthians 13:4, are actually used as a verb, and so should be translated as *love is being kind* or *love is showing acts of kindness*.

The reason this etymology is discussed is to highlight the fact that being kind is accompanied by zeal and enthusiasm. It is not meant to be for the exclusive domain of the quiet and elderly. When we are being kind our purpose is to improve the lives of those around us by providing them some tangible benefit. When we are described as being a kind person, our life in part serves to benefit others. It goes without saying that a kind person is a selfless person. It is hard to be self-absorbed and yet still plan our daily activities so that we will be a blessing to others. How can we remove our self from our burdens so that we will be able to remove burdens from others? That is a good question. It is answered in kindness.

The Ezra 7:10 Plan — 1st Love   DISCOVERY   God's Love for Me

It is answered in a simple question we can ask ourselves every day. How can I benefit another person today?

Developing kindness is a process, and the following will help us start. First, meditate on the following verse from Philippians:

Philippians 2:3-4 *Do nothing from selfishness or empty conceit, but with humility of mind regard one another as more important than yourselves; do not merely look out for your own personal interests, but also for the interests of others.*

To be truly kind we need to put our own personal interests in their proper priority. The Lord always comes first; that is a given. What happens after that often becomes fuzzy. Although we go to the Lord for our help and sustenance, it is not meant to be a closed loop. While we are being helped we need to be on the lookout to help others. This is easy to do with some and much harder with others. Do we think the Lord puts people in our paths to *stretch* our capacity for kindness? Absolutely. Note that *kindness*, like *patience* we just studied, is a fruit of the Spirit as detailed in Galatians 5:22.

We should not say we will never be kind to someone who is unkind to us, for the Lord experiences this every day. We should aspire to be like Christ. If He sends blessings and healings on the unjust and unloving, so should we. Consider the many people Jesus healed and yet did not show Him any appreciation. What motivated Jesus to help them? It was kindness. It was His way of showing us, do as I do, even to ungrateful people.

Kindness demands no thanks but seeks its reward in the blessing it bestows on its recipients. Kindness is no doormat but rather a willing enthusiastic servant. Kindness is Joseph who made himself blind to his surroundings and benefited his fellow prisoners. Kindness is Ruth who left all to be a blessing to her mother-in-law. When we seek only our own interests our life is like a closed pool of water that becomes more stagnant as each year passes. We can become stingy and unsympathetic, completely oblivious to the opportunities we have to benefit others.

The Ezra 7:10 Plan 1st Love   DISCOVERY   God's Love for Me

When we seek to live also for the benefit of others, the dam will break and refreshing waters of life will continually pour forth from our soul, enriching the lives of many and ours as well.

John 7:38 *He who believes in Me, as the Scripture said, 'From his innermost being will flow rivers of living water.'*

Consider the following verses as well.

God's Kindness Toward Us	
Psalm 106:7 *Our fathers in Egypt did not understand Your wonders; They did not remember Your abundant kindnesses,*	Psalm 145:17 *The Lord is righteous in all His ways And kind in all His deeds.*
Luke 6:35 *But love your enemies, and do good, and lend, expecting nothing in return; and your reward will be great, and you will be sons of the Most High; for He Himself is kind to ungrateful and evil men.*	

God Requests Our Kindness	
Galatians 5:22 *But the fruit of the Spirit is love, joy, peace, patience, kindness, goodness, faithfulness,*	Colossians 3:12 *So, as those who have been chosen of God, holy and beloved, put on a heart of compassion, kindness, humility, gentleness and patience;*
Ephesians 4:32 *Be kind to one another, tender-hearted, forgiving each other, just as God in Christ also has forgiven you.*	Micah 6:8 *He has told you, O man, what is good; And what does the Lord require of you But to do justice, to love kindness, And to walk humbly with your God?*

Examples of Our Kindness Toward Others	
2 Samuel 9:1 *Then David said, "Is there yet anyone left of the house of Saul, that I may show him kindness for Jonathan's sake?*	Proverbs 31:26 *She opens her mouth in wisdom, And the teaching of kindness is on her tongue.*
2 Timothy 2:24 *The Lord's bond-servant must not be quarrelsome, but be kind to all, able to teach, patient when wronged,*	

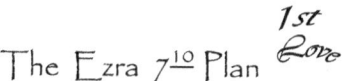

By reading the verses above, we may reach a few conclusions about kindness. It is very clear that kindness is to be shown to all people whether they are deserving of it or not. The Bible abounds in examples of God's kindness toward us. If we are to be like Him, we must be kind as He is kind. Another conclusion can be drawn in that kindness is given for many purposes, one of which is salvation. Kindness benefits others — salvation being the biggest benefit. For those teachers and parents out there kindness is essential. For those in ministry it is basically a pre-requisite. In the Old and New Testaments mention is made of good and bad shepherds. One qualification of good shepherds is kindness. Bad shepherds were described as wolves. Wolves do not seek the best in others, but rather are self-seeking, scattering the flock, not protecting, preserving and benefiting it.

We start each day with a pocketful of benefits. We need to be on the lookout to empty our pockets by day's end.

Perhaps these final words will also inspire us to be a kind person!

Quotes

Tolstoy, the great Russian writer, was passing along a street one day when a begger stopped him and pleaded for alms. The great Russian searched through his pockets for a coin, but finding none he regretfully said, "Please don't be angry with me, my brother, but I have nothing with me. If I did I would gladly give it to you." The beggar's face flamed up, and he said, "You have given me more than I asked for. You have called me brother." — Evangelistic Illustration

It is said that when Mrs. Booth, who even more than her husband, was the life of the Salvation Army, was a little girl, running along the road with hoop and stick, she saw a prisoner dragged away by a constable to the lockup. A mob was hooting at the unfortunate culprit, and his utter loneliness appealed at once to her heart. It seemed to her that he had not a friend in the world. Quick as thought she sprang to his side and marched down the street with him, determined that he should know that there was one soul that felt for him whether he suffered for his own fault or that of another.

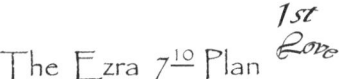

Who has not been thrilled by Beethoven's "Moonlight Sonata?" It is a master interpretation in sound of the unspeakable glory of a moonlit night. This beautiful piece of music was created because the composer wanted to give something of himself and his talent to a blind girl. This lady could not see the beauties of a moonlit night: blind was she to the silver sheen on trees and shrub and grass; blind was she to the silver covering on the lake; blind was she to the world of milky white in the sky. So the thoughtful and selfless Beethoven put his genius to work. He would tell her not merely in words, but in sound, of the beauty her eyes could not behold. As a result the world has been enriched. He gave the best of his talent in a selfless act of kindness. — Tonne

Lord Palmerston, Queen Victoria's Prime Minister, was crossing Westminster Bridge when a little girl ahead dropped a jug of milk. The jug broke into fragments, and she dissolved into tears. Palmerston, having no money with him dried her eyes by telling her that if she came to the same spot next day at that hour he would pay for both jug and milk. The following morning, in the midst of a cabinet meeting, he suddenly remembered his promise to the little girl, left the bewildered ministers, dashed across the bridge, popped half a crown into the waiting child's hand and hurried back. — All Nations Missionary Review

Many years ago Dwight W. Morrow, the father of Anne Lindbergh, told a group of friends that Calvin Coolidge had real presidential possibilities. They disagreed, saying that Coolidge was too quiet, and lacked color and political personality. "No one would like him," objected one of the group. But up piped little Anne, then aged six: "I like Mr. Coolidge." Then she displayed a finger with a bit of adhesive tape on it. "He was the only one who asked me about my sore finger." Mr. Morrow nodded. "There's your answer," he said.

The teacher asked the pupils to tell the meaning of loving-kindness. A little boy jumped up and said, "Well, if I was hungry and someone gave me a piece of bread that would be kindness. But if they put a little jam on it, that would be loving-kindness."

To ease another's heartache is to forget one's own. — Abraham Lincoln

The Ezra 7:10 Plan — 1st Love   DISCOVERY   God's Love for Me

XOgesis

Annie: "How is your Bible study on kindness coming?"

Ned: "Well it's a one-of-a-kind study, but it's kind of hard to figure out the kind of kindness I am the kind for, but I know I'll benefit in kind."

Annie: "Huh?"

Ned: "It's going well. Kind of you to ask."

From KJ & Friends ™ © *2010 by G Doulos*

The Ezra 7:10 Plan 1st Love 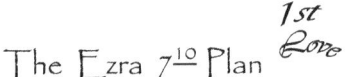 DISCOVERY God's Love for Me

OLD TESTAMENT EXAMPLES [Gen 39] [Psalm 106:7]

Describe how the LORD displays **Kindness** in these passages.

Describe how the LORD has been **Kind** to you and/or someone that you know.

The Ezra 7:10 Plan — *1st Love*   DISCOVERY   God's Love for Me

List a way you will be **Kind** this week. Prepare a concise teaching on **Kindness**.

My Application:

My Lesson Plan

Extra Credit – Pick any of the 10 commandments and think about how being **Kind** will help you fulfill the commandment.

CHARACTERISTIC OF LOVE

Discussion

Now that we have the first two positive characteristics down, we start a series of negative characteristics. These are actions that we should avoid if we are to emulate the love of God. This is similar to the Ten Commandments, where we have actions to perform, and actions to avoid. Inherent in an action to avoid is an action to take its place. As Jesus points out, it is not enough not to murder someone in order to fulfill the sixth commandment. We should pray for those we consider enemies, "turn the other cheek," and avoid calling them names or thinking ill of them. In the same way, we will discover some positive things we can do instead of not being jealous, not bragging, not being arrogant, etc. We want to go on the offensive to promote love instead of just trying to suppress bad actions. Let us now look at jealousy.

Both the Hebrew and the Greek words for being jealous can more aptly be translated as *being zealous*. The Greek verb translated as *to be jealous* even sounds like zealous, ζηλόω (*zēloō*). Being zealous, however, has its good side and its bad side. Think of being zealous or exhibiting zeal as a single-minded focus on an object, cause, person, etc. The Old Testament often refers to God as a jealous God. In fact a better translation would be that God is a zealous God, since jealousy has a negative connotation. However, let us dive into the definition of

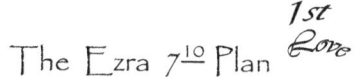

jealous and perhaps we can see how jealousy can be a good thing as well as a bad thing.

We can define jealousy as anger or fear that others will take what we have. Couple this definition with what we have stated about zeal as being a single-minded devotion and we can clearly see how God can be both zealous and jealous over His children. God zealously protects His children from bad influences, because He is concerned (jealous), that the *enemy* will lead them astray from the blessings of the Promised Land. So that is what being zealous or exhibiting *good* jealousy is about. Another great example is when Jesus chased the money changers and profiteers from the temple area. His single-minded devotion to His Father's house moved him to remove anything that would bring dishonor to His Father. He fulfilled the scripture:

Psalm 69:9 *For zeal for Your house has consumed me, And the reproaches of those who reproach You have fallen on me.*

Now let us look at the *bad* side of jealousy. It is interesting to note that many of the modern translations translate *zēloō* as *to envy*, instead of *to be jealous*. This has to do with the blending of the terms in our modern usage. Let us look at *Merriam-Webster's* definitions for jealous and envy.

Jealous is defined as: *intolerant of rivalry or unfaithfulness; hostile toward a rival or one believed to enjoy an advantage and; vigilant in guarding a possession.* Envy is defined as: *painful or resentful awareness of an advantage enjoyed by another joined with a desire to possess the same advantage and; an object of envious notice or feeling.*

The Theological Wordbook of the Old Testament has a good comparison of the two as follows: *It may prove helpful to think of "zeal" as the original sense from which derived the notions:*

"zeal for another's property" = *"envy"*
and *"zeal for one's own property"* = *"jealousy."*

199

Or still another simplistic view of the two:

Envy = Anger / Resentment that others have what we want
Jealousy = Anger / Fear others will take what we have

It is clear from the above that many situations exist where both definitions will fit. Also we can see how covetousness (the Tenth Commandment) would be a subset of envy. There is one thing that is common to both jealousy and envy. Feelings of hostility and resentment are present toward another person. So what is the root cause? What positive action(s) can we take so that we will not be jealous? Let us look at the following scriptures:

God's Zeal Toward Us	
Nahum 1:2 *A jealous and avenging God is the Lord; The Lord is avenging and wrathful. The Lord takes vengeance on His adversaries, And He reserves wrath for His enemies.*	1 Corinthians 12:6,7 *There are varieties of effects, but the same God who works all things in all persons. But to each one is given the manifestation of the Spirit for the common good.*
Luke 10:17-21 *The seventy returned with joy, saying, "Lord, even the demons are subject to us in Your name." And He said to them, "I was watching Satan fall from heaven like lightning. "Behold, I have given you authority to tread on serpents and scorpions, and over all the power of the enemy, and nothing will injure you. "Nevertheless do not rejoice in this, that the spirits are subject to you, but rejoice that your names are recorded in heaven." At that very time He rejoiced greatly in the Holy Spirit, and said, "I praise You, O Father, Lord of heaven and earth, that You have hidden these things from the wise and intelligent and have revealed them to infants. Yes, Father, for this way was well-pleasing in Your sight."*	Exodus 34:24 *For I will drive out nations before you and enlarge your borders, and no man shall covet your land when you go up three times a year to appear before the Lord your God.*

The Ezra 7:10 Plan — 1st Love   DISCOVERY   God's Love for Me

God Forbids Our Jealousy / Envy / Covetousness	
Luke 9:49-50 *John answered and said, "Master, we saw someone casting out demons in Your name; and we tried to prevent him because he does not follow along with us." But Jesus said to him, "Do not hinder him; for he who is not against you is for you."*	Deuteronomy 7:25 *The graven images of their gods you are to burn with fire; you shall not covet the silver or the gold that is on them, nor take it for yourselves, or you will be snared by it, for it is an abomination to the Lord your God.*
Job 5:2 *For anger slays the foolish man, And jealousy kills the simple.*	James 3:16 *For where jealousy and selfish ambition exist, there is disorder and every evil thing.*
Proverbs 23:17 *Do not let your heart envy sinners, But live in the fear of the Lord always.*	Deuteronomy 5:21 *You shall not covet your neighbor's wife, and you shall not desire your neighbor's house, his field or his male servant or his female servant, his ox or his donkey or anything that belongs to your neighbor.*

Examples of Our Zeal Toward Others	
Numbers 25:11 *Phinehas the son of Eleazar, the son of Aaron the priest, has turned away My wrath from the sons of Israel in that he was jealous with My jealousy among them, so that I did not destroy the sons of Israel in My jealousy.*	2 Corinthians 11:2 *For I am jealous for you with a godly jealousy; for I betrothed you to one husband, so that to Christ I might present you as a pure virgin.*
Hebrews 10:24 *and let us consider how to stimulate one another to love and good deeds,*	Numbers 11:29 *But Moses said to him, "Are you jealous for my sake? Would that all the Lord's people were prophets, that the Lord would put His Spirit upon them!"*

It is clear that God is zealous for us. He wants us to be protected from bad influences so that we can follow his Word and flourish. Then we can use our God-given gifts for His glory. So, how can we single-handedly stop coveting, envying, and being jealous? We can prevent their growth in us if we are zealous about ourselves and others in the same way God is zealous about us.

If we think about it, all three of the above-mentioned *badnesses* (not sure that is even a word) are caused by thinking that God has not sufficiently provided for us. We create this wrong thinking by comparing ourselves to others. God's provision includes material things as well as gifts and talents. We can envy someone's possessions, even where they were born. We can also envy their skills, their knowledge, their looks, their popularity, etc.

So to eliminate jealousy, envy and covetousness, our eyes must be focused on God, our hearts must be content and thankful for what He has given us, and we must serve Him with what we are and what we have.

If we are content with what He has given us, and are using it wisely (remember the parable of the talents – Matthew 25:14-30), then comparisons to others are useless and really serve no purpose. And in fact, once we get a handle on this, we will also be able to spot those people who perhaps have little or no self-esteem because they are comparing themselves when they should be sharing themselves.

There will always be people who try to make us envious and jealous. But, if we are zealous for God, and zealous about using what He has given us to serve Him, then those people will hold no sway over us.

So we count our blessings (one by one), maximize our spiritual gifts, and look for ways to encourage others to do the same. Remember, we are the apple of God's eye.

Perhaps these final words will also inspire us to be zealous (the good kind)!

The Ezra 7:10 Plan — 1st Love   DISCOVERY   God's Love for Me

Quotes

   F. B. Meyer told the following experience to a few personal friends: "It was easy," he said, "to pray for the success of G. Campbell Morgan when he was in America. But when he came back to England and took a church near to mine, it was something different. The old Adam in me was inclined to jealousy, but I got my heel upon his head, and whether I felt right toward my friend, I determined to act right." "My church gave a reception for him, and I acknowledged that if it was not necessary for me to preach Sunday evenings I would dearly love to go and hear him myself. Well, that made me feel right toward him. But just see how the dear Lord helped me out of my difficulty. There was Charles Spurgeon preaching wonderfully on the other side of me. He and Mr. Morgan were so popular, and drew such crowds, that our church caught the overflow, and we had all we could accommodate." — *Ministers' Research Service*

   The counselors of Florence asked Leonardo da Vinci, then Italy's most celebrated artist, to submit sketches for the decorations of the grand hall at Florence. One of the counselors had heard of a young and little-known artist who had done good work, Michelangelo, and asked him to submit sketches also. The sketches of Leonardo were superb, in keeping with his genius, but when the counselors saw the sketches of Michelangelo there was a spontaneous expression of wonder and enthusiasm. News of this reached Leonardo. He also heard that one of the counselors had said, "Leonardo is getting old." He was never able to get over the eclipse of his fame by Michelangelo, and the remaining years of his life were clouded with gloom and sorrow.
  — C. E. Macartney

   The man who keeps busy helping the man below him won't have time to envy the man above him—and there may not be anybody above him anyway.
  — Henrietta C. Mears

The Ezra 7:10 Plan — 1st Love   DISCOVERY   God's Love for Me

XOgesis

KJ: "Hey, Annie, have you heard of a story written by some guy named Asap, where a dog has a piece of meat in his mouth…"

Annie: "Yeah. By the way, it's Aesop."

KJ: "anyway, this dog is crossing a stream, sees his reflection and thinks it's another dog and starts barking 'cause he wants the other dog's meat…"

Annie: " …and when he barks, the meat in his mouth falls out and floats away."

KJ: "Yeah. My mom says there is something called a moral in that story. She says a moral is a good lesson that teaches you right from wrong."

Annie: "There are lots of good morals in that story like, be content with what you have, don't be jealous or envious of what others have…"

KJ: "… and don't talk with your mouth full!"

From KJ & Friends ™ © 2010 by G Doulos

The Ezra 7:10 Plan *1st Love*

DISCOVERY   God's Love for Me

OLD TESTAMENT EXAMPLES [Isaiah 37:30-35] [Psalm 69]

Describe how the LORD displays ***Zeal*** in these passages

Describe how the LORD has been ***Zealous*** for you and/or someone that you know.

The Ezra 7:10 Plan — 1st Love

DISCOVERY — God's Love for Me

List a way you will be **Zealous** this week. Prepare a concise teaching on combating **Jealousy**.

My Application:

My Lesson Plan

Extra Credit – Pick any of the 10 commandments and think about how not being **Jealous** will help you fulfill the commandment.

The Ezra 7:10 Plan — 1st Love   DISCOVERY   God's Love for Me

CHARACTERISTIC OF LOVE

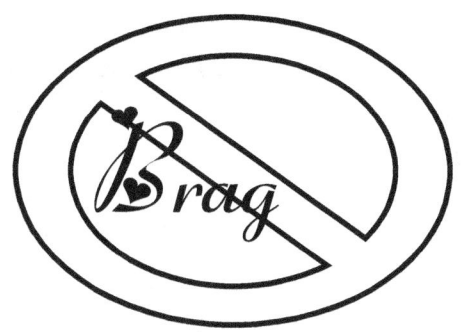

Discussion

The word used in the Greek here for *brag*, περπερεύεται (*perpereuetai*), basically means *to brag* or *boast* and has as its noun form the meaning, *braggart*. In *Vincent's Word Studies in the New Testament*, this word is defined as, *used of one who sounds his own praises*. *Merriam-Webster's Collegiate Dictionary* echoes this: *to talk boastfully,* and to *engage in self-glorification*. The Greek has a separate word for boasting. Boasting is something that can be good or bad, and the boast may not necessarily be about one's own accomplishments.

Boasting in things other than ourselves can be quite beneficial, as the apostle Paul says:

1 Corinthians 1:27-31 *but God has chosen the foolish things of the world to shame the wise, and God has chosen the weak things of the world to shame the things which are strong, and the base things of the world and the despised God has chosen, the things that are not, so that He may nullify the things that are, so that no man may boast before God. But by His doing you are in Christ Jesus, who became to us wisdom from God, and righteousness and sanctification, and redemption, so that, just as it is written, "Let him who boasts, boast in the Lord."*

But the word (περπερεύεται) used here for bragging makes it clear that this is not *good* boasting. It literally means *being a braggart*. It means that our boasting is about our self. The timing of this characteristic of love following *do not be jealous* is perfect. Let us follow the train of thought. We are commanded not to be covetous or envious about another person's property, skills or achievements. This will create ill feelings and prevent us from having good relationships with others. It may also make us feel bad and promote a low self-esteem within us. Now, what happens when we brag about ourselves, our property, our skills, and our achievements? It tempts people to be jealous, and envious, and covetous of us. It may contribute to their having a low self-esteem. It is putting a stumbling block in front of others that is entirely unnecessary.

We as zealous Christians want to encourage others to use the gifts and talents that God has given to them. We do not want to try and make them feel bad that they are not as successful as we are with our gifts and talents. Bragging does not elevate others; it puts them down, as we seek to elevate ourselves above them. To put it succinctly, we are commanded to not be jealous of others, and to not cause jealousy in others. We are commanded to not be envious of others, and to not cause envy in others by our bragging.

So what is the correct way to handle acknowledging our accomplishments? How can we prevent ourselves from being a braggart? Let us look at the following scriptures:

The Ezra 7:10 Plan — 1st Love   DISCOVERY   God's Love for Me

God Boasts on Us	
Matthew 19:28,29 *And Jesus said to them, "Truly I say to you, that you who have followed Me, in the regeneration when the Son of Man will sit on His glorious throne, you also shall sit upon twelve thrones, judging the twelve tribes of Israel. And everyone who has left houses or brothers or sisters or father or mother 1or children or farms for My name's sake, will receive many times as much, and will inherit eternal life."*	Luke 10:41,42 *But the Lord answered and said to her, "Martha, Martha, you are worried and bothered about so many things; but only one thing is necessary, for Mary has chosen the good part, which shall not be taken away from her."*
Matthew 8:10 *Now when Jesus heard this, He marveled and said to those who were following, "Truly I say to you, I have not found such great faith with anyone in Israel."*	Isaiah 43:4 *Since you are precious in My sight, Since you are honored and I love you, I will give other men in your place and other peoples in exchange for your life.*

God Requests Us to not Brag	
Matthew 6:3-4 *But when you give to the poor, do not let your left hand know what your right hand is doing, so that your giving will be in secret; and your Father who sees what is done in secret will reward you.*	Judges 7:2 *The Lord said to Gideon, "The people who are with you are too many for Me to give Midian into their hands, for Israel would become boastful, saying, 'My own power has delivered me.'"*
Proverbs 27:2 *Let another praise you, and not your own mouth; A stranger, and not your own lips.*	Galatians 5:26 *Let us not become boastful, challenging one another, envying one another.*
Jeremiah 9:23,24 *Thus says the Lord, "Let not a wise man boast of his wisdom, and let not the mighty man boast of his might, let not a rich man boast of his riches; but let him who boasts boast of this, that he understands and knows Me, that I am the Lord who exercises lovingkindness, justice and righteousness on earth; for I delight in these things," declares the Lord.*	

Examples of Our Good Boasting	
Psalm 20:7 *Some boast in chariots and some in horses, But we will boast in the name of the Lord, our God.*	Psalm 34:2 *My soul will make its boast in the Lord; The humble will hear it and rejoice.*
2 Corinthians 7:4 *Great is my confidence in you; great is my boasting on your behalf. I am filled with comfort; I am overflowing with joy in all our affliction.*	2 Corinthians 12:9 *And He has said to me, "My grace is sufficient for you, for power is perfected in weakness." Most gladly, therefore, I will rather boast about my weaknesses, so that the power of Christ may dwell in me.*

From the verses above it is clear that we can boast in the Lord and boast on others. It is also clear that the Lord is very proud of us. He will always have great things to say about any and all of our victories and sacrifices for His sake. Remember this always.

The Lord will always be our greatest source of encouragement. He wants us to succeed. He loves us and loves to boast about us to the angels. Remember Job. God really thought he was amazing. Job had his faults, but he was dearly loved.

So how do we handle speaking about our own accomplishments? Well this one is easy — just be quiet about it. Do not be a show-off. The Bible is extremely clear on this. Two things to remember: Let others recount our victories, and we should not let our left hand know what our right hand is doing. We will explain that one a little further.

On the surface of Matthew 6:3,4 (see above verses) we may wonder how we can do one thing with one hand that the other hand may not even know about. We can assume that this is an expression emphasizing that we should do good things without expecting anyone to give us any credit; and that it would be done in such secrecy that we would not be aware of it if that were possible. This would be a reasonable assumption and recent discoveries in how the brain functions make this verse quite an interesting statement. Scientists have relatively recently discovered that different parts of the brain control different parts of the body.

The Ezra 7:10 Plan — 1st Love   DISCOVERY   God's Love for Me

And you guessed it, the left hand and the right hand are in fact controlled by different sides of the brain. The left hand is controlled by the right side of the brain and the right hand is controlled by the left side of the brain. The left side of the brain tends to manage our verbal, analytical, rational, logical sides, while the right side of the brain runs our nonverbal, synthetic, non-rational, and intuitive sides. Thus the more we dwell on our accomplishments the more we engage both sides of our brain, and allow the left and right sides of the brain to fully know what we have done. If we spend almost no time thinking about how *great* we are, or what we have done, then perhaps only one side of our brain will truly know what we have done. Perhaps then truly the one hand will not know what the other has done.

From a practical standpoint this is really not that possible, but you get the idea. The less time we dwell on our past accomplishments the better for us. God will make sure we are encouraged. Count on it. It is better that others praise us anyway. If someone praises us for something we did in the past, we should always be gracious and say *thank you*. We can rejoice in our victories each day, but as a new day dawns we have a big zero on our good deeds list. So at the start of each day we should start out by boasting in the Lord and in others, and not dwell on our past deeds.

Looking at this in another way it may appear that the antidote for stopping jealousy and bragging may be the exact opposite of each other. Let us compare and contrast these.

For envy / jealousy *the cure* is to not to compare ourselves to others, but rather be zealous in our attention to using our gifts and talents to serve the Lord. For bragging *the cure* is to think of others rather than ourselves and boast in them and build them up, and not think too highly of our gifts, talents and accomplishments as we serve the Lord. Remember that measuring and comparing ourselves to others invariably leads to either envy / jealousy or bragging.

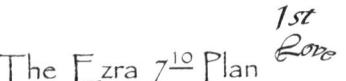

Jealousy and envy try to bring others down to our level, while bragging tries to bring us up to what we perceive is the level of others or beyond. In both cases, where we are in relationship to another person is completely unimportant. All that matters is our walk with God. The only measure we need to worry about is the distance between us and the Lord. The question we can ask at the close of every day, *Are we closer to or farther away from the Lord?* Remember, let other people praise us, and let us not be too enamored with our good deeds. We should concentrate on praising the accomplishments of others. We will close with one additional verse from the Lord Jesus Christ.

Luke 17:10 *So you too, when you do all the things which are commanded you, say, 'We are unworthy slaves; we have done only that which we ought to have done.'*

Perhaps these final words will also inspire us to refrain from bragging but concentrate on proper boasting!

Quotes

In basic training, our first sergeant made things very clear. He told us, "Don't question anything I say or tell you to do. Don't worry—I hardly ever make mistakes. Matter of fact, I've made only one mistake in my life. I once thought I was wrong about something. It turned out I wasn't." — Dalex J. LeBlanc

A minister who was walking along a road saw a crowd of boys surrounding a dog. "What are you doing with the dog?" asked the kindly minister. "Whoever tells the biggest lie, he wins the dog." "Oh, my, my, my," exclaimed the minister, "when I was a little boy like you here I never told a lie." There was a moment's silence. "Here," said one of the little fellows, "you win the dog."

We always weaken whatever we exaggerate. — Jean Francois De Laharpe

Few people need voice lessons to sing their own praise. — E. C. Mckenzie

The Ezra 7:10 Plan *1st Love*   DISCOVERY   God's Love for Me

Do you wish men to speak well of you? Then never speak well of yourself.
— *Pascual*

If a fish escapes, it was a big one. — *Malay Proverb*

Sign in front of an Atlanta restaurant featuring fried chicken: "If the Colonel Had Our Chicken Recipe He'd Be a General." — *Atlanta Journal*

XOgesis

Annie:	"Thanks for the loan of a dollar but why are you giving it to me with your left hand behind your back?"
KJ:	"This way my left hand doesn't know what my right hand is doing so I won't become a braggart!"
Annie:	"Does that work?"
KJ:	"Yeah! Yesterday I gave $2 away with my right hand, before that I accepted a trophy with my left hand, then I washed the dishes with only my right hand, was a bit difficult, but I did great, then before that with only one hand I beat someone in doing push ups, then before that..."
Annie:	"So this is not bragging ??? I think one of your hands must be peeking!"

From KJ & Friends ™ © 2010 by G Doulos

The Ezra 7:10 Plan — 1st Love   DISCOVERY   God's Love for Me

OLD TESTAMENT EXAMPLES [Job 1:8] [Judges 7 and 8]

Describe how the LORD displays *good* **Boasting** or prevents us from **Bragging,** in these passages.

Describe how the LORD has been **Boasting** on you and/or someone that you know.

The Ezra 7¹⁰ Plan — 1st Love   DISCOVERY   God's Love for Me

List a way you will **Boast** (good) this week. Prepare a concise teaching on combating **Bragging**.

My Application:

My Lesson Plan

Extra Credit – Pick any of the 10 commandments and think about how not **Bragging** will help you fulfill the commandment.

CHARACTERISTIC OF LOVE

Discussion

The word used in the Greek here for *arrogant*, φυσιοῦται (*phusioutai*), basically means *to be arrogant* or *proud*. In *Vincent's Word Studies in the New Testament*, this word is defined as *to be puffed up* and it is used only by the apostle Paul in the books of Corinthians and Colossians. It may be derived from another Greek word φῦσα (*phusa*), meaning *a pair of bellows*. *Merriam-Webster's Collegiate Dictionary* echoes this, saying, *exaggerating or disposed to exaggerate one's own worth or importance in an overbearing manner.*

While bragging as previously discussed may boast of many deeds, arrogance is more an attitude that inflates our self-worth out of proportion. It can be argued that a janitor of a school and the principal of a school are jobs differing in value. However, both the janitor and the principal can still be arrogant. It is not the job or position that makes us arrogant but our perspective on our worth compared to others. There is that same problem again!! Comparing ourselves — aaghh!! Arrogance also has to do with the thought that we do not need others. Not only are the arrogant more lofty in their estimation of themselves, but they convince themselves that they do not need what others can give because they undervalue (even dismiss) the contributions of others.

The Ezra 7:10 Plan 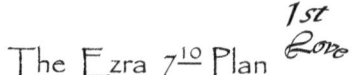   DISCOVERY   God's Love for Me

So how does one become arrogant? What does God say about it? What is the remedy? Perhaps we can start with the opposite of arrogance, which would be humility. Let's compare the two.

Merriam-Webster's Collegiate Dictionary displays the following information about the word *humble*.

> Humble
>
> [Middle English, from Old French, from Latin humilis low, humble, from humus earth; akin to Greek chthōn earth, chamai on the ground] (13th century)
>
> 1 : not proud or haughty : not arrogant or assertive
> 2 : reflecting, expressing, or offered in a spirit of deference or submission
>   ⟨a humble apology⟩
> 3 a: ranking low in a hierarchy or scale : insignificant, unpretentious
>   b: not costly or luxurious ⟨a humble contraption⟩

So if we compare the lowliness of the humble being akin to the humus of the earth, to the inflated (by bellows) position of the arrogant, we see the stark contrast of these two individuals. Most people start somewhere in between these two levels. So how do we lower ourselves to obtain true humility; and conversely, how do we inflate ourselves to become arrogant and full of pride? Start with the verses below, and then read on.

The Ezra 7:10 Plan — 1st Love

DISCOVERY God's Love for Me

God's View of Arrogance
James 3:13-18 *Who among you is wise and understanding? Let him show by his good behavior his deeds in the gentleness of wisdom. But if you have bitter jealousy and selfish ambition in your heart, do not be arrogant and so lie against the truth. This wisdom is not that which comes down from above, but is earthly, natural, demonic. For where jealousy and selfish ambition exist, there is disorder and every evil thing. But the wisdom from above is first pure, then peaceable, gentle, reasonable, full of mercy and good fruits, unwavering, without hypocrisy. And the seed whose fruit is righteousness is sown in peace by those who make peace.*

1 Corinthians 8:1 *Now concerning things sacrificed to idols, we know that we all have knowledge. Knowledge makes arrogant, but love edifies.*	1 Corinthians 1:27, *but God has chosen the foolish things of the world to shame the wise, and God has chosen the weak things of the world to shame the things which are strong,*
Proverbs 14:16 *A wise man is cautious and turns away from evil, But a fool is arrogant and careless.*	Proverbs 28:25 *An arrogant man stirs up strife, But he who trusts in the Lord will prosper.*

God Requests Us to Not be Arrogant

Ezekiel 16:49 *Behold, this was the guilt of your sister Sodom: she and her daughters had arrogance, abundant food and careless ease, but she did not help the poor and needy.*	Obadiah 1:3 *The arrogance of your heart has deceived you, You who live in the clefts of the rock, In the loftiness of your dwelling place, Who say in your heart, 'Who will bring me down to earth?'*

1 Corinthians 4:5-7 *Therefore do not go on passing judgment before the time, but wait until the Lord comes who will both bring to light the things hidden in the darkness and disclose the motives of men's hearts; and then each man's praise will come to him from God. Now these things, brethren, I have figuratively applied to myself and Apollos for your sakes, so that in us you may learn not to exceed what is written, so that no one of you will become arrogant in behalf of one against the other. For who regards you as superior? What do you have that you did not receive? And if you did receive it, why do you boast as if you had not received it?*

The Ezra 7:10 Plan — 1st Love   DISCOVERY   God's Love for Me

Examples of Our Humility Towards Others	
Matthew 19:13,14 *Then some children were brought to Him so that He might lay His hands on them and pray; and the disciples rebuked them. But Jesus said, "Let the children alone, and do not hinder them from coming to Me; for the kingdom of heaven belongs to such as these."*	1 Peter 5:5 *"You younger men, likewise, be subject to your elders; and all of you, clothe yourselves with humility toward one another, for God is opposed to the proud, but gives grace to the humble.*
Romans 12:3-5 *For through the grace given to me I say to everyone among you not to think more highly of himself than he ought to think; but to think so as to have sound judgment, as God has allotted to each a measure of faith. For just as we have many members in one body and all the members do not have the same function, so we, who are many, are one body in Christ, and individually members one of another.*	Ephesians 5:22, 25 *"Wives, be subject to your own husbands, as to the Lord.* *Husbands, love your wives, just as Christ also loved the church and gave Himself up for her,* Ephesians 6:5,9 *Slaves, be obedient to those who are your masters according to the flesh, with fear and trembling, in the sincerity of your heart, as to Christ;* *And masters, do the same things to them, and give up threatening, knowing that both their Master and yours is in heaven, and there is no partiality with Him.*

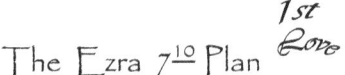

We have listed some observations about arrogance from the above verses. Let us see if we can figure out how one inflates this monster.

Arrogant traits	Humble traits
know it all	reasonable
bitter jealousy	peacemaker
selfish ambition	full of mercy
lying	without hypocrisy
disorderly	unwavering
stirs up strife	gentle
pride	peaceable
boasting	righteous
deceived by pride	good fruits

Without going into too much analysis a couple of thoughts are offered. Arrogance is characterized by self-glorification and results in the destruction of people, plans and purposes, through strife, disorder, bitter jealousy, etc. Humility, however is contrasted in that it seeks not glory for itself; rather, it promotes the well-being of others and results in the continual growth of people, plans and purposes through gentle, peaceful, unwavering, and righteous behavior. The results or effects of the two are in stark contrast to each other.

Perhaps we can picture the difference between these contrasting qualities by reflecting on people in the Bible who had these traits. Moses was the most humble man in the Bible. Though he had his faults, he was highly esteemed by God. No one else could have possibly done a better job leading thousands of people through the wilderness, while patiently teaching, encouraging and admonishing everyone about the ways of the Lord. John the Baptist spent his whole life preparing people to receive salvation from the Messiah who was to come. And then at the height of his ministry, he simply said, *He must increase, and I must decrease.* He gradually faded into the background, until he was murdered by King Herod. We could go on about others, such as King David, who

The Ezra 7:10 Plan — 1st Love   DISCOVERY   God's Love for Me

in true humility waited until the Lord had dealt with Saul before he assumed the reins of his kingdom.

The arrogant folks in the Bible would include the likes of Cain, Pharaoh, and King Saul. So how did these folks become arrogant? By looking at a few episodes of their lives we can get an inkling of how this might have occurred. The next time we read the books Genesis and First and Second Samuel we should keep this in mind.

Perhaps these final words will also inspire us to refrain from being arrogant and concentrate on being humble!

Quotes

A rich man once invited many honored guests for a feast. His own chair, richly decorated, was placed at one end of the long table. While he was away, each guest seated himself according to his own esteem of his position in sight of the master. When time came and all were seated, the master moved his chair to the other end of the table!

One of Spurgeon's students went into a pulpit with every expression of confidence but he had an extremely difficult time. He came down distressed, almost brokenhearted, and he went to Spurgeon about it. The words of Spurgeon to him were these, "If you had gone up as you came down, you would have come down as you went up." — Al Bryant

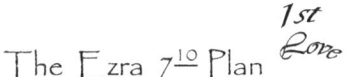

XOgesis

KJ: "I was elected class president today, and that goofy old Richard was elected as vice-president. Why do you need a vice-president anyway? The president is the one who makes all the decisions. My first action as president will be to abolish all the other lesser positions like vice-president, secretary, and …"

Ned: "You do know they will have a vote on that action."

KJ: "What?! I guess my first action will have to be to abolish voting rights for everyone except me."

Ned: "But they will have a vote on that, too."

KJ: "Oh well I guess I am stuck with them. Being president is turning out to be harder than I thought."

From KJ & Friends ™ © 2010 by G Doulos

The Ezra 7:10 Plan *1st Love* DISCOVERY   God's Love for Me

OLD TESTAMENT EXAMPLES [Gen 19:1-22]

Describe how the LORD has shown **Humility** or dealt with the **Arrogant** in this passage.

Describe how the LORD has shown **Humility** toward you and/or someone that you know or has dealt with your **Arrogance**.

The Ezra 7:10 Plan 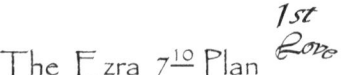 1st Love

DISCOVERY   God's Love for Me

List a way you will show **Humility** this week. Prepare a concise teaching on combating **Arrogance**.

My Application:

My Lesson Plan

Extra Credit – Pick any of the 10 commandments and think about how being **Humble** will help you fulfill the commandment.

CHARACTERISTIC OF LOVE

Discussion

The word used in the Greek here for *acting unbecomingly*, ἀσχημονεῖ (*aschēmonei*), basically means *to act indecently, to be rude* or *to behave in a disgraceful or shameful manner*. The word in the Greek has a negative prefix *a*, which is negating the word *schēmonei*, that can be translated as *form, conduct*, or *character*. So literally translated it means *without character*. Depending on the degree of our actions when we act unbecomingly, people may say that we are not conducting ourselves well or our behavior is downright shameful and disgraceful. To act unbecomingly is to not care about our reputation or our character. Once we cease to worry about conducting ourselves properly, any lewd, degrading or shameful actions are open to tempt us. We want to be an example of decency not indecency. We want to be known as a decent person.

There are a variety of examples in the New Testament on this character quality. We will look at these one at a time. Read the verses that follow.

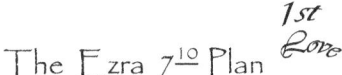

1 Corinthians 7:36,37 If anyone thinks he is acting improperly toward the virgin he is engaged to, and if she is getting along in years and he feels he ought to marry, he should do as he wants. He is not sinning. They should get married. But the man who has settled the matter in his own mind, who is under no compulsion but has control over his own will, and who has made up his mind not to marry the virgin—this man also does the right thing. (NIV)

The word *improperly* used in this New International Version (NIV) of the verse is the Greek word *aschēmonein* (translated as *unbecomingly* in the NASB95). The connotation based on this particular context is that the improper behavior is of a physical or sensual nature. This is one characteristic of indecent behavior. When we are not in control of our sensual passions it may lead to behavior that is indecent. It is indecent to want to satisfy our own desires at the expense of others.

Another use of this word for indecent (*shame*) is found in the following verses:

Jude 12,13 These are the men who are hidden reefs in your love feasts when they feast with you without fear, caring for themselves; clouds without water, carried along by winds; autumn trees without fruit, doubly dead, uprooted; wild waves of the sea, casting up their own shame like foam; wandering stars, for whom the black darkness has been reserved forever.

The people being described here pretend to be believers who attend *love feasts,* which may represent church fellowships gathering over a meal. These pretenders (*trees without fruit*) care only for themselves and display their shameful behavior like foam on the sea. Sea foam is composed of many things including wastes from plants and fish and other things that are decomposing. This includes the dregs on the sea floor that get churned up to the top of the water.

So the illustration is a great one. Wastes and foul-smelling objects are disgraceful and distasteful and should be kept buried or even incinerated. But in this case these indecent things are actually on display. Such is one characteristic of an indecent person: not caring if what is deemed indecent is on display.

The Ezra 7:10 Plan 1st Love   DISCOVERY   God's Love for Me

An Old Testament verse that conveys indecent behavior is found in Ezekiel.

Ezekiel 23:29 *They will deal with you in hatred, take all your property, and leave you naked and bare. And the nakedness of your harlotries will be uncovered, both your lewdness and your harlotries.*

In this verse and in Ezekiel chapters sixteen and twenty-three, indecent behavior is related to being naked or nakedness, which is used as a metaphor for indecent behavior. Again the message is clear. It is not appropriate to go around naked or view nakedness in others (e.g., the episode of Ham and Noah, Genesis 9:22,23).

One final verse on this topic:

Ephesians 5:3,4 *But immorality or any impurity or greed must not even be named among you, as is proper among saints; and there must be no filthiness and silly talk, or coarse jesting, which are not fitting, but rather giving of thanks.*

The specific indecent behavior mentioned is when we talk about indecent things. The three words sum up indecent talking very well: filthiness, silly talk and coarse jesting.

So we see that indecent behavior can be what we do ourselves, how we behave with others, and what we talk about. Indecency can be mild but also can be horrible. An easy way to remember this is that indecent behavior encompasses the following actions: *rude, crude and lewd.*

Thus while lewd behavior is indecent and can get us arrested, rude behavior is also indecent and will arrest our good reputation and testimony for Christ. Let us now look at the following additional scriptures.

The Ezra 7:10 Plan — 1st Love

DISCOVERY — God's Love for Me

God's View of Being Indecent	
Deuteronomy 23:14 *Since the LORD your God walks in the midst of your camp to deliver you and to defeat your enemies before you, therefore your camp must be holy; and He must not see anything indecent among you or He will turn away from you.*	*Isaiah 47:3 Your nakedness will be uncovered, Your shame also will be exposed; I will take vengeance and will not spare a man.*
Romans 1:27 and in the same way also the men abandoned the natural function of the woman and burned in their desire toward one another, men with men committing indecent acts and receiving in their own persons the due penalty of their error.	

God Requests Us to Not be Indecent	
Ephesians 4:29 Let no unwholesome word proceed from your mouth, but only such a word as is good for edification according to the need of the moment, so that it will give grace to those who hear.	*1 Timothy 2:9,10 Likewise, I want women to adorn themselves with proper clothing, modestly and discreetly, not with braided hair and gold or pearls or costly garments, but rather by means of good works, as is proper for women making a claim to godliness.*

Examples of Our Decent Behavior Toward Others	
Gen 9:23 *But Shem and Japheth took a garment and laid it upon both their shoulders and walked backward and covered the nakedness of their father; and their faces were turned away, so that they did not see their father's nakedness.*	Matthew 1:19 *And Joseph her husband, being a righteous man and not wanting to disgrace her, planned to send her away secretly.*

Perhaps these final words will also inspire us to refrain from acting unbecomingly and concentrate on being decent!

The Ezra 7:10 Plan — 1st Love   DISCOVERY   God's Love for Me

Quotes

In 1974, the research firm of Daniel Yankelovich, Inc., surveyed thirty-five hundred young people, ages sixteen to twenty-five. The interviews sought to learn what these selected individuals felt about "every important value" in today's world.

The study indicated that only 31 percent considered premarital sexual relations as morally wrong, compared with 52 percent in a 1969 survey. Opposition to abortion dropped from 58 percent to 45 percent in the same period. The proportion who considered "Living a clean moral life a very important value" fell from 71 percent to 52 percent. It would seem that standards are shifting into the patterns that existed in the days of Noah.
  — *Bible Expositor*

In the United States 21% of all first babies are conceived before marriage, and 10% of all births are illegitimate. In some countries the rate is as high as 70% illegitimate.

Disney looked around for a worthy male star to play in "Mary Poppins." He settled on Dick Van Dyke—"my only choice"—when he heard that Van Dyke taught Sunday school and prayed with his children at bedtime. Disney also learned that Van Dyke had said, "I won't appear in a movie that I can't take my children to see." Van Dyke gave a great performance. The picture got thirteen Academy Award nominations.

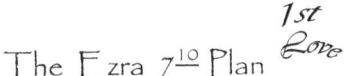

XOgesis

Ned: "What are you looking up in the dictionary?"

KJ: "…rude, crude and socially inaccessible. Mom said that I was acting like that. I wanted to know what it meant so she said to look it up. I get that crude means doing shameful stuff, but all I get for socially inaccessible is being a hermit. Do hermits do shameful stuff?"

Ned: "Yeah. Haven't you heard about the hermit crab? If you are crabby you do shameful stuff, and a hermit crab is the worst. And remember in the book of Jude, where it says that some bad people were like *wild waves of the sea casting up their own shame like foam?* What do you think was in that sea foam? Hermit crabs of course!"

KJ: "Is that really true?"

Ned: "KJ, I'm just joking. Your mom probably said you were socially unacceptable, not inaccessible."

KJ: "That's a relief, because I have a pet hermit crab and he seems nice."

Ned: ">>Sigh<<"

From KJ & Friends ™ © 2010 by G Doulos

The Ezra 7:10 Plan *1st Love*   DISCOVERY   God's Love for Me

OLD TESTAMENT EXAMPLES [Ps 25:3] [Prov 13:18] [Lev 20:26]

Describe how the LORD displays **Decency** or prevents us from **Acting Unbecomingly,** in these passages.

Describe how the LORD has been encouraging you and/or someone that you know to act **Decently.**

The Ezra 7:10 Plan 1st Love   DISCOVERY   God's Love for Me

List a way you will behave **Decently** this week. Prepare a concise teaching on **Indecency**.

My Application:

My Lesson Plan

Extra Credit – Pick any of the 10 commandments and think about how being **Decent** will help you fulfill the commandment.

The Ezra 7:10 Plan *1st Love*   DISCOVERY   God's Love for Me

CHARACTERISTIC OF LOVE

Discussion

The expression used in the Greek here for *does not seek its own*, οὐ ζητεῖ τὰ ἑαυτῆς (*ou zētei ta heautēs*), is translated literally word for word as: *not — it seeks — things — of herself* (herself being our subject *Love*). It is written very generically so that we can examine all of the *things* that pertain to ourselves, to see if our seeking *these things* is preventing us from seeking those same *things* for others. It does not mean that we should not take care of ourselves. A good corollary to this would be the following verse:

Philippians 2:4, *do not merely look out for your own personal interests, but also for the interests of others.*

This aspect of love is reminding us of the second greatest commandment:

Matthew 22:39 *The second is like it, 'You shall love your neighbor as yourself.'*

As we plan our day, our week, our year, our life, we need to ask if we are consumed with seeking those things that pertain primarily to ourselves, to our own interests, or to our own benefit.

This simple expression (*does not seek its own*) has a surprisingly wide variety of interpretative nuances as the differing Bible translations of our study text 1 Corinthians 13:5 illustrate:

NAS: *...it does not seek its own...* NET: *...it is not self-serving...*
NIV: *...it is not self-seeking...* KJV: *...seeketh not her own...*
RSV: *...Love does not insist on its own way...*

Paul uses a similar expression employing the same Greek words as above:

1Corinthians 10:24 *Let no one seek his own good but that of his neighbor.*

The other Bible translations are much more in-synch on this passage:

NAS: *Let no one seek his own good, but that of his neighbor.*
NIV: *Nobody should seek his own good, but the good of others.*
RSV: *Let no one seek his own good, but the good of his neighbor.*
NET: *Do not seek your own good, but the good of the other person.*
KJV: *Let no man seek his own, but every man another's wealth.*

It is very interesting that in the Greek for 1 Corinthians 10:24 the word for *good* is not actually used. The expression literally translated would be, *Let no one seek that of himself, but that of the other*. The words that the other translations use such as, *good, neighbor* or *wealth* are not found in the Greek. The translators picked those words to try and convey the sense of the verse. As an aside, from these simple examples we can see that sometimes translators use words that too narrowly confine the meaning of the text. Sometimes the words they choose can actually subtly change the basic meaning.

For example, the RSV for 1 Corinthians 13:5 uses *insist on its own way*. That can be confusing especially if we actually do need to insist on a way that is clearly better. The other translations better convey the meaning of not being absorbed with seeking one's own things by using words such as self-seeking or self-serving. Also, as an example, the KJV for 1 Corinthians 10:24 intimates that we are to seek to make others wealthy instead of ourselves. That is too narrow a thought and thus changes the sense of the text too much.

From these verses it is clear that the priority in life is not us. How difficult this is for some to grasp. I am not number one, I am not the most important thing, and I am not the only thing that matters.

However, the Lord knows our interests and goals in life and what we want to accomplish. He has a unique way of ensuring our success. By making our interests and goals subservient to the interest and goals of others, this will help ensure that our (God-given) goals are accomplished. This is similar to:

Matthew 6:33, *But seek first His kingdom and His righteousness, and all these things will be added to you;*

and

Matthew 10:39 *He who has found his life will lose it, and he who has lost his life for My sake will find it.*

The Ezra 7:10 Plan 1st Love   DISCOVERY   God's Love for Me

Let us now look at the following additional scriptures:

God's View of Being Self-Centered	
Matthew 23:25 *Woe to you, scribes and Pharisees, hypocrites! For you clean the outside of the cup and of the dish, but inside they are full of robbery and self-indulgence.*	Romans 6:6 *knowing this, that our old self was crucified with Him, in order that our body of sin might be done away with, so that we would no longer be slaves to sin;*
James 3:16 *For where jealousy and selfish ambition exist, there is disorder and every evil thing.*	

God Requests Us to Not be Self-Centered	
Titus 1:7 *For the overseer must be above reproach as God's steward, not self-willed, not quick-tempered, not addicted to wine, not pugnacious, not fond of sordid gain,*	Philippians 2:3 *Do nothing from selfishness or empty conceit, but with humility of mind regard one another as more important than yourselves;*

Examples of Our Selfless Behavior Toward Others	
1 Samuel 19:1–7 Jonathan risks the ire of his father King Saul to put in a good word for David so that his father would not seek to kill David anymore. It worked this time.	1 Kings 18:3–4 *Ahab called Obadiah who was over the household. (Now Obadiah feared the LORD greatly; for when Jezebel destroyed the prophets of the LORD, Obadiah took a hundred prophets and hid them by fifties in a cave, and provided them with bread and water.)*

Perhaps these final words will also inspire us to refrain from being self-centered and concentrate on others.

The Ezra 7:10 Plan — 1st Love

DISCOVERY — God's Love for Me

Quotes

Dear Friend:

Our church membership	1400
Nonresident membership	75
Balance left to do the work...	1325
Elderly folks who have done their share in the past	25
Balance left to do the work...	1300
Sick and shut-in folks	25
Balance left to do the work...	1275
Membership who did not pledge	350
Christmas and Easter members	300
Balance left to do the work...	625
Members who are too tired and overworked	300
Balance left to do the work...	325
Alibiers	200
Balance left to do the work...	125
Members who are too busy somewhere else	123
Balance left to do the work...	2

Just you and me—and brother, you'd better get busy, for it's too much for me!
— *Progress*

A small boy and his sister were riding on the back of the new wooden horse given to them as a present. Suddenly the boy turned to his sister and said: "If one of us would get off there would be more room for me."

"Be Yourself!" is about the worse advice you can give to some people.

My idea of an agreeable person is one who agrees with me. – Samuel Johnson

Admiration: Our polite recognition of another person's resemblance to ourselves.

The Ezra 7:10 Plan — 1st Love   DISCOVERY   God's Love for Me

XOgesis

Ned: "KJ, why are you staring into the refrigerator?"

KJ: "I am trying to decide if I should eat the last piece of pie or let my sister have it."

Ned: "Well you should follow the golden rule, you know, do unto others, love your neighbor as yourself."

KJ: "Thanks that settles it!"

<< Later >>

Ned: "So, I bet your sister was happy you saved that piece of pie for her."

KJ: "Well, actually she was mad because I ate it. But I told her that I was following your advice."

Ned: "My advice?! What! I didn't tell you …"

KJ: "You said love your neighbor as yourself. But she's my sister not my neighbor, so it was OK for me to eat it, 'cause I wasn't doing anything bad to my neighbor."

Ned: "But that's not what… I mean… your sister is still your… well she's … you should of… Oh forget it!"

From KJ & Friends ™ © 2010 by G Doulos

The Ezra 7:10 Plan *1st Love*

DISCOVERY God's Love for Me

OLD TESTAMENT EXAMPLES [Numbers 16]

Describe how the LORD displays **Selfless** behavior or prevents us from being **Self-centered,** in this passage.

Describe how the LORD has been **Selfless** on your behalf and/or someone that you know.

The Ezra 7:10 Plan — 1st Love   DISCOVERY   God's Love for Me

List a way you will be **Selfless** this week. Prepare a concise teaching on combating **Self-Centeredness**.

My Application:

My Lesson Plan

Extra Credit – Pick any of the 10 commandments and think about how not being ***Self-Centered*** will help you fulfill the commandment.

The Ezra 7:10 Plan — 1st Love   DISCOVERY   God's Love for Me

CHARACTERISTIC OF LOVE

Discussion

The word used in the Greek here for *provoked*, παροξύνεται *(paroxunetai)*, has a variety of similar meanings including: *to be spurred, urged, stimulated, provoked* or *stirred (to anger)*. In a similar way to boasting or being zealous, this word can have positive or negative connotations. We can spur people on to good works, or we can provoke people by doing things we know they hate. We can make somebody feel angry or indignant, provoke an argument, and yet our actions can also provoke creativity, sympathy, courage, and even bravery.

When the Bible commands us not to be provoked, the idea is that we will not allow ourselves to lose control when provoked by others. This quality of not allowing ourselves to be provoked is different then the character quality of exhibiting patience. This difference is best described by looking at different scenarios.

We use patience when we are trying to teach others new skills. Our students may take a long time to master the skill, which may try our patience, but they are certainly not trying to provoke us. On the other hand, this same student may constantly talk in class, not stand still in line, do the things that he or she knows we do not like, which will provoke us and tempt us to become very upset. Also we may like to have our class organized in a very particular way and our students may take some liberties and rearrange a few things. This will really, truly provoke us and tempt us to be very upset indeed.

Note that some provocations deserve punishment, but it must be the right punishment at the right time. We are not called to allow injustice to continue, but we are called to administer justice in the proper way. When we lose control of our emotions we may be tempted to act rashly and incorrectly. When we can take a quick breath that can allow provoking without losing our cool, it is a great asset. We can then deal properly with a given situation. We do not want to act rashly and then create a worse situation.

By not allowing ourselves to be provoked it can help us to be calm and clear and deal properly with the situation. Call it having a thick skin. Call it not having a chip on your shoulder. It is the practice of self-control. So how do we stimulate ourselves to stay above the fray and the fracas? How do we provoke ourselves to be provoke-proof? How do we become a self-controlled person, not overly sensitive and easily irritated?

First we need to examine the ways that we are provoked. We need to know our weaknesses. Not everyone is provoked in the same way. We need to separate what provocations that need to be dealt with later and those that we need to let slide. In all cases we need to handle the initial provocation with love.

As we stated above we need to separate those things that provoke us that we can tolerate to a point, and those things that should not be tolerated, but dealt with in an appropriate way.

So what are things or circumstances that provoke us but are not necessarily inherently or overtly evil? How about our pet peeves? How about all the times that we say ours is the best way and we do not want to hear another way? Certain situations or people (sometimes quite innocently) may bother us to a point where we become upset. In these cases we need to deal with ourselves, not the situation or the people. Some examples follow:

The Ezra 7:10 Plan — 1st Love   DISCOVERY   God's Love for Me

We may share an office and our co-worker may like it one temperature and we like it another. The way people drive their car may push us to the verge of road rage. We may get upset based on the weather ("rainy days and Mondays always get us down"). Arguments over our favorite subjects, people or family, may tempt us to lose it. Our children may do a lot of little things that annoy us. The common theme here is that people are doing things that we do not like or we are in situations that we do not like. It is provoking us because we do not like it when things do not go our way. In some of these cases we do not even have an opportunity to express our displeasure, which can make us even more upset. In other cases, we are being provoked by an opinion, which may not be evil or immoral, but it is different from our own, and we may not be able to hear it without being upset.

We need to employ understanding and compassion in order to keep ourselves from getting upset. We need to keep the right perspective on the situation. In some cases if we seek to understand why certain situations or other people bother us, and if we can step back or give them a break (compassion), we remove our own feelings, stubbornness and pride from the equation. What once seems so annoying to us perhaps we can now view as trivial. We have effectively dealt with the problem — us.

There are situations where the people who provoke us do actually need to be talked to, admonished, disciplined, or possibly rebuked and punished. But even in these cases, our initial reaction is not anger and vengeance, but understanding and compassion. The Old Testament abounds in examples. Even though people constantly provoked the Lord by their actions, He exhibited the same consistent compassion and understanding. He desired that they would eventually see the error of their ways and repent. He did not zap people right away but gave them room. That is our model as well. Only when it was clear that the people had no intention of repenting or had become mired in a bad habit did He administer any punishment. For those people who wanted to turn their life around, He administered any chastisement in small doses, increasing it only if needed. For those who were brazenly rebellious, the discipline was more severe and administered more often. In every case because the Lord starts with love, He is able to administer the perfect discipline to turn our lives around for the better, assuming we take our medicine.

Let us now look at the following additional scriptures:

God Requests Us to Not Provoke Him	
Proverbs 14:31 *He who oppresses the poor taunts his Maker, But he who is gracious to the needy honors Him.*	Proverbs 17:5 *He who mocks the poor taunts his Maker; He who rejoices at calamity will not go unpunished.*

Examples of Being Provoked and Handling it Well	
Psalm 106:28-31 *They joined themselves also to Baal-peor, And ate sacrifices offered to the dead. Thus they provoked Him to anger with their deeds, And the plague broke out among them. Then Phinehas stood up and interposed, And so the plague was stayed. And it was reckoned to him for righteousness, To all generations forever.*	Job 2:6-10 *So the LORD said to Satan, "Behold, he is in your power, only spare his life." Then Satan went out from the presence of the LORD and smote Job with sore boils from the sole of his foot to the crown of his head. And he took a potsherd to scrape himself while he was sitting among the ashes. Then his wife said to him, "Do you still hold fast your integrity? Curse God and die!" But he said to her, "You speak as one of the foolish women speaks. Shall we indeed accept good from God and not accept adversity?" In all this Job did not sin with his lips.*
2 Samuel 16:5-6 and 9-12 *When King David came to Bahurim, behold, there came out from there a man of the family of the house of Saul whose name was Shimei, the son of Gera; he came out cursing continually as he came. He threw stones at David and at all the servants of King David; and all the people and all the mighty men were at his right hand and at his left. Then Abishai the son of Zeruiah said to the king, "Why should this dead dog curse my lord the king? Let me go over now and cut off his head." But the king said, "What have I to do with you, O sons of Zeruiah? If he curses, and if the LORD has told him, 'Curse David,' then who shall say, 'Why have you done so?' " Then David said to Abishai and to all his servants, "Behold, my son who came out from me seeks my life; how much more now this Benjamite? Let him alone and let him curse, for the LORD has told him. "Perhaps the LORD will look on my affliction and return good to me instead of his cursing this day."*	

The Ezra 7:10 Plan — 1st Love   DISCOVERY   God's Love for Me

> Deuteronomy 9:16-21 *And I saw that you had indeed sinned against the LORD your God. You had made for yourselves a molten calf; you had turned aside quickly from the way which the LORD had commanded you. I took hold of the two tablets and threw them from my hands and smashed them before your eyes. I fell down before the LORD, as at the first, forty days and nights; I neither ate bread nor drank water, because of all your sin which you had committed in doing what was evil in the sight of the LORD to provoke Him to anger. For I was afraid of the anger and hot displeasure with which the LORD was wrathful against you in order to destroy you, but the LORD listened to me that time also. The LORD was angry enough with Aaron to destroy him; so I also prayed for Aaron at the same time. I took your sinful thing, the calf which you had made, and burned it with fire and crushed it, grinding it very small until it was as fine as dust; and I threw its dust into the brook that came down from the mountain.*

Examples of Being Provoked and Handling it Poorly

> Psalm 106:32-33 *They also provoked Him to wrath at the waters of Meribah, So that it went hard with Moses on their account; Because they were rebellious against His Spirit, He spoke rashly with his lips.*

Perhaps these final words will also inspire us to maintain our cool when we are provoked.

Quotes

The neat middle-aged executive peers out from the television screen. "Hello," he says, his face crinkling into a sheepish grin. "I'm from General Telephone." Boos and hisses explode off-camera. "Now, I'm aware that General Telephone provides less than adequate service." Plop. A rotten tomato slides down his chin. "But we're spending $200 million in California this year on improving our service." He is hit with an egg. "Cables, switches, personnel, everything." A cream pie splatters over his face. "Thank you for your patience," he mumbles through the goo.

In another commercial, a woman at a crowded cocktail party asks her husband to say something funny. "General Telephone," he replies, and everyone falls into paroxysms of laughter. The punch line: "We know some people think our service is laughable, but we're spending $200 million in California this year to improve it. What's so funny about that?"

These vignettes have appeared on Los Angeles television as part of a zany General Telephone of California. By tacitly conceding the company's mistakes, the admen hope that the campaign will win sympathy and understanding among the system's many disgruntled users.

John Wesley tells of a man whom year after year he thought of contemptuously as covetous. One day when he contributed to one of Wesley's charities a gift that seemed very small, Wesley's indignation knew no bounds, and he raked him fore and aft with blistering condemnation.

Wesley tells in his diary that the man quietly said: "I know a man who at each week's beginning goes to market and buys a penny's worth of parsnips and takes them home to boil in water, and all that week he has parsnips for his food and water for his drink; and food and drink alike cost him a penny a week." The man had been skimping in order to pay off debts contracted before his conversion. —Christ's Ambassadors Herald

Several years ago a Santa Fe train was speeding through Oklahoma. In one of the coaches sat a young woman desperately trying to take care of a restless baby, whose crying was evidently annoying some of the passengers.

Across the aisle sat a stout fellow, a picture of comfort and rich living. He glowered over at the woman and shouted: "Can't you keep that child quiet?" On taking a further look at the young lady, he noticed that her dress was one of mourning.

Then he heard her say gently: "I cannot help it. The child is not mine. I am doing my best."

"Where is its mother?" asked the portly passenger.

"In her coffin, sir," answered the young lady, "in the baggage car up ahead."

The steely eyes of the fat fellow filled with tears. He got up, took the babe in his arms, kissed it, and then walked up and down the aisle with the child, trying his best to soothe the motherless little one and make up for his harshness.
—Selected

The Ezra 7¹⁰ Plan 1st Love   DISCOVERY   God's Love for Me

XOgesis

Ned: "KJ in trouble again?"

KJ: "My sister keeps saying that I am provoking her, but I don't know what she is talking about and I don't even know what that means."

Ned: "Why don't you just turn the other cheek?"

KJ: "No thanks. That will really make her mad."

Ned: "Huh?!"

KJ: "I was just very innocently painting a little sign when she was sleeping…"

Ned: "So you weren't bothering her?"

KJ: "I was very careful while I was painting on her face and it was going to look really cool and I was only half finished when she just woke up and yelled at me. So you see doing the other cheek would not really be a good idea here…"

From KJ & Friends ™ © 2010 by G Doulos

The Ezra 7:10 Plan — 1st Love   DISCOVERY   God's Love for Me

OLD TESTAMENT EXAMPLES [Deut 9] [Isaiah 65]

Describe how the LORD handles being **Provoked** or prevents us from acting poorly after being **Provoked,** in these passages.

Describe how the LORD has been nice to you even after He has been **Provoked** by you or by someone you know.

The Ezra 7:10 Plan 1st Love   DISCOVERY   God's Love for Me

List a way you will handle being **Provoked** this week. Prepare a concise teaching on combating being **Provoked**.

My Application:

My Lesson Plan

Extra Credit – Pick any of the 10 commandments and think about how not losing control after being **Provoked** will help you fulfill the commandment.

The Ezra 7¹⁰ Plan *1st Love*   DISCOVERY   God's Love for Me

CHARACTERISTIC OF LOVE

Take into Account a Wrong Suffered (crossed out)

Discussion

The word used in the Greek here for *take into account*, λογίζεται (*logizetai*), basically means *to keep a record of events or actions for the sake of some future purpose*. A secular use of this word would be *to reckon* or *charge*. Reckoning has to do with settling accounts and has to do with calculations. We can reconcile a bank account by making sure we have meticulously accounted for all expenses and deposits. We can reckon the height of a building by estimating how many floors it contains. We can reckon one's exact age by counting the days since their birth date. Reckon also has the idea of thoughtful musings as in, "I reckon I have been fortunate to work at a job I love." And of course we all know about the *Day of Reckoning*, where we give an accounting of our actions to God. So this word is innocent enough in its uses unless it is used for hurtful purposes.

Let us look at the rest of the verse. Now while the NASB mentions that love does not take into account *a wrong suffered*, the Greek for *a wrong suffered*, is simply, τὸ κακόν (*to kakon*), *the bad*. We can translate this aspect of love succinctly as *love does not record bad*.

In today's modern society we are very familiar with recording things. Cameras which take still pictures have been around for a long time. Nowadays there are video recorders, voice recorders, music recorders, analog, digital — you name it.

Even cell phones now can record voice, as well as take still pictures and videos. Most of us are familiar with recording our favorite TV shows and movies. In our digital world it is easy to record and store information on our computer's hard drive or on a small digital media card or thumb drive. Those Old Testament scribes would be so jealous (in a good way).

But in the realm of love with regard to recording and remembering other people's sins and faults we are told to not hit the record button. The human brain has a tremendous capacity for remembering things and although we are not in the same league as a computer, our total memory capacity and processing speed is none too shabby. Plus, we have several advantages over computers. We do not need a new operating system or hard drive every three or four years, and our hard drive (actually the brain is kind of soft) lasts for up to one hundred years. We do not need a power supply, and with a little work we can have instant recall of our favorite information.

In an article by Ralph C. Merkle, first appearing in *Foresight Update No. 4*, in October 1988, he details an experiment involving human memory capability. The remarkable result of this work was that human beings remembered very nearly two bits per second under all the experimental conditions. The type of learning: visual, verbal, musical, or whatever did not seem to matter. That corresponds to about fifteen bytes per minute, and about one kilobyte per hour.

One kilobyte of information for example would be the text of the first seven verses of 1 Corinthians chapter thirteen (our study chapter). Thus if we carefully reviewed these verses for about one hour they would be initially committed to memory, and subsequent review sessions would keep them in our memory.

Well that is quite nice. So now we have instant recall of our favorite scripture verses. And if we dwell on them over the next months and years they will always be with us in an instant to refresh our heart, soul, mind and strength. But what happens when we dwell on the wrong type of information?

The Ezra 7:10 Plan *1st Love*   DISCOVERY God's Love for Me

Unfortunately when we put to memory the sins of others and we dwell on these unforgiven injustices, they are committed to memory also and are instantly available. How easily we can see this. These memorized transgressions, these fault accounts, are recited word for word when we become upset with a person that may have the misfortune to have a sin account with us.

It is unfair to this person to recite his or her past faults, and unhealthy and sinful for us to do so. A legal term related to this is called *double jeopardy,* and can be defined as a procedural defense that forbids a defendant from being tried twice for the same crime on the same set of facts. In many countries the guarantee against being twice put in jeopardy is a constitutional right.

So how can we forgive and forget? The key is not recording, not reciting, not dwelling on the sins of others. The less we dwell on the sins of others, the more those old memories will eventually fall out of our memory. Another way to remove imbedded sin accounts from our brains is to replace them with accounts full of good thoughts. To use computer terminology, these new good accounts will be copied over the sin accounts and thus will replace them and remove them from our brain into the trash can. This is very biblical as Philippians 4:8 states,

Finally, brethren, whatever is true, whatever is honorable, whatever is right, whatever is pure, whatever is lovely, whatever is of good repute, if there is any excellence and if anything worthy of praise, dwell on these things.

Keeping account of the sins of others is preventing something really important from happening. What is that? It is preventing the ministry of reconciliation. How important is reconciliation? Read the following:

2 Corinthians 5:16–19 *Therefore from now on we recognize no one according to the flesh; even though we have known Christ according to the flesh, yet now we know Him in this way no longer. Therefore if anyone is in Christ, he is a new creature; the old things passed away; behold, new things have come. Now all these things are from God, who reconciled us to Himself through Christ and gave us the ministry of reconciliation,*

The Ezra 7:10 Plan 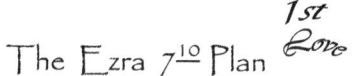   DISCOVERY   God's Love for Me

namely, that God was in Christ reconciling the world to Himself, not counting their trespasses against them, and He has committed to us the word of reconciliation.

Wow! We are actually ministers of reconciliation. However, we cannot be involved with the ministry of reconciliation if we are counting, recording, reciting and holding transgressions against others. Our ministry will fail miserably. It is hoped this helps clean up some troublesome relationships. Remember each day we need to wipe everyone's slate clean. We can be thankful that God does this for us! Think good thoughts and do not record the bad.

Remember the goal — reconciliation. Our constant mentioning of people's failings (even if it is not to their face) is just what the devil does. Satan is the accuser of the brethren. So repeating someone else's sin is doing Satan's job for him. It is not that we should never share with others how we have been treated. After we share our story, however, perhaps we should also mention that we have forgiven the person. If we cannot bring ourselves to forgive someone completely just yet, we need to be very careful to control our tongue. We do not want to turn into a bitter person who is constantly holding grudges against others.

Proverbs 17:9 *He who conceals a transgression seeks love, But he who repeats a matter separates intimate friends.*

If we are having trouble letting go of the past sins of others, try these symbolic (albeit simplistic) actions. We can try putting down all the faults of the person we are constantly upset with on a board or piece of paper. Then we pray and once and for all truly forgive that person as we wipe the board clean, or we can burn the paper, removing their faults from our memory for all time. Our God will surely give us the strength to do this! His mercies towards us are new every morning, and He can give us the ability to extend those same tender mercies through forgiveness to others we know. What a burden will be removed. We will be as light as a feather. Praise God! Besides, we have more important and exciting things to keep in our memory as we embark on our ministry of reconciliation!

Let us now look at the following additional scriptures:

The Ezra 7:10 Plan 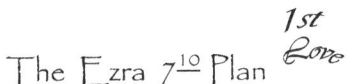 1st Love   DISCOVERY   God's Love for Me

God's View of Reconciliation	
Jeremiah 18:8 *if that nation against which I have spoken turns from its evil, I will relent concerning the calamity I planned to bring on it.*	Matthew 18:21–22 *Then Peter came and said to Him, "Lord, how often shall my brother sin against me and I forgive him? Up to seven times?" Jesus said to him, "I do not say to you, up to seven times, but up to seventy times seven.*
Psalm 32:1–2 *How blessed is he whose transgression is forgiven, Whose sin is covered! How blessed is the man to whom the LORD does not impute iniquity, And in whose spirit there is no deceit!*	Romans 4:8 *Blessed is the man whose sin the Lord will not take into account.*

Examples of Reconciliation
Luke 15:11-24 *And He said, "A man had two sons. The younger of them said to his father, 'Father, give me the share of the estate that falls to me.' So he divided his wealth between them. And not many days later, the younger son gathered everything together and went on a journey into a distant country, and there he squandered his estate with loose living. Now when he had spent everything, a severe famine occurred in that country, and he began to be impoverished. So he went and hired himself out to one of the citizens of that country, and he sent him into his fields to feed swine. And he would have gladly filled his stomach with the pods that the swine were eating, and no one was giving anything to him. But when he came to his senses, he said, 'How many of my father's hired men have more than enough bread, but I am dying here with hunger!' I will get up and go to my father, and will say to him, 'Father, I have sinned against heaven, and in your sight; I am no longer worthy to be called your son; make me as one of your hired men.' So he got up and came to his father. But while he was still a long way off, his father saw him and felt compassion for him, and ran and embraced him and kissed him. And the son said to him, 'Father, I have sinned against heaven and in your sight; I am no longer worthy to be called your son.' But the father said to his slaves, 'Quickly bring out the best robe and put it on him, and put a ring on his hand and sandals on his feet; and bring the fattened calf, kill it, and let us eat and celebrate; for this son of mine was dead and has come to life again; he was lost and has been found.' And they began to celebrate."*

The Ezra 7:10 Plan 1st Love 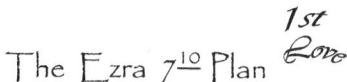 DISCOVERY   God's Love for Me

Examples of Reconciliation
Genesis 50:15–21 *When Joseph's brothers saw that their father was dead, they said, "What if Joseph bears a grudge against us and pays us back in full for all the wrong which we did to him!" So they sent a message to Joseph, saying, "Your father charged before he died, saying, 'Thus you shall say to Joseph, Please forgive, I beg you, the transgression of your brothers and their sin, for they did you wrong.' And now, please forgive the transgression of the servants of the God of your father." And Joseph wept when they spoke to him. Then his brothers also came and fell down before him and said, "Behold, we are your servants." But Joseph said to them, "Do not be afraid, for am I in God's place? As for you, you meant evil against me, but God meant it for good in order to bring about this present result, to preserve many people alive. So therefore, do not be afraid; I will provide for you and your little ones." So he comforted them and spoke kindly to them.*

Examples of Taking into Account a Wrong Suffered	
Genesis 27:41 *So Esau bore a grudge against Jacob because of the blessing with which his father had blessed him; and Esau said to himself, "The days of mourning for my father are near; then I will kill my brother Jacob."*	Esther 3:5–6 *When Haman saw that Mordecai neither bowed down nor paid homage to him, Haman was filled with rage. But he disdained to lay hands on Mordecai alone, for they had told him who the people of Mordecai were; therefore Haman sought to destroy all the Jews, the people of Mordecai, who were throughout the whole kingdom of Ahasuerus.*
Acts 15:36–39 *After some days Paul said to Barnabas, "Let us return and visit the brethren in every city in which we proclaimed the word of the Lord, and see how they are." Barnabas wanted to take John, called Mark, along with them also. But Paul kept insisting that they should not take him along who had deserted them in Pamphylia and had not gone with them to the work. And there occurred such a sharp disagreement that they separated from one another, and Barnabas took Mark with him and sailed away to Cyprus.*	

Perhaps these final words will also inspire us to not keep accounts of the faults and sins of others, and treat each other with a clean slate each day.

Quotes

David H. Fink, author of <u>Release From Nervous Tension</u>, wrote an article for the <u>Coronet Magazine</u>, in which he made a striking suggestion as to how we can overcome mental and emotional tensions.

As a psychiatrist for the Veterans Administration he was familiar with 10,000 case histories in this field. Thousands of people, who were mentally and emotionally "tied up," had asked Dr. Fink for some short, magic-button cure for nervousness. In his search for such a cure he studied two groups; the first group was made up of thousands of people who were suffering from mental and emotional disturbances; the second group contained only those, thousands of them, who were free from such tensions.

Gradually one fact began to stand out: those who suffered from extreme tension had one trait in common—they were habitual faultfinders, constant critics of people and things around them, whereas the men and women who were free of all tensions were the least faultfinding. It would seem that the habit of criticizing is a prelude or mark of the nervous and of the mentally unbalanced.

A preacher had on his desk a special book labeled "Complaints of members against one another." When one of his people called to tell him the faults of another he would say, "Well, here's my complaint book. I'll write down what you say, and you can sign it. Then when I have to take up the matter officially I shall know what I may expect you to testify to." The sight of the open book and the ready pen had its effect, "Oh, no, I couldn't sign anything like that!" and no entry was made. The preacher said he kept the book for forty years, opened it probably a thousand times, and never wrote a line in it.

The Ezra 7:10 Plan — 1st Love   DISCOVERY   God's Love for Me

This story was told of General Robert E. Lee: Hearing General Lee speak in the highest terms to President Davis about a certain officer, another officer, greatly astonished, said to him, "General, do you know that the man of whom you speak so highly to the President is one of your bitterest enemies, and misses no opportunity to malign you?" "Yes," replied General Lee, "but the President asked my opinion of him; he did not ask for his opinion of me."
— Sunshine Magazine

I will speak ill of no man, not even in the matter of truth, but rather excuse the faults I hear, and, upon proper occasions, speak all the good I know of everybody. —Benjamin Franklin

King Henry VI of England had it said of him: "He never forgot anything but injuries." Of Cranmer it was said: "If you want to get a favor from him, do him a wrong." Emerson said of Lincoln: "His heart was as great as the world, but there was no room in it for the memory of a wrong." Spurgeon gives this advice: "Cultivate forbearance till your heart yields a fine crop of it. Pray for a short memory as to unkindness." —Rev. David L. Currens

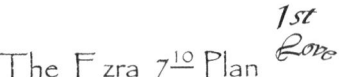

XOgesis

Naz: "KJ, why are you erasing those check marks on your white board?"

KJ: "I was keeping a record of every time this kid Richard did something bad to me."

Naz: "Why don't you just forgive him like the Bible says?"

KJ: "I did, but I didn't want to forget how many times he's been mean to me."

Naz: "Don't you know forgetting the wrongs people do to you is part of forgiveness? If you don't forget the past wrongs, then when that same person wrongs you, you will be upset for that and everything else he has ever done to you. That weight of sin will drag you down. And you will be punishing people over and over again for something that they thought was forgiven…"

KJ: "Well, that is why I am erasing these marks and because …"

Naz: "Well now that is very nice of you… hey, is that a black eye ???"

KJ: "Yup. Richard found out about my check marks and he told me I didn't need them 'cause he would give me something to remember his faults better."

From KJ & Friends ™ © 2010 by G Doulos

The Ezra 7:10 Plan *1st Love*   DISCOVERY God's Love for Me

OLD TESTAMENT EXAMPLES [Neh 9:1-31] [Jer 31:31-34] [Isa 6:1-8]

Describe how the LORD **Seeks Reconciliation** in these passages.

Describe how the LORD has been **Reconciling** you or someone that you know.

The Ezra 7:10 Plan *1st Love*   DISCOVERY   God's Love for Me

List a way you will **Not Record the Bad** this week. Prepare a concise teaching on **Reconciliation**.

My Application:

My Lesson Plan

Extra Credit – Pick any of the 10 commandments and think about how not ***Taking into Account a Wrong Suffered*** will help you fulfill the commandment.

DISCOVERY   God's Love for Me

CHARACTERISTIC OF LOVE

Discussion

The phrase used in the Greek here for *does not rejoice in unrighteousness*, οὐ χαίρει ἐπὶ τῇ ἀδικίᾳ (*ou chairei epi tē adikia*) translated word for word would be: *not it rejoices in the unrighteousness*. Before we tackle the implications behind the word *unrighteousness* let us delve into this simple word *rejoice*.

The noun forms related to the verb would include χαρά (*chara*) and χάρις (*charis*), joy and grace. Joy is more than happiness as it is more independent of happenings. It is more of a state of mind or being although it may ebb and flow. The verb form of grace includes the idea of bestowing favor and blessing. Rejoice is also used as a greeting. So if someone comes to our door we can say *Rejoice*, meaning *hey good to see you, come right in, we welcome you with favor and blessing!* We are commanded to rejoice in the Lord and the idea is that we should embrace Him spiritually and bestow favor and blessing on Him. Also, what we consider a blessing is what brings us joy.

What brings out the joy in us, what we welcome with open arms into our lives, what we bless and bestow favor upon is very important. It can define who we are. It can show us how we have defined our priorities in life. Again, we hate to beat a dead horse but this word, like jealousy and zealousness, can be good for us or bad for us depending on what we decide to embrace. The joy of the Lord can be our strength, but the joy derived by embracing the world can lead to big trouble.

So what does the Bible tell us concerning unrighteousness? Why should we not bestow favor on and embrace unrighteousness? In the New Testament a person who embraces unrighteousness is termed *unrighteous*. We can see how the Bible contrasts a person who rejoices in unrighteousness versus a person who does not in the following verses.

Matthew 5:45: *so that you may be sons of your Father who is in heaven; for He causes His sun to rise on the evil and the good, and sends rain on the righteous and the unrighteous.*

1 Corinthians 6:1 *Does any one of you, when he has a case against his neighbor, dare to go to law before the unrighteous and not before the saints?*

1 Corinthians 6:9–10 *Or do you not know that the unrighteous will not inherit the kingdom of God? Do not be deceived; neither fornicators, nor idolaters, nor adulterers, nor effeminate, nor homosexuals, nor thieves, nor the covetous, nor drunkards, nor revilers, nor swindlers, will inherit the kingdom of God.*

Based on these and other verses we can put together a table of attributes that describes the righteous versus the unrighteous.

Unrighteous		**Righteous**
Evil		Good
Fornicators	Idolaters	Saints
Adulterers	Effeminate	Just
Homosexuals	Thieves	Godly
Covetous	Drunkards	Faithful
Revilers	Swindlers	True
Unjust		

The Ezra 7:10 Plan — 1st Love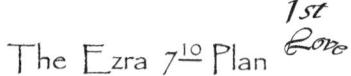

DISCOVERY   God's Love for Me

From the previous table we can clearly see the distinction between what is righteous and what is not righteous. For now we will skip the theological discussion of righteousness as it pertains to right standing with God. For now we need to grasp what we should not rejoice in.

Another facet we need to mention is that it is possible to rejoice in something without outwardly identifying with it. We will discuss this even more fully when we discuss the next portion of our study verse (1 Corinthians 13:6). While we may not overtly or consistently behave in the manner of the unrighteous, we may also not be upset about the behavior either. We need to be careful about the books we read and the shows we watch. In some cases, most likely our weak areas, we may secretly rejoice in the bad behavior as well. Our attitude about certain behavior is important because it can lead to action. We may think to ourselves that we do not always participate in a certain behavior, but if we still see nothing really wrong with it, we may find that we are soon becoming a frequent flyer. We may not outwardly associate ourselves with people who are unrighteous, but inwardly we may embrace some of their sinful attributes. We need to catch ourselves before this becomes a habit. Otherwise the Lord may have to use discipline in order to modify our behavior or attitude. We need to be pure in heart and not compromise God's moral code of righteousness.

Let us now look at the following additional scriptures:

God's View of Unrighteousness	
2 Samuel 7:14 *I will be a father to him and he will be a son to Me; when he commits iniquity, I will correct him with the rod of men and the strokes of the sons of men,*	2 Chronicles 19:7 *Now then let the fear of the LORD be upon you; be very careful what you do, for the LORD our God will have no part in unrighteousness or partiality or the taking of a bribe.*
Psalm 66:18 *If I regard wickedness in my heart, The Lord will not hear;*	Psalm 92:15 *To declare that the LORD is upright; He is my rock, and there is no unrighteousness in Him.*

The Ezra 7:10 Plan — 1st Love   DISCOVERY   God's Love for Me

Examples of Unrighteous Behavior	
Psalm 52:2 *Your tongue devises destruction, Like a sharp razor, O worker of deceit.*	Lamentations 2:14 *Your prophets have seen for you False and foolish visions; And they have not exposed your iniquity So as to restore you from captivity, But they have seen for you false and misleading oracles.*
Ezekiel 12:2 *Son of man, you live in the midst of the rebellious house, who have eyes to see but do not see, ears to hear but do not hear; for they are a rebellious house.*	

Examples of Not Rejoicing in Unrighteousness	
Psalm 17:3 *You have tried my heart; You have visited me by night; You have tested me and You find nothing; I have purposed that my mouth will not transgress.*	Psalm 119:29 *Remove the false way from me, And graciously grant me Your law.*
Proverbs 11:5 *The righteousness of the blameless will smooth his way, But the wicked will fall by his own wickedness.*	

Perhaps these final words will also inspire us to avoid rejoicing in unrighteousness.

Quotes

Billy Sunday, the baseball evangelist and reformer, never spared himself nor those he wanted to help in the vigor of his attacks on sin. He thundered against evil from the Gay Nineties through the Great Depression. He preached Christ as the only answer to man's needs until his death in 1935.

"I'm against sin," he said. "I'll kick it as long as I've got a foot, and I'll fight it as long as I've got a fist. I'll butt it as long as I've got a head. I'll bite it as long as I've got a tooth. When I'm old and fistless and footless and toothless, I'll gum it till I go home to Glory and it goes home to perdition."

The Ezra 7:10 Plan 1st Love   DISCOVERY   God's Love for Me

A flippant youth asked a preacher, "You say that unsaved people carry a weight of sin. I feel nothing. How heavy is sin? Is it ten pounds? Eighty pounds?" The preacher replied by asking the youth, "If you laid a four-hundred-pound weight on a corpse, would it feel the load?" The youth replied, "It would feel nothing, because it is dead." The preacher concluded, "That spirit, too, is indeed dead which feels no load of sin or is indifferent to its burden and flippant about its presence." The youth was silenced!

- *We sing "Sweet Hour of Prayer" and are content with 5–10 minutes a day.*
- *We sing "Onward Christian Soldiers" and wait to be drafted into His service.*
- *We sing "O for a Thousand Tongues to Sing" and don't use the one we have.*
- *We sing "There Shall be Showers of Blessing" but do not come when it rains.*
- *We sing "Blest Be the Tie That Binds" and let the least little offense sever it.*
- *We sing "Serve the Lord With Gladness" and gripe about all we have to do.*
- *We sing "I Love to Tell the Story" and never mention it at all.*
- *We sing "We're Marching to Zion" but fail to march to worship or church school.*
- *We sing "Cast Thy Burden on the Lord" and worry ourselves into a nervous breakdown.*
- *We sing "The Whole Wide World for Jesus" and never invite our next-door neighbor.*
- *We sing "O Day of Rest and Gladness" and wear ourselves out traveling, cutting grass or playing golf on Sunday.*
- *We sing "Throw Out the Lifeline" and content ourselves with throwing out a fishing line.*

The Ezra 7:10 Plan — 1st Love   DISCOVERY   God's Love for Me

XOgesis

Naz: "KJ, you are all dressed up. Who are you pretending to be?"

KJ: "I am Zack Powers international hunter of evil."

Naz: "Zack Powers. He does some really bad stuff too."

KJ: "Yeah, but all the good he does is more than the bad."

Naz: "You should be careful not to idolize someone like that because you are promoting the bad as well as the good."

KJ: "But the good is gooder than the bad."

Naz: "You can never do enough good so that your bad is excused."

KJ: "Even if I catch a million bad guys and maybe just cheat on one test question at school, the bad isn't wiped out?"

Naz: "Nope."

KJ: "What if I rescue a billion people from being captured by bad guys and just say a few bad words???"

Naz: "Nope."

KJ: "What good is it being an international hunter of evil if you don't get any breaks?"

From KJ & Friends ™ © 2010 by G Doulos

The Ezra 7:10 Plan 1st Love

DISCOVERY God's Love for Me

OLD TESTAMENT EXAMPLES [2 Chron 19:1-7] [Mal 2:1-9]

Describe how the LORD does not ***Rejoice in Unrighteousness*** or prevents us from doing so in these passages.

Describe how the LORD has been asking you to not ***Rejoice In Unrighteousness*** and/or someone that you know.

The Ezra 7:10 Plan 1st Love   DISCOVERY   God's Love for Me

List a way you will not **Rejoice in Unrighteousness** this week. Prepare a concise teaching on combating **Rejoicing in Unrighteousness**.

My Application:

My Lesson Plan

Extra Credit – Pick any of the 10 commandments and think about how not **Rejoicing in Unrighteousness** will help you fulfill the commandment.

The Ezra 7:10 Plan 1st Love   DISCOVERY   God's Love for Me

CHARACTERISTIC OF LOVE

Rejoices with the Truth

Discussion

The phrase used in the Greek here for *rejoices with the truth*, συνχαίρει δὲ τῇ ἀληθείᾳ (*sunchairei de tē alētheia*) basically means *but it rejoices with the truth*. In addition or perhaps even more emphatically, this phrase means *to become associated with and identified in connection with the truth*. If we look at the whole of verse six together we may ask ourselves why the verse did not say *love does not rejoice in unrighteousness, but rejoices in righteousness*. Let us look at the very subtle yet challenging reason why the verse is framed as it is.

First we can look at the first part of the verse and ask ourselves a few questions. Is it easier to say we do not approve of any unrighteousness, or is it easier to say that we will never be part of an evil gang? Well, for most of us it is easier to say we will not be part (action) of a gang of evildoers, than it is to say that we will go on record as saying we despise (attitude) all unrighteousness.

Jesus alluded to this when He talked about committing adultery in our heart. It may be easy for some people to say, "Oh no I have never committed adultery" (action). However, have they actually committed adultery in their heart (attitude)? In a similar passage, Jesus says one may say that he has never actually killed someone, but perhaps in his mind, he has called the person very vile names and wished for his death. So He forbids killing people, the outward action, but also forbids rejoicing inwardly in the unrighteous thoughts of slander and wishing harm on others. This underlines the message in our previously studied characteristic that states *Loves does not rejoice in unrighteousness.*

But to go on the holy offensive we must not limit ourselves in saying that we believe in the Ten Commandments and in being good. That would be just rejoicing *in* righteousness. We must identify ourselves with these beliefs by actively living them out and taking a stand for them even if it is unpopular. We need to be a person of integrity, of honor, and leave cowardly ways behind. We must *rejoice with the truth.* To follow this exhortation we must do more than just meekly identify ourselves with truth. We must completely embrace the truth, including rejoicing at the thought of being persecuted for the truth. When we think of what brings us joy in the Christian life, one of those things should be associating with and identifying with the truth. Joy is also a fruit of the Spirit. The following statements taken from various passages in the Bible will illustrate other sources of joy for the believer.

- When we are persecuted because our reward is great in heaven
- In affliction
- When demons are subjugated
- When a sinner repents
- When miracles are seen
- Upon hearing and following God's commandments
- In seeing Jesus risen from the dead
- When the Kingdom of God is described as *righteousness and peace and joy in the Holy Spirit*
- The people we disciple
- Discipline
- Standing firm
- Festivals
- Taking refuge in God
- God's presence
- Singing, shouting, and playing songs
- Being a counselor of peace

The Ezra 7:10 Plan *1st Love*   DISCOVERY   God's Love for Me

Let us now look at the following additional scriptures:

God's View of Rejoicing with the Truth	
Joshua 24:14 *Now, therefore, fear the LORD and serve Him in sincerity and truth; and put away the gods which your fathers served beyond the River and in Egypt, and serve the LORD.*	1 Samuel 12:24 *Only fear the Lord and serve Him in truth with all your heart; for consider what great things He has done for you.*
Psalm 51:6 *Behold, You desire truth in the innermost being, And in the hidden part You will make me know wisdom.*	

Examples of Rejoicing with the Truth	
Psalm 40:10 *I have not hidden Your righteousness within my heart; I have spoken of Your faithfulness and Your salvation; I have not concealed Your lovingkindness and Your truth from the great congregation.*	John 17:17–19 *Sanctify them in the truth; Your word is truth. As You sent Me into the world, I also have sent them into the world. For their sakes I sanctify Myself, that they themselves also may be sanctified in truth.*

Examples of Not Rejoicing with the Truth	
Acts 5:1–3 *But a man named Ananias, with his wife Sapphira, sold a piece of property, and kept back some of the price for himself, with his wife's full knowledge, and bringing a portion of it, he laid it at the apostles' feet. But Peter said, "Ananias, why has Satan filled your heart to lie to the Holy Spirit and to keep back some of the price of the land?*	Isaiah 48:1 *Hear this, O house of Jacob, who are named Israel And who came forth from the loins of Judah, Who swear by the name of the LORD And invoke the God of Israel, But not in truth nor in righteousness.*
Galatians 2:14 *But when I saw that they were not straightforward about the truth of the gospel, I said to Cephas in the presence of all, "If you, being a Jew, live like the Gentiles and not like the Jews, how is it that you compel the Gentiles to live like Jews?"*	

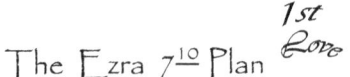

The Ezra 7:10 Plan 1st Love   DISCOVERY   God's Love for Me

Perhaps these final words will also inspire us to rejoice with the truth.

Quotes

It is said that when Grover Cleveland was a boy he insisted upon returning the egg that a neighbor's hen daily laid on the Cleveland side of the fence. Thus he early began to give proof of the honesty that marked him as a man and a future President of the United States. Faithfulness to high principles in such little things leads to honesty in matters of greater importance.

When he was 24 years old, Abraham Lincoln served as the postmaster of New Salem, Illinois, for which he was paid an annual salary of $55.70. Even then, 24 years before he entered the White House, the rail-splitter was showing the character that earned him the title of "Honest Abe." The New Salem post office was closed in 1836, but it was several years before an agent arrived from Washington to settle accounts with ex-postmaster Lincoln, who was a struggling lawyer not doing too well. The agent informed him that there was $17 due the government. Lincoln crossed the room, opened an old trunk and took out a yellowed cotton rag bound with string. Untying it, he spread out the cloth and there was the $17. He had been holding it untouched for all the years. "I never use any man's money but my own," he said.

When the father of the great Emmanuel Kant was an old man he made a perilous journey through the forests of Poland to his native country of Silesia. On the way he encountered a band of robbers who demanded all his valuables, finally asking: "Have you given us all?" and only letting him go when he answered, "All." When safely out of their sight his hand touched something hard in the hem of his robe. It was his gold, sewn there for safety and quite forgotten by him in his fear and confusion.
At once he hurried back to find the robbers, and having found them, he said meekly: "I have told you what was not true; it was unintentional. I was too terrified to think. Here, take the gold in my robes." Then to the old man's astonishment nobody offered to take his gold. Presently one went and brought

back his purse. Another restored his book of prayer, while still another led his horse toward him and helped him to mount. They then unitedly entreated his blessing, and watched him slowly ride away. Goodness had triumphed over evil.
– J.A. Clark

An American vessel named Nancy, suspected of carrying contraband, was seized by a British revenue cutter in 1799 and taken into Port Royal. Before it was boarded, however, the crew disposed of the forbidden part of the cargo and the captain likewise threw overboard the ship's papers, substituting a faked set he had prepared for such an emergency.

At the trial he and the officers were about to be acquitted of the charge of smuggling, for lack of evidence, when the master of another cutter walked into the court with the Nancy's original papers. His men had discovered them in the stomach of a shark they had harpooned that morning. Consequently, the defendants were convicted.

Today, these documents, called "The Shark's Papers," are on exhibition in the Institute of Jamaica in Kingston, and the shark's head is preserved in the Royal United Service Institution in London. —Selected

In my youth, science was more important to me than either man or God. I worshipped science. Its advance had surpassed man's wildest dreams. It took many years for me to discover that science, with all its brilliance, lights only a middle chapter of creation.

I saw the aircraft I love destroying the civilization I expected it to save. Now I understand that spiritual truth is more essential to a nation than the mortar in its cities' walls. For when the actions of a people are undergirded by spiritual truths, there is safety. When spiritual truths are rejected, it is only a matter of time before civilization will collapse.

We must understand spiritual truths and apply them to our modern life. We must draw strength from the almost forgotten virtues of simplicity, humility, contemplation and prayer. It requires a dedication beyond science, beyond self, but the rewards are great and it is our only hope. —Charles Lindbergh

The Ezra 7:10 Plan — 1st Love    DISCOVERY   God's Love for Me

Few international celebrities have been so baffling as Charles Lindbergh. It was unreasonable to many—yet remarkable to others—why he did not capitalize more on his flight across the Atlantic in 1927. But commercializing the flight was the last thing he wanted. One friend estimated that Lindbergh could have made five million dollars in one week if he would have accepted the hundreds of offers to sign testimonials, write books, or go into the movies.

William Randolph Hearst offered Lindbergh five hundred thousand dollars if he would star in a film about aviation. He declined a vaudeville contract to which was attached a one-million-dollar guarantee. A movie company made him another million-dollar offer; it was turned down. Another movie company upped its offer to five million. Money came to him as gifts, but it was always returned. An associate summed it up: "Lindbergh won't take money he hasn't earned."

When the citizens of High Wycombe, England, elect a new mayor, all the town councilors are weighed in public, following an ancient custom. Those whose weight is less than or at least not more than when they took office are warmly applauded—they have not grown fat at public expense. —Ospitalita Albergh

Once when the famous Bishop Warren A. Candler was preaching to a large audience, he used as his text the story of Ananias and Sapphira, who told a lie to God and were struck dead. The old bishop roared: "God doesn't strike people dead for lying like He used to. If He did, where would I be?" When his audience snickered a bit, he roared back, "I tell you where I would be. I would be right here preaching to an empty house!"—Optimist Magazine

The Ezra 7:10 Plan 1st Love   DISCOVERY   God's Love for Me

XOgesis

Ned: "KJ, you are back from your soccer tournament?"

KJ: "Yep, we got 2nd place, but we did win the sportsmanship award."

Ned: "Well that's great because that's the best award. Your zeal for what is honest and true is more important than winning or losing a game."

KJ: "Yeah, that's what coach said, but I would rather get the 1st place trophy."

Ned: "That's not a good attitude. What if your whole team thought that, then how…"

KJ: "Everyone on the team does think that."

Ned: "Then how did your team win the sportsmanship award?"

KJ: "Because we were the only team that shook the hands with the players and referees after every game."

Ned: "Well, at least that is something."

KJ: "Yeah, if we didn't, coach said we'd be running sprints for the next ten practices."

Ned: "So you won the sportsmanship award because you were threatened with punishment?"

KJ: "You mean there are actually people out there that want to be good sports without getting rewards or fearing punishments?"

From KJ & Friends ™ © 2010 by G Doulos

The Ezra 7:10 Plan — 1st Love

DISCOVERY — God's Love for Me

OLD TESTAMENT EXAMPLES [Exodus 18:21-23] [Malachi 4]

Describe how the LORD ***Rejoices with the Truth*** or prevents us from not ***Rejoicing with the Truth,*** in these passages.

Describe how the LORD has been teaching you or someone you know to ***Rejoice with the Truth.***

The Ezra 7:10 Plan *1st Love*

DISCOVERY   God's Love for Me

List a way you will **Rejoice with the Truth** this week. Prepare a concise teaching on how to **Rejoice with the Truth**.

My Application:

My Lesson Plan

Extra Credit – Pick any of the 10 commandments and think about how **Rejoicing with the Truth** will help you fulfill the commandment.

CHARACTERISTIC OF LOVE

ears

Discussion

The word used in the Greek here for *bears*, στέγει (*stegei*), comes from a stem meaning *to cover, to conceal*. It is a relatively rare term but exists in both Greek prose and common speech. Its basic meaning is *to keep covered*, but this gives it such senses as *to protect, to ward off, to hold back, to resist,* to *support*, to be *watertight*, to *bear*, and to *sustain*. It can also mean *to keep secret, to keep silent*, and *to keep a confidence*. The noun form literally means *a roof*. The meaning, then, is perhaps that love *covers* all things. The NIV translates this word as *protects*. This love keeps silent about unfavorable matters while it withstands the storms that rage on the outside. And yet the soul is quieted and is kept safe under the roof of this love that is bearing up under all things.

What may be the motivation for this all-bearing love? Let us look at another verse from Corinthians.

1 Corinthians 9:12 *If others share the right over you, do we not more? Nevertheless, we did not use this right, but we endure all things so that we will cause no hindrance to the gospel of Christ.*

In this case the reason this love is bearing all things is so that the Gospel of Christ would be spread without any hindrances. It is important that we bear up under all things for the right reasons and motivation. Parents who work hard and

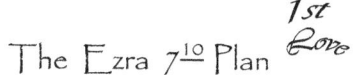

bear many hardships for the sake of meeting their children's needs (not necessarily all their wants) are good examples of bearing all things. Another good example would be a Christian bearing up under ridicule and prejudice, not becoming angry or seeking revenge, when verbally attacked just for taking a stand for the truth. Bearing unlawful or vicious physical abuse is a different story. Bringing perpetrators of crimes to justice is the better act of love than allowing ourselves to be mistreated, and allowing the transgressors to go unpunished.

We may ask what the difference may be between bearing all things and enduring all things. It can be a little confusing, as even in the above verse 1Corinthians 9:12, the Greek word στέγομεν (*stegomen* (*we bear*)), is translated as *we endure*. And to make things even foggier, another aspect of love that we will cover in our current study verse of 1 Corinthians 13:7 is that love endures (the Greek word being ὑπομένει (*hupomenei*)) all things.

So what is the difference between bearing and enduring? Perhaps a construction metaphor and the Greek etymology will help us out here. If bearing all things is related to the roof of a structure, then enduring all things is perhaps best related to the walls of the structure. The possible definitions of *hupomenei* are *to stand firm, to stay, to remain firm,* and *to wait*. Another way to look at enduring is that it represents a courageous resistance to hostile attacks.

The two terms are similar, just as a roof and the walls of a structure do similar things, and yet there are distinctions. Both offer protection and both withstand hostile forces. The way they provide stability is slightly different. The walls represent the more enduring stability of the structure and even hold the roof in place. However, the roof actually handles the brunt of the bad weather. It helps to withstand, divert and distribute the effects of the wind, lightning, rain, hail, sleet, snow and falling trees. The roof needs the walls, but the walls need the protection of the roof to be able to continue to stand firm. As we silently bear all things in love it prevents us from being known as a complainer, or worse, as a gossip.

Let us now look at the following additional scriptures:

God's View of Bearing all Things	
Galatians 6:2 *Bear one another's burdens, and thereby fulfill the law of Christ.*	Psalm 68:19 *Blessed be the Lord, who daily bears our burden, The God who is our salvation. Selah.*
Romans 15:1 *Now we who are strong ought to bear the weaknesses of those without strength and not just please ourselves.*	

Examples of Bearing all Things	
Psalm 89:50 *Remember, O Lord, the reproach of Your servants; How I bear in my bosom the reproach of all the many peoples,*	Jeremiah 10:19 *Woe is me, because of my injury! My wound is incurable. But I said, "Truly this is a sickness, And I must bear it."*
Mark 15:21–22 *They pressed into service a passer-by coming from the country, Simon of Cyrene (the father of Alexander and Rufus), to bear His cross.*	Exodus 18:22 *Let them judge the people at all times; and let it be that every major dispute they will bring to you, but every minor dispute they themselves will judge. So it will be easier for you, and they will bear the burden with you.*

Examples of Not Bearing all Things	
Genesis 4:13 *Cain said to the Lord, "My punishment is too great to bear!*	Luke 11:46 *But He said, "Woe to you lawyers as well! For you weigh men down with burdens hard to bear, while you yourselves will not even touch the burdens with one of your fingers.*

Perhaps these final words will also inspire us to bear all things in love.

The Ezra 7:10 Plan — 1st Love　　　　　DISCOVERY　God's Love for Me

Quotes

> *I counted dollars while God counted crosses.*
> *I counted gains while He counted losses!*
> *I counted my worth by the things gained in store.*
> *But He sized me up by the scars that I bore.*
> *I coveted honors and sought for degrees;*
> *He wept as He counted the hours on my knees.*
> *And I never knew 'til one day at a grave,*
> *How vain are these things that we spend life to save!*   —Selected

There are no crownwearers in Heaven that were not crossbearers here below.
—Spurgeon

When the late Bishop of Madras was visiting Travancore, there was introduced to him a little slave girl called "The Child Apostle." She had won this title by the zeal with which she talked of Christ to others. Her quiet, steady persistence in this had won several converts to Christ. But she had suffered persecution too brutal to relate. When she was introduced to the Bishop, her face, neck and arms were disfigured and scarred by stripes and blows. As he looked at her, the good man's eyes filled, and he said, "My child, how could you bear this?"

She looked up at him in surprise and said, "Don't you like to suffer for Christ, sir?" —Choice Gleanings

Adoniram Judson, the renowned missionary to Burma, endured untold hardships trying to reach the lost for Christ. For 7 heartbreaking years he suffered hunger and privation. During this time he was thrown into Ava Prison, and for 17 months was subjected to almost incredible mistreatment. As a result, for the rest of his life he carried the ugly marks made by the chains and iron shackles which had cruelly bound him.

Undaunted, upon his release he asked for permission to enter another province where he might resume preaching the Gospel. The godless ruler

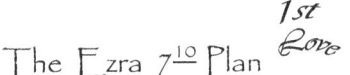

indignantly denied his request, saying, "My people are not fools enough to listen to anything a missionary might SAY, but I fear they might be impressed by your SCARS and turn to your religion!" —Henry G. Bosch

John Wesley was riding along a road one day when it dawned on him that three whole days had passed in which he had suffered no persecution. Not a brick or an egg had been thrown at him for three days.

Alarmed, he stopped his horse, and exclaimed, "Can it be that I have sinned, and am backslidden?"

Slipping from his horse, Wesley went down on his knees and began interceding with God to show him where, if any, there had been a fault.

A rough fellow, on the other side of the hedge, hearing the prayer, looked across and recognized the preacher. "I'll fix that Methodist preacher," he said, picking up a brick and tossing it over at him. It missed its mark, and fell harmlessly beside John. Whereupon Wesley leaped to his feet joyfully exclaiming, "Thank God, it's all right. I still have His presence." —J. G. Morrison

A young man was trying to establish himself as a peach grower. He had worked hard and invested his all in a peach orchard which blossomed wonderfully—then came a frost. He did not go to church the next Sunday, nor the next, nor the next. His minister went to see him to find the reason. The young fellow exclaimed: "I'm not coming any more. Do you think I can worship a God who cares for me so little that He will let a frost kill all my peaches?"

The old minister looked at him a few moments in silence, then said kindly: "God loves you better than He does your peaches. He knows that while peaches do better without frosts, it is impossible to grow the best men without frosts. His object is to grow men, not peaches." —Christian Worker's Magazine

The Ezra 7:10 Plan *1st Love*   DISCOVERY   God's Love for Me

XOgesis

Ned: "KJ, looks like you are building card houses to house dinosaurs?"

KJ: "The dinosaurs are monsters knocking the cavemen houses over."

Ned: "How come some of the cards are so bent?"

KJ: "Well, uh, heh, heh, I guess my friend sort of got mad and he started to bend and rip the cards."

Ned: "What did you do?"

KJ: "He started it by saying his card houses were stronger than mine. And when I threw a stegosaurus and knocked his over, I told him that if they were really strong even a stegosaurus couldn't knock them over."

KJ: "Then he turned into some kind of animal and started to step on my cards, and chew them and rip them. It was pretty gross how he acted. I would never do that."

Ned: "Hmmm, don't you think you could have just let that first comment slide. You know, just grin and bear it? You know, if you acted like a stegosaurus you could have avoided that argument."

KJ: "Huh?"

Ned: "Did you know that stegosaurus actually means *roof lizard* or *covered lizard* from the Greek word, *stego*. And when the Bible says love *bear all things*, the Greek word for *bear* is *stego*. So if you would have acted like a stegosaurus instead of throwing a stegosaurus your friend would probably still be here playing with you."

KJ: "I don't know. If I acted like a stegosaurus my friend would probably have turned into a T-rex and eaten me and the cards."

From KJ & Friends ™ © 2010 by G Doulos

The Ezra 7:10 Plan *1st Love*   DISCOVERY   God's Love for Me

OLD TESTAMENT EXAMPLES [1 Samuel 26] [The Book of Exodus]

Describe how the LORD **Bears all Things** or prevents us from not **Bearing all Things** in these passages.

Describe how the LORD has been **Bearing with** you and/or with someone that you know.

The Ezra 7:10 Plan *1st Love*   DISCOVERY   God's Love for Me

List a way you will **Bear all Things** this week. Prepare a concise teaching on **Bearing all Things.**

My Application:

My Lesson Plan

Extra Credit – Pick any of the 10 commandments and think about how **Bearing all Things** will help you fulfill the commandment.

CHARACTERISTIC OF LOVE

Believes

Discussion

The word used in the Greek here for *believes*, πιστεύει *(pisteuei)*, basically means *to trust or believe.* The noun form also has the meaning of *faith*. However, the use of the word *faith* in the context of 1 Corinthians 13 in verses two and thirteen makes it clear that the word used here in verse seven (*believes*) denotes more of a trust or confidence in people. While our own personal faith can move mountains, and though faith is one of the *big three* character qualities to seek after (faith, hope and love being the greatest), this use of belief/faith is not about what we have but how we think of others and what we instill in them.

Believing in another person does not mean that we will be naïve or gullible. We are not advocating what Proverbs warns us against.

Proverbs 14:15 *The naive believes everything, But the sensible man considers his steps.*

We can be fully aware of someone's past track record, but we also want to share in the person's future track record. We want to elevate people to higher levels, not remind them of where they are or have been. We can believe well of others before they are fully trustworthy or one hundred percent reliable. The fact that we may not have seen this person exhibit faithfulness is no reason for believing that the person is incapable of it.

The Ezra 7:10 Plan 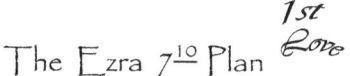 DISCOVERY   God's Love for Me

Most people want to do a good job and be thought of as a person that can be trusted. People fail, sometimes miserably. People sometimes lose heart. People sometimes wonder themselves if they will be able to go on and turn failure into success. People wonder if they will be able to turn fear into courage. Amidst all of this uncertainty what really helps is a boost of trust, of belief, and of confidence. This is where we take our part in believing in others. We want to be used as an encouragement to people. We do not want to slip into skeptical, critical, fault-finding behavior that does nothing but decimate others. Elevate, do not decimate.

Now it is one thing to say that we believe in someone and another to give them some actual responsibility to prove our confidence in them. Sometimes it is a test of our faith to put faith in others and yet trust is one step beyond faith. Do we want to see people succeed? Trust in them. Do we want to see people move past the pain of failure? Trust in them. Do we want people to move past the numbness of fear? Trust in them. Do we want people to be at peace with God again? Give them a chance. Then give them another chance and another until the fire of the Holy Spirit is rekindled afresh in them. Simply put — believe in them.

Let us now look at the following additional scriptures:

God's View of Believing all Things
John 21:15-17 *So when they had finished breakfast, Jesus said to Simon Peter, "Simon, son of John, do you love Me more than these?" He said to Him, "Yes, Lord; You know that I love You." He said to him, "Tend My lambs." He said to him again a second time, "Simon, son of John, do you love Me?" He said to Him, "Yes, Lord; You know that I love You." He said to him, "Shepherd My sheep." He said to him the third time, "Simon, son of John, do you love Me?" Peter was grieved because He said to him the third time, "Do you love Me?" And he said to Him, "Lord, You know all things; You know that I love You." Jesus said to him, "Tend My sheep."*

Isaiah 35:3,4 *Encourage the exhausted, and strengthen the feeble. Say to those with anxious heart, Take courage, fear not. Behold, your God will come with vengeance; The recompense of God will come, But He will save you.*	Hebrews 3:13 *But encourage one another day after day, as long as it is still called "Today," so that none of you will be hardened by the deceitfulness of sin.*

Examples of Believing all Things	
Proverbs 31:11 *The heart of her husband trusts in her, And he will have no lack of gain.*	
1Samuel 23:16 *And Jonathan, Saul's son, arose and went to David at Horesh, and encouraged him in God.*	Acts 14:22 *strengthening the souls of the disciples, encouraging them to continue in the faith, and saying, "Through many tribulations we must enter the kingdom of God."*

Examples of Not Believing all Things	
Ezekiel 13:22 *Because you disheartened the righteous with falsehood when I did not cause him grief, but have encouraged the wicked not to turn from his wicked way and preserve his life,*	Acts 15:38 *But Paul kept insisting that they should not take him along who had deserted them in Pamphylia and had not gone with them to the work.*
1Kings 13:11 – 32 (an example of being gullible)	

Perhaps these final words will also inspire us to believe all things.

Quotes

As a boy, Marshall Rommel, later known as "the Desert Fox," was the laziest and most indolent student in his class. His teachers said he would never amount to anything. One schoolteacher said, "If Rommel ever shows up with a dictation without mistake we'll hire a band and go off for a day in the country."

At this the boy promptly sat up and soon turned in a dictation without one single error, showing that he could do it if there was sufficient inducement to spur him to the effort. But when the promised award was not forthcoming he promptly fell back into his old, indolent ways. But later on, fired by ambition to rise above the ranks, he became a bundle of driving energy and one of the ablest military men in the world. —Evangelistic Illustration

The Ezra 7:10 Plan — 1st Love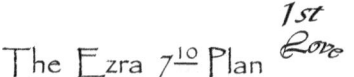

DISCOVERY   God's Love for Me

Courage is not the absence of fear; it is the mastery of it.

Oh, do not pray for easy lives. Pray to be stronger men. Do not pray for tasks equal to your powers. Pray for powers equal to your tasks.

It is a fine thing to have ability, but the ability to discover ability in others is the true test. —Elbert Hubbard

A good leader inspires other men with confidence in him; a great leader inspires them with confidence in themselves.

XOgesis

Ned: "Isn't fishing great! Hey, KJ, do you need help?"

KJ: "I can't figure this out!"

Ned: "Let me help you learn how to use your rod and reel to cast your lure."

KJ: "I can't do it, I am too afraid. What if I get it caught or hook myself or break the pole."

Ned: "I think you can do it. You just need practice to build your confidence."

KJ: "Why don't you just cast the line and then I'll hold it until a fish bites, then you reel the fish in?"

Ned: "But then you won't learn to be a confident fisherman."

KJ: "I'd rather have fish than confidence."

From KJ & Friends ™ © 2010 by G Doulos

The Ezra 7:10 Plan — 1st Love

DISCOVERY — God's Love for Me

OLD TESTAMENT EXAMPLES [Exodus 3-4:17] [1Kings 19]

Describe how the LORD **Believes** in us or displays His trust in us in these passages.

Describe how the LORD has been **building up your confidence** and/or someone that you know.

The Ezra 7:10 Plan — 1st Love

DISCOVERY   God's Love for Me

List a way you will **Believe** in someone this week. Prepare a concise teaching on **Believing** in others.

My Application:

My Lesson Plan

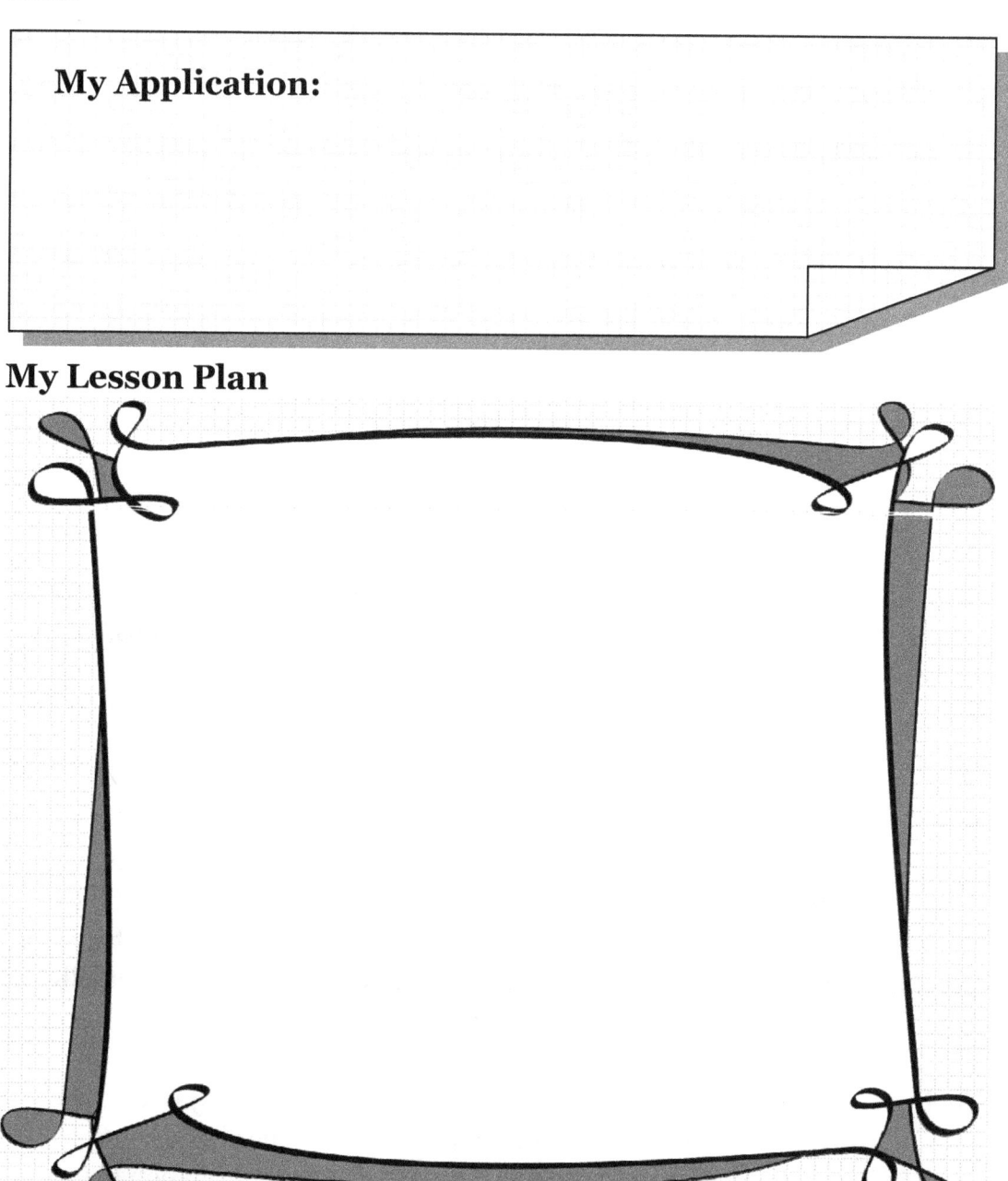

Extra Credit – Pick any of the 10 commandments and think about how **Believing** in others will help you fulfill the commandment.

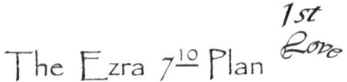

The Ezra 7:10 Plan — 1st Love DISCOVERY God's Love for Me

CHARACTERISTIC OF LOVE

Hopes

Discussion

The word used in the Greek here for *hopes*, ἐλπίζει *(elpizei)*, basically means *to hope* or *to expect*. The implication is that which is hoped for is of a good and beneficial nature. Thus the idea behind this quality is that we would hope for the best in others and we would hope the best would happen to others. Most of the verses in the Bible use hope in reference to hoping in the Lord. By extension, we can say that the same favor and blessing we expect by hoping in the Lord, we can desire for others. Thus we hope for the Lord to bless them. Note that hoping in God is often translated as trusting in God or taking refuge in God.

When we hope for the best in others it leaves no room for unhealthy competition. Now we can spur others on by our example and our desire to do more for the Lord. We can do as the apostle Paul says, run the race to win. However, while we run the race to win, we also do not begrudge others that same victory. Even more than not begrudging people good things, hope will actually exhort others to achieve their (God-given) goals.

Hoping for the best for others is found in the family, in the workplace, in the church, and on the athletic field to name a few locations. When hope is not present it fosters sibling rivalry, a lack of sharing skills and information that could better people's careers, promotes internal church strife, and the unhealthy "i" in *win* (there is no "i" in *team*).

The Ezra 7:10 Plan *1st Love* DISCOVERY   God's Love for Me

How do we adopt an attitude that promotes another's welfare (possibly literally a promotion, in the case of the workplace) as much or even above our own? One of the keys is to first recognize our own unique position and place in God's kingdom. While our goal may be to climb the ladder of dominance in terms of spiritual success, we should not be pushing people off the same ladder in order to get higher. Hoping in others is a top quality for disciple makers. We simply cannot make disciples if our goal is to make our selves look spiritually good and make others look spiritually not so good.

This can be subtle. Do we make derogatory comments (to others or just to ourselves) about those we do not like, respect or get along with? Do we secretly wish for or are just a little bit happy when we see the failure of some people? Or do we decide each day that we are going to help everyone we can get one step higher on the ladder? Or do we discuss among ourselves who is the greatest? That would not happen? What does Jesus say about this?

Mark 9:33-35 *They came to Capernaum; and when He was in the house, He began to question them, "What were you discussing on the way?" But they kept silent, for on the way they had discussed with one another which of them was the greatest. Sitting down, He called the twelve and said to them, "If anyone wants to be first, he shall be last of all and servant of all.*

So some of the keys to recognizing our own unique position and place in God's kingdom are to humble ourselves (before the Lord does), and to make it a priority to know Him, follow Him, deny ourselves and serve others. That will occupy so much of our time that we will not have much time left to worry about how high we are on the ladder compared to others. We have the right balance between being overly competitive and having a low self-esteem.

And in fact, if we are at the bottom of the ladder helping as many people get on as possible, is that not the highest position of all? Some of us may need to quit trying to be the first to get to the top and start helping people find that first and second rung on the ladder.

The Ezra 7:10 Plan 1st Love   DISCOVERY   God's Love for Me

Hope will be the way. Hope will give us strength. Hope will keep our eyes on what is important. Hope is what we will instill in others. Hope is what will characterize our life.

Let us now look at the following additional scriptures:

God's View of Hoping all Things	
Jeremiah 29:11 *For I know the plans that I have for you, declares the Lord, plans for welfare and not for calamity to give you a future and a hope.*	
Psalm 31:24 *Be strong and let your heart take courage, All you who hope in the LORD.*	Psalm 32:10 *Many are the sorrows of the wicked, But he who trusts in the LORD, lovingkindness shall surround him.*

Examples of Hoping all Things	
1 Samuel 20 Jonathan, Saul's son encourages and protects David and recognizes him as the future king of Israel, despite the fact that he would be next in line to be king if Saul had his way.	John 3:30 *He must increase, but I must decrease.* – What John the Baptist said in relation to his ministry compared to the ministry of Jesus.
2 Kings 5:1-14 An Israelite slave girl captured by the Arameans when hearing of her mistress' husbands's (Naaman, captain of the army) leprosy, she still seeks his best by recommending that he go to see the prophet Elisha for healing.	Ruth Ruth, a Moabite, decides to stay with her mother-in-law, Naomi, an Israelite, after the death of both their husbands, and travel back to Israel in order to help and take care of Naomi.
Psalm 34:8 *O taste and see that the LORD is good; How blessed is the man who takes refuge in Him!*	Psalm 42:5 *Why are you in despair, O my soul? And why have you become disturbed within me? Hope in God, for I shall again praise Him For the help of His presence.*

The Ezra 7:10 Plan *1st Love* DISCOVERY God's Love for Me

Examples of Not Hoping all Things	
1 Kings 12:25-33	Mark 9:38-40
Jeroboam decides to create rival worship centers at Bethel and Dan because he fears losing his kingship (and his life) and would rather Israel not worship together at Jerusalem if it means he gets what he wants.	The disciple John and others when seeing a "rival" doing miracles told Jesus that they actually tried to stop him because he was not part of their group. Of course Jesus says no, as He states, "He who is not against us is for us…"
1 Samuel 18:5 - 27:4	Genesis 4
Saul tries repeatedly to kill David because he fears that David will soon become king despite the fact that David has only helped him and served him well.	The Lord has regard for Abel's offering and not Cain's. Instead of learning from Abel and admiring his ways, he decides to get rid of the competition.

Perhaps these final words will also inspire us to hope all things.

Quotes

A small boy was given two apples and told to divide them with his sister, and in doing so to be generous in giving her the larger one. He said finally, "Look Ma, you give her the apples and ask her to be generous."

In an old monastery near Bebenhausen, Germany, one may see two pairs of deer horns interlocked. They were found in that position many years ago. The deer had been fighting; their horns got jammed together and could not be separated; so they died. Dr. Kerr, who first told the story, added, "I would like to carry those horns into every house and school." We might add, "And into every church." —Harold P. Barker

The Ezra 7:10 Plan *1st Love* DISCOVERY   God's Love for Me

XOgesis

KJ: "Great soccer game, Annie, but you should have crushed them even more. You were beating them three to nothing at half time. How come your coach switched everyone around?"

Annie: "She wants others to learn different positions and doesn't really care too much about the score. I'm glad she did 'cause I felt sorry for the other team."

KJ: "Felt sorry?! They are the enemy, they must be crushed or they will crush you."

Ned: "KJ has been playing too much World War III again. You know, there is a real world out there, where you can encourage and hope for good behavior instead of just shooting bad guys."

Annie: "Yeah, in your video game maybe you can talk to the bad guys and try and make friends with them instead of just shooting them."

KJ: "Well my goal is to make as many points as I can, and I don't score points by making friends."

Annie: "Maybe you should change your goals."

KJ: "Maybe your team should score more goals!!!"

Annie: "Hmmph, you are hopeless."

Ned: "Annie don't give up hope. KJ is still learning."

Annie: "Fine, you teach him."

From KJ & Friends ™ © 2010 by G Doulos

The Ezra 7:10 Plan *1st Love*   DISCOVERY   God's Love for Me

OLD TESTAMENT EXAMPLES [1Kings 3:6-14] [Nehemiah 1:1-2:8]

Describe how the LORD shows that He is **Hoping** for the best for you, in these passages.

Describe how the LORD has been giving you **Hope** and/or someone that you know.

The Ezra 7:10 Plan 1st Love   DISCOVERY   God's Love for Me

List a way you will **Hope** for the best for someone this week. Prepare a concise teaching on **Hoping** for the best in others.

My Application:

My Lesson Plan

Extra Credit – Pick any of the 10 commandments and think about how **Hoping** for the best in others will help you fulfill the commandment.

The Ezra 7:10 Plan — 1st Love   DISCOVERY   God's Love for Me

CHARACTERISTIC OF LOVE

Endures

Discussion

The word used in the Greek here for *endures*, ὑπομένει (*hupomenei*), has many senses such as: *stay behind, stay alive, stand firm, endure,* and *suffer*. This type of endurance is independent of reward or recognition and is instead motivated by love or honor or duty.

Nuances of this word include waiting for God with expectancy, and standing fast and persevering against worldly trials. And yet these two are one and the same, for how can we stand fast against Satan and his devices unless we await the direction and power of the Holy Spirit to provide our guidance, our deliverance and our victory.

Enduring is courage in the face of fire. Enduring is holding out until the bitter end. Enduring is staying in formation even when everything tells us to flee in fear. Enduring is cleaving to God. We cannot take up our cross daily unless we decide to endure all things. We can not consider it all joy when we fall into various trials unless we endure all things. We cannot rejoice when we are persecuted unless we resolutely decide to endure all things. We cannot put our hand to plow and never look back unless we endure all things.

If our motivation is not to be found in any personal rewards, then what will possess us to commit to such radical endurance of all that the world may throw our way to knock us down and out? What will keep us clinging to God as to a mast of a boat amidst a hurricane? What will enable us to endure all things? Let us review the following scriptures.

2 Timothy 2:10 *For this reason I endure all things for the sake of those who are chosen, so that they also may obtain the salvation which is in Christ Jesus and with it eternal glory.*

It is clear in this passage that Paul is enduring all things so that he may be used of God to spread the Gospel message. His desire for others to experience salvation is greater than any hardship he may face. Now that is dedication. His desire to see people make peace with God is what motivates him to endure.

Matthew 5:9 *Blessed are the peacemakers for they shall be called sons of God.*

Let us continue with some verses from the book of Hebrews.

Hebrews10:32-36 *But remember the former days, when, after being enlightened, you endured a great conflict of sufferings, partly by being made a public spectacle through reproaches and tribulations, and partly by becoming sharers with those who were so treated. For you showed sympathy to the prisoners and accepted joyfully the seizure of your property, knowing that you have for yourselves a better possession and a lasting one. Therefore, do not throw away your confidence, which has a great reward. For you have need of endurance, so that when you have done the will of God, you may receive what was promised.*

In this passage folks are reminded how they have endured persecutions for following Christ. These folks were also actively ministering and identifying with other fellow believers/prisoners who were being put to public spectacle. The desire to minister to others was more compelling than the accumulation of worldly possessions. We have good examples of this in Paul's fellow workers. Paul states in Philippians that he sent Timothy and Epaphroditus to them because they were genuinely concerned with their welfare. In fact, he states that Epaphroditus literally endured risking his life to minister to them. Timothy and Epahproditus viewed their own lives of little value compared to the value of others' lives. They were reliable, anything but lazy, *can-do* Christians!

The Ezra 7:10 Plan — 1st Love   DISCOVERY   God's Love for Me

Matthew 16:25 *For whoever wishes to save his life will lose it; but whoever loses his life for My sake will find it.*

And finally, we have one more good reason why we may be motivated to endure all things. Let us continue in Hebrews.

Hebrews 12:7 *It is for discipline that you endure; God deals with you as with sons; for what son is there whom his father does not discipline?*

While the reason we endure in the above passage is stated as *for discipline*, in reality, it is to please God. We allow God to shape our character through many things, both pleasant and painful. As we seek to stay within the will of God we have our rough edges sanded smooth. That friction can be tough to endure at times. Paul states in Philippians, chapter three, that he *suffered the loss of all things, and counted them but rubbish so that* he *may gain Christ*.

So what is the common thread throughout these three examples? Is the light bulb above our head shining?! The key to enduring all things is to be consumed with God and others. Are we beginning to understand what God meant for us to do when He gave us the two greatest commandments in the Old Testament? Jesus often repeated these as well. These commandments follow:

Deuteronomy 6:4,5 *"Hear, O Israel! The Lord is our God, the Lord is one! "You shall love the Lord your God with all your heart and with all your soul and with all your might.*

Leviticus 19:18 *You shall not take vengeance, nor bear any grudge against the sons of your people, but you shall love your neighbor as yourself; I am the Lord.*

Matthew 22:36-40 *"Teacher, which is the great commandment in the Law?" And He [Jesus] said to him, " 'You shall love the Lord your God with all your heart, and with all your soul, and with all your mind.' "This is the great and foremost commandment. "The second is like it, 'You shall love your neighbor as yourself.' "On these two commandments depend the whole Law and the Prophets."*

The Ezra 7:10 Plan *1st Love* DISCOVERY God's Love for Me

Let us now look at the following additional scriptures:

God's View of Enduring all Things	
James 1:12 *Blessed is a man who perseveres under trial; for once he has been approved, he will receive the crown of life which the Lord has promised to those who love Him.*	Isaiah 40:31 *Yet those who wait for the LORD Will gain new strength; They will mount up with wings like eagles, They will run and not get tired, They will walk and not become weary.*
Lamentations 3:25 *The Lord is good to those who wait for Him, To the person who seeks Him*	Job 22:21 *Yield now and be at peace with Him: Thereby good will come to you.*

Examples of Enduring all Things			
Hebrews 12:2 *fixing our eyes on Jesus, the author and perfecter of faith, who for the joy set before Him endured the cross, despising the shame, and has sat down at the right hand of the throne of God.*		1 Peter 2:20 *For what credit is there if, when you sin and are harshly treated, you endure it with patience? But if when you do what is right and suffer for it you patiently endure it, this finds favor with God.*	
Job	Noah	Jeremiah	Daniel

Examples of Not Enduring all Things
Acts 15:38 *But Paul kept insisting that they should not take him [Mark] along who had deserted them in Pamphylia and had not gone with them to the work.*
1 Samuel 13:10-14 *As soon as he finished offering the burnt offering, behold, Samuel came; and Saul went out to meet him and to greet him. But Samuel said, "What have you done?" And Saul said, "Because I saw that the people were scattering from me, and that you did not come within the appointed days, and that the Philistines were assembling at Michmash, therefore I said, 'Now the Philistines will come down against me at Gilgal, and I have not asked the favor of the LORD.' So I forced myself and offered the burnt offering." Samuel said to Saul, "You have acted foolishly; you have not kept the commandment of the LORD your God, which He commanded you, for now the LORD would have established your kingdom over Israel forever. "But now your kingdom shall not endure. The LORD has sought out for Himself a man after His own heart, and the LORD has appointed him as ruler over His people, because you have not kept what the LORD commanded you."*

The Ezra 7:10 Plan *1st Love*   DISCOVERY   God's Love for Me

Examples of Not Enduring all Things
Jeremiah 38:17-19   Then Jeremiah said to Zedekiah, "Thus says the LORD God of hosts, the God of Israel, 'If you will indeed go out to the officers of the king of Babylon, then you will live, this city will not be burned with fire, and you and your household will survive. 'But if you will not go out to the officers of the king of Babylon, then this city will be given over to the hand of the Chaldeans; and they will burn it with fire, and you yourself will not escape from their hand.' " Then King Zedekiah said to Jeremiah, "I dread the Jews who have gone over to the Chaldeans, for they may give me over into their hand and they will abuse me.

Perhaps these final words will also inspire us to endure all things.

Quotes

The bee has been aptly described as "busy." To produce one pound of honey, the bee must visit 56,000 clover heads. Since each head has 60 flower tubes, a total of 3,360,000 visits are necessary to give us that pound of honey for the breakfast table. Meanwhile, that worker bee has flown the equivalent of three times around the world.

To produce one tablespoon of honey for our toast, the little bee makes 4,200 trips to flowers. He makes about ten trips a day to the fields, each trip lasting twenty minutes average and four hundred flowers. A worker bee will fly as far as eight miles if he cannot find a nectar flow that is nearer. Therefore, when you feel that persistence is a difficult task ... think of the bee.

William Wilberforce early became enflamed with the idea of stopping the slave trade and slavery in England. He succeeded in becoming a member of Parliament. Goaded by William Pitt, he spoke often against slavery and the slave trade but suffered repeated defeats in Parliament.

In 1807 he persuaded his colleagues to ban the slave trade. Not until 1833 did both houses of Parliament finally abolish slavery in Britain. The news of total victory came to Wilberforce on his deathbed. He was motivated in his life's career by an idea whose time finally came.

On a tablet in a church of Algiers is the name of "Devereux Spratt, 1641." The traveler inquires what that means, and he is told that Devereux Spratt, an Englishman, was captured with one hundred and twenty others in 1641 by the Algerian pirates. He was put to work with his fellow-slaves on the fortifications around Algiers. Cut off from congenial company, he looked to God for sympathy and strength, and God's grace proved, as always, sufficient.

Finding his fellow-captives full of despair, he began to cheer them with words of faith and hope; and soon he had gathered about him, through his faithful testimony, a little band of praying and worshipping Christians. Through the influence of his brother in England, after several years, Devereux Spratt was ransomed, and the order for his release was brought to the fortifications.

His fellow-captives rejoiced with tears at his good fortune, but expressed regret that their leader was to leave them. Devereux Spratt refused to accept the ransom, and remained until he died, a slave among slaves, that he might continue to comfort those whom God had brought to Christ through him.
—Current Anecdotes

When we give our final account to God, Let us only recount these ...

> *How much we counted on Him*
> *How much others counted on us*
> *What we counted as gain*
> *What we counted as loss*

— G Doulos

The Ezra 7¹⁰ Plan ~~Love~~ *1st Love*   DISCOVERY   God's Love for Me

XOgesis

Naz: "So, looks like you've been to your church's trick-or-treatin' party. Are you supposed to be some type of a soldier?"

KJ: "I am a soldier for Christ, and now I know how tough it is."

Naz: "What do you mean?"

KJ: "I mean the whole time I was running around playing, and then having to lug tons of candy around, it was exhausting."

Naz: "Hmmm, well you look like a soldier, and talk like a soldier, but I doubt when the apostle Paul penned those words he had this in mind. Hey can I have one of those licorice candy things?"

KJ: "Back off."

Naz: "Whoa. Sorry. Geez!"

KJ: "A soldier always protects his prize."

Naz: "I thought you were a soldier for Christ."

KJ: "I am. I am pretending that the candy is the Gospel. So I must protect it."

Naz: "Actually shouldn't you be sharing this candy Gospel instead of protecting it?"

KJ: "Oh, OK. See what I mean? Being a soldier of Christ is tough. I do all the work and you get free candy."

Naz: "You are on to something!"

From KJ & Friends ™ © 2010 by G Doulos

The Ezra 7:10 Plan   1st Love   DISCOVERY   God's Love for Me

OLD TESTAMENT EXAMPLES [1Peter 3:18-20] [Malachi 3&4]

Describe how the LORD **Endures all things** for us in these passages.

Describe how the LORD has been **Enduring all things** for you and/or someone that you know.

The Ezra 7:10 Plan — 1st Love   DISCOVERY   God's Love for Me

List a way you will **Endure all things** this week. Prepare a concise teaching on how to **Endure all things**.

My Application:

My Lesson Plan

Extra Credit – Pick any of the 10 commandments and think about how **Enduring all things** will help you fulfill the commandment.

CHARACTERISTIC OF LOVE

Discussion

The word used in the Greek here for *fails*, πίπτει (*piptei*), basically means *to fall*. It can also be used to mean *to go under*, *to perish* and *to cease*. It is used to describe buildings that collapse due to earthquakes, the falling of crumbs from a table, the falling of stars from heaven, the literal falling of people (including being slain in battle) and animals. It can also be used in figurative senses as when a lot falls on someone, or when someone commits a sin, or falls away from following the truth.

In this verse the sense is akin to *not being defeated*, *not being brought to the ground*, and (using a double negative, not, not) *being able to stand*. Thus since love does *not fall* it does *not fail*. It should be noted that the Greek does not merely say that love *should* not fail, but in fact that love *never* fails. So we see a beautiful crescendo to our list of the characteristics of love. In all things or circumstances love bears, believes, hopes and endures, and in no circumstances will love ever fail. Thus we have reached the perfection in love that Jesus was talking about.

The Ezra 7:10 Plan — 1st Love

DISCOVERY — God's Love for Me

Matthew 5:43-48 *"You have heard that it was said, "You shall love your neighbor and hate your enemy." But I say to you, love your enemies and pray for those who persecute you, so that you may be sons of your Father who is in heaven; for He causes His sun to rise on the evil and the good, and sends rain on the righteous and the unrighteous. For if you love those who love you, what reward do you have? Do not even the tax collectors do the same? If you greet only your brothers, what more are you doing than others? Do not even the Gentiles do the same?" Therefore you are to be perfect, as your heavenly Father is perfect."*

Perhaps these final words will also inspire us to exhibit never failing love.

Quotes

I remember one precious experience with Henrietta Mears when we were having a sandwich in a hotel restaurant in St. Louis during a Christian bookseller's convention.

She began to reminisce about the wonderful things God had done in her life. She talked of the Lord Jesus as simply and genuinely as a new convert possessed by first love.

The tears flowed down her cheeks. It was thrilling to be with a Christian worker who had not become a pro. She really loved Jesus Christ, and she lived to make Him known.   —Russell Hitt, Editor of Eternity

A little boy declared that he loved his mother "with all his strength." He was asked to explain what he meant by "with all his strength." He said: "Well, I'll tell you. You see, we live on the fourth floor of this tenement; and there's no elevator, and the coal is kept down in the basement. Mother is busy all the time, and she isn't very strong; so I see to it that the coal hold is never empty. I lug the coal up four flights of stairs all by myself. And it's a pretty big hold. It takes all my strength to get it up here...."   —Gospel Herald

The Ezra 7:10 Plan — *1st Love* DISCOVERY God's Love for Me

Dr. Alexander Maclaren used to tell of a man of great intellectual power whom he longed to win. To do so the famous preacher preached a whole series of sermons dealing with intellectual difficulties. To the doctor's delight, the man came shortly afterward and said he had become a convinced Christian and he wanted to join the church.

Overjoyed, the doctor said, "And which of my sermons was it that removed your doubts?" "Your sermons?" said the other. "It wasn't any of your sermons. The thing that set me thinking was that a poor woman came out of your church beside me and stumbled on the steps. When I put out my hand to help her, she smiled and said 'thank you' and then added, 'Do you love Jesus Christ my blessed Saviour? He means everything to me.' I did not then, but I thought about it. I found I was on the wrong road. I still have many intellectual difficulties, but now He means everything to me, too." —Leslie D. Weatherhead

A gentleman who was a professed Christian was taken seriously ill. He became troubled about the little love he felt in his heart for God, and spoke of his experience to a friend. This is how the friend answered him.

"When I go home from here, I expect to take my baby on my knee, look into her sweet eyes, listen to her charming prattle, and tired as I am, her presence will rest me; for I love that child with unutterable tenderness. But she loves me little. If my heart were breaking it would not disturb her sleep. If my body were racked with pain, it would not interrupt her play. If I were dead, she would forget me in a few days. Besides this, she had never brought me a penny, but was a constant expense to me. I am not rich, but there is not money enough in the world to buy my baby. How is it? Does she love me, or do I love her? Do I withhold my love until I know she loves me? Am I waiting for her to do something worthy of my love before extending it?"

This practical illustration of the love of God for His children caused the tears to roll down the sick man's face. "Oh, I see," he exclaimed, "it is not my love to God, but God's love for me, that I should be thinking of. And I do love Him now as I never loved Him before." —Gospel Herald

The Ezra 7:10 Plan *1st Love*   DISCOVERY   God's Love for Me

XOgesis

Teacher: "OK class let's see how you all did in using the letters of the word *love* as an acronym to describe what love means to you. Annie?"

Annie: "Leaving Others Very Encouraged."

Teacher: "Very nice! How about you KJ?"

KJ: "I have two. Like to Own Every Video game, and Laughing Obout ripping Video action Enemies!!"

Teacher: "Uh well, KJ, the acronym was only supposed to have the letters L-O-V-E and it was about love *itself*, not what *you* love."

Classmate
Sid: "Yeah, ya goof. Besides Obout starts with an A. So your acronym would spell LARVAE which is a bunch of baby bugs. What a goofus."

KJ: "Well that makes sense because another thing I love to do is squash big *babies* who *bug* me like you, Sid."

Sid: "I can beat you in any video game."
KJ: "No, you can't."
Sid: "Yes, I can."
KJ: "No, you can't."

Teacher: "I had such good intentions..."

Sid: "Yes, I can."
KJ: "No, you can't."

From KJ & Friends ™ © 2010 by G Doulos

The Ezra 7:10 Plan *1st Love* DISCOVERY God's Love for Me

OLD TESTAMENT EXAMPLES [You Find One !!!]

Describe how the LORD's **Love Never Fails** or prevents us from **Failing,** in the selected passage(s).

Describe how the LORD is showing His **Never Failing Love** for you and/or someone that you know.

The Ezra 7:10 Plan — 1st Love   DISCOVERY   God's Love for Me

List a way you will show **Never Failing Love** this week. Prepare a concise teaching on **Love that Never Fails.**

My Application:

My Lesson Plan

Extra Credit – Review the table, *Love's Sweet Sixteen Summary* that follows. See if you can memorize all sixteen attributes of love (the first column).

Encore

Now that we have covered all of the characteristics of love we may be tempted to back-pedal a little and try and excuse ourselves from achieving the perfection that Jesus asks of us. We may say things like, *well, I am never going to be like that*, or *it is too hard for me to change*, or *I was born this way*.

Relatively recently, personality studies and leadership style studies have come into prominence. Based on research and how we answer certain questions we are categorized as a certain type of a personality, with the potential for exhibiting good and bad character qualities. Now while it is very obvious that two people can be completely different, for example, one can be quite extroverted (choleric and sanguine types) and the other quite introverted (melancholy and phlegmatic types), nevertheless the Lord would have all of us strive to imitate His example of perfect love.

As we look over the sixteen characteristics of love from our study, it may be intuitively obvious that some people with different personality traits may have an easier time mastering some of the aspects of love than others. Now in some senses that may be true, as those who have been given a special gifting from God may be a little more equipped to serve as a leader and as an example in that area. But the question needs to be asked: a leader or example for what purpose? One advantage of having spiritual leaders is that we have a living example that we can emulate. We may not all excel to the same degree in all sixteen characteristics of love, but we should be practicing all of them until they become perfected in our life. It is too easy to say, *well, I am just not going to get there*, or *it is too late for me*. Or we could say, *that other person is such a good example I do not need to be one*.

Wrong-o (old fashioned saying meaning *one is clearly mistaken*). There is a bumper sticker that says something like, *Jesus said it, I believe it, that settles it*. That needs to be our attitude as well with respect to treasuring our *First Love*, Jesus Christ, and reflecting that love in our lives.

The Ezra 7:10 Plan *1st Love* DISCOVERY God's Love for Me

The *measure of the pleasure in what we treasure* defines what is important to us. We must constantly be on guard to makes sure our treasure box is full of heavenly pursuits and not full of worldly items or pursuits. It is often the very pursuit of worldly items that limits the success in our spiritual pursuits. Jesus said we cannot serve God and mammon and so it is with love. Worldly pursuits will crowd out our love for God and our desire to serve Him.

1 John 2:15,16 *Do not love the world nor the things in the world. If anyone loves the world, the love of the Father is not in him. For all that is in the world, the lust of the flesh and the lust of the eyes and the boastful pride of life, is not from the Father, but is from the world.*

For young and old alike our first priority in life must always be our relationship with God, our *First Love*. Whether we are renewing or establishing a lifelong commitment; we are all seeking the same close relationship with God. God will never give up on us. His relationship with us is His first priority. And finally, as the Lord perfects His love in us, He will use us to perfect His love in others as well. So, do we want to change the world for Christ? We will, as Christ changes us into His definition of love. A key point of this study is that God's love for us empowers us to imitate that love to others.

The following table, *Love's Sweet Sixteen Summary,* summarizes the sixteen studies that we have gone through. We can come back to this well often to measure our progress and be amazed by all the many qualities of love that make our God so awesome! As a bonus, we have also included a table that compares our *sweet sixteen* to the nine *Fruit of the Spirit* and the *Ten Commandments*. Perhaps it can be improved upon. As an optional homework assignment, discuss other possible groupings for columns two and three. We have also summarized the positive teaching and corresponding negative admonitions into a paragraph in the form of a prayer. We can use the prayer each week to remind us of God's love for us and to review our path to becoming perfected in His love. Or even better (as another optional homework assignment), we can write out our very own prayer based on this study — dedicated to our *First Love! He would love it!*

Love's Sweet Sixteen Summary

NASB Wording	Alternate Word or Phrase	Without this quality we may become…
Is patient	Slow to anger	Insensitive, angry, unreasonable
Is kind	Beneficent, sympathetic	Stingy, unsympathetic
Is not jealous	Content, zealous for others	Envious, angry others have what we want or fearful they will take what we have, distrustful
Does not brag	Boasts on others, builds up others	Show-offs, tempting others to be jealous of us
Is not arrogant	Humble	Prideful, focused on our way of doing things, exaggerating our importance and self worth
Does not act unbecomingly	Decent	Rude, crude and lewd, socially insensitive and offensive
Does not seek its own	Selfless, a willing helper	Self absorbed, consumed with own problems
Is not provoked	Self-controlled	Overly sensitive, easily irritated
Does not take into account a wrong suffered	Seeks reconciliation	Bitter, someone who holds grudges, not truly forgiving
Does not rejoice in unrighteousness	Pure in heart	Double-minded, moral compromiser
Rejoices with the truth	Integrity	Dishonorable, corruptible, cowardly
Bears	Protects	A complainer, a gossip
Believes	Encourages	Skeptic, constant critic, fault-finder
Hopes	Exhorts	Overly competitive, low self-esteem
Endures	Suffers willingly, resolute	Not reliable, lazy, can't do attitude
Never fails	Perfect	Complacent

The Ezra 7:10 Plan — 1st Love   DISCOVERY   God's Love for Me

Love's Sweet Sixteen Compared

NASB Wording	Fruit of the Spirit	Ten Commandments
Is patient	Patience	Do not murder
Is kind	Kindness	Honor father and mother
Is not jealous	Gentleness	Do not covet
Does not brag	Gentleness	Do not covet
Is not arrogant	Gentleness	Honor father and mother
Does not act unbecomingly	Self-control	Do not commit adultery
Does not seek its own	Self-control	Do not steal
Is not provoked	Self-control	Do not murder
Does not take into account a wrong suffered	Peace	Do not murder
Does not rejoice in unrighteousness	Goodness	Do not bear false testimony
Rejoices with the truth	Joy	Remember the Sabbath
Bears	Faithfulness	Do not take God's name in vain
Believes	Faithfulness	Do not take God's name in vain
Hopes	Faithfulness	No idols
Endures	Faithfulness	No idols
Never fails	Love	No other Gods

The Ezra 7:10 Plan — 1st Love   DISCOVERY   God's Love for Me

Love. What I Want to Become.

I, Love, am patient and slow to anger. I am sensitive and willing to work with others without becoming overbearing or unreasonable. **I am kind**, beneficent, and sympathize with the plight of others and always generous. **I am never jealous**, envious or automatically mistrustful of anybody. I am extremely content with my life so far and yet zealous for others. **I never brag**, but rather build up and boast on others. I refrain from showing off because I do not want others to ever be jealous of my abilities. **I avoid arrogant** thoughts that exaggerate my own importance, while I live humbly and remind myself that I can always learn from others. **I do not act unbecomingly** but seek to be thought of as a decent human being. I avoid rude and crude talk and behavior and do not even joke about things that are socially insensitive. **I do not only seek my own** desires and needs. I am always willing to help others and not totally absorbed in solving my problems. I am selfless. **I am not easily provoked** but self-controlled so that I am not overly sensitive and do not get irritated at the drop of a hat. There is no chip on my shoulder. **I do not take into account a wrong suffered**. In fact, I try to forget the wrongs that people do because I seek reconciliation. I do not want to become a bitter, unforgiving person who holds grudges. However, **I never rejoice in unrighteousness** or view with pleasure things that go against God's Word. I do not compromise God's morals for anything and desire to be pure from the inside out. **I do rejoice in truth** found in God's Word. I am not afraid to associate myself with Christ and live out His Word in my life. I am integrity and honor, and will never corrupt His Holy Word. I am not a coward. **I bear** gladly hardships and other things so I can protect and serve. I do all of this quietly without complaint and would never think to complain about others behind their back. In fact, I am a great **believe**r in people and will always seek to encourage them every chance I get. I avoid being a skeptic, a critic and a fault-finder. I have great **hopes** for people and I exhort them to achieve their goals every chance I get. I have a positive self-image and am goal-oriented. However, I am not competitive to a point where I am glad others fail. **I endure** and suffer willingly all circumstances — for Christ's love compels me. I am resolute because it is Christ who strengthens me. I will never be thought of as an unreliable, lazy person who is always trying to get out of doing things. I am not only a *can-do* person but a *will-do* person. With all my heart, with all my soul, with all my mind, and with all my strength **I will** strive to **never fail** my Lord, my *First Love*. And, finally, I will never quit until Christ's love is perfected in me.

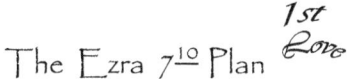

Bibliography

Aland, K., Black, M., Martini, C. M., Metzger, B. M., Robinson, M., & Wikgren, A. (1993; 2006). *The Greek New Testament, Fourth Revised Edition (Interlinear with Morphology)*. Deutsche Bibelgesellschaft.

Biblia Hebraica Stuttgartensia : With Westminster Hebrew Morphology. 1996 (electronic ed.). Stuttgart; Glenside PA: German Bible Society; Westminster Seminary.

Biblical Studies Press. (2006; 2006). *The NET Bible First Edition; Bible. English. NET Bible.; The NET Bible*. Biblical Studies Press.

Brenton, L. C. L. (1844). *The Septuagint Version of the Old Testament Translated into English*. London: Samuel Bagster and Sons.

Brown, F., Driver, S. R., & Briggs, C. A. (2000). *Enhanced Brown-Driver-Briggs Hebrew and English Lexicon* (electronic ed.). Oak Harbor, WA: Logos Research Systems.

Canne, J., Browne, Blayney, B., Scott, T., & Torrey, R. (2009). *The Treasury of Scripture Knowledge*. Bellingham, WA: Logos Research Systems, Inc.

Harris, R. L., Harris, R. L., Archer, G. L., & Waltke, B. K. (1999). *Theological Wordbook of the Old Testament* (electronic ed.). Chicago: Moody Press.

Kittel, G., Friedrich, G., & Bromiley, G. W. (1995). *Theological Dictionary of the New Testament*. Grand Rapids, MI: W.B. Eerdmans.

Liddell, H. (1996). *A Lexicon : Abridged from Liddell and Scott's Greek-English Lexicon*. Oak Harbor, WA: Logos Research Systems, Inc.

Louw, J. P., & Nida, E. A. (1996). *Greek-English Lexicon of the New Testament : Based on Semantic Domains* (electronic ed. of the 2nd edition.). New York: United Bible societies.

Merriam-Webster, I. (1996). *Merriam-Webster's Collegiate Dictionary*. (10th ed.). Springfield, Mass., U.S.A.: Merriam-Webster.

New American Standard Bible : 1995 update. 1995. LaHabra, CA: The Lockman Foundation.

Robertson, A. (1997). *Word Pictures in the New Testament.* Oak Harbor: Logos Research Systems.

Strong, J. (1996). *Enhanced Strong's Lexicon* (electronic ed.). Ontario: Woodside Bible Fellowship.

Strong, J., S.T.D., LL.D. (2009). *A Concise Dictionary of the Words in the Greek Testament and The Hebrew Bible.* Bellingham, WA: Logos Research Systems, Inc.

Swanson, J. (1997). *Dictionary of Biblical Languages with Semantic Domains : Greek (New Testament)* (electronic ed.). Oak Harbor: Logos Research Systems, Inc.

Swete, H. B., D.D. (2009). *The Old Testament in Greek: According to the Septuagint (Text).* Bellingham, WA: Logos Research Systems, Inc.

Tan, P. L. (1996, c1979). *Encyclopedia of 7700 Illustrations* : A treasury of illustrations, anecdotes, facts and quotations for pastors, teachers and Christian workers. Garland TX: Bible Communications.

Tan, R., deSilva, D. A., & Logos Research Systems, I. (2009; 2009). *The Lexham Greek-English Interlinear Septuagint.* Logos Research Systems, Inc.

The Holy Bible: King James Version. 2009 (Electronic Edition of the 1900 Authorized Version.). Bellingham, WA: Logos Research Systems, Inc.

The Holy Bible: New International Version. 1996 (electronic ed.). Grand Rapids, MI: Zondervan.

Theological Dictionary of the New Testament. 1964- (G. Kittel, G. W. Bromiley & G. Friedrich, Ed.) (electronic ed.). Grand Rapids, MI: Eerdmans.

The Revised Standard Version. 1971. Oak Harbor, WA: Logos Research Systems, Inc.

Thomas, R. L. (1998). *New American Standard Hebrew-Aramaic and Greek Dictionaries : Updated Edition.* Anaheim: Foundation Publications, Inc.

Vincent, M. R. (2002). *Word Studies in the New Testament.* Bellingham, WA: Logos Research Systems, Inc.

The Ezra 7:10 Plan 1st Love   DISCOVERY   God's Love for Me

Walvoord, J. F., Zuck, R. B., & Dallas Theological Seminary. (1983-). *The Bible Knowledge Commentary: An Exposition of the Scriptures.* Wheaton, IL: Victor Books.

Wiersbe, W. W. (1996). *The Bible Exposition Commentary.* Wheaton, Ill.: Victor Books.

Wuest, K. S. (1997). *Wuest's Word Studies from the Greek New Testament : For the English Reader.* Grand Rapids: Eerdmans.

How Many Bytes in Human Memory? by Ralph C. Merkle
This article first appeared in Foresight Update No. 4, October 1988.

www.ingramcontent.com/pod-product-compliance
Lightning Source LLC
Chambersburg PA
CBHW080331170426
43194CB00014B/2527